I0138182

# The Complete Story

## of the

# Galveston Horror

### As Told by the Survivors

Compiled by John Coulter in the Year 1900

Edited by Michelle M. Haas

Copano Bay Press
2018

New material, copyright Copano Bay Press 2018

ISBN 978-1-941324-15-8

# Contents

## UPDATE TO THE 2018 TRADE EDITION

I re-read my 2010 Publisher's Note while preparing this edition to go to print. A few things occurred to me:

1) Wow. I was a *horrible* writer eight years ago!

2) I stand by my 2010 idea that Mark was nuts for not wanting to swim in the Gulf because he was thinking about the victims of the Galveston storm. When he sees a grand lake, does he think of the *Edmund Fitzgerald* and refuse to swim? I've asked. He says he doesn't swim in lakes but does enjoy Gordon Lightfoot.

3) In my Note, I mentioned the fearful question that had plagued me all of my adult life: "If I have to go, what can I take and what will I leave behind to the wind and the rain?" A year ago, Hurricane Harvey made me answer that question in a hurry. The answer was surprisingly simple:

PARENTS

BUSINESS BASICS

DOG

FAMILY PICTURES

It turned out that everything else—things I viewed as irreplaceable before that monster was in the Gulf— was negligible, including the house and most everything in it. I'm writing this in a different town, in a different office, as a different person. The things that I miss most about what I called "home" aren't things I can buy...my garden and my trees. Someday, I'll nurture another garden and maybe live somewhere with ancient trees. For now, what I walked away with is honestly all I needed and I find a lot of comfort in that having learned that.

*Michelle*
*North Padre Island, 2018*

## PUBLISHER'S NOTE

In the intervening years between 1900 and 2010, I was born. I've been a resident of the Texas Gulf coast every minute since and fear of the inevitable big windstorm is very much a part of my sense of place. Among my prominent childhood memories are scattered images of my mother picking up the free hurricane tracking map at the local grocery store and sticking it to the fridge with magnets. We'd plot the coordinates of storms on the map as the weatherman gave them to us on the news. As a kid, I longed for the excitement of a change of scenery that fleeing from a storm would provide. The prospect of a big change in weather, in addition to an excused September school absence and a road trip, was very intriguing to me.

Time marches on, though, and most of us become adults with responsibilities...houses, children, pets, family heirlooms, art, furniture, business assets. The Internet gives us the ability to glare at a little cluster of thunderstorms in the Caribbean for a week or more, awaiting its development and wondering if our little patch of earth will be in the dreaded "Cone of Uncertainty." The long ago excitement I once associated with hurricane season has evolved into fear. "If I have to go, what can I take and what will I leave behind to the wind and the rain?" Every year I ask myself this, as do most residents of the Gulf coast. Preparedness has come a long way since Galveston's 1900 blow but I'm not certain any of us can fully prepare for such a catastrophic and disruptive event.

During the summer and early fall, I like to take the ferry over to Port Aransas for a moonlight swim once month. One September, I invited my oldest and dearest friend (a native Houstonian and Texas history buff) to accompany me. Who, after all, would not be awed by the sight of the full moon rising over the Gulf of Mexico while immersed in its warm waters? As far as I'm concerned, this is one of the biggest perks of living near the Gulf. My friend seemed keen on the idea, suited up and took the ride with me to Port A. After selecting a spot on the beach and putting the car in park, I did what I've done since I was old enough to walk—jumped out of the car as though it were filling with fire ants and made for the water.

I was already waist-deep in the swirling waters, preparing to frolic, when I noticed my friend lagging far behind, barely getting his feet wet. I gave him the customary lecture about respecting the water and the critters in it, that shark attacks aren't nearly as common as car crashes and so forth. But he just wouldn't budge. He just stood there, seemingly paralyzed. He wanted out of the water. So I asked the party-pooper what his problem was. His answer was one that I could not have guessed if my life had depended upon it. He couldn't swim in the Gulf at night, he said, because he couldn't help but imagine the horror the victims of the Galveston storm experienced in their last moments in the dark of night in that water, listening to the screams of their spouses and children grow farther and father away. At the time I thought he was a little bit insane. After working on this book, I no longer feel that way. I will not curtail my evening swims but will, however, enjoy them with more reverence than before.

I volunteered at the Astrodome following Hurricane Katrina because I could not get into New Orleans to render any assistance there. What I saw and heard in Houston both reiterated my fear of hurricanes and gave me a healthy swelling of Texan pride in the City of Houston. Working with this material gave me the same sense of pride—different storm, different era, same response. Thank you, Houston.

*-Michelle M. Haas, Managing Editor*
*Windy Hill, 2010*

## CHAPTER ONE:
### WEST INDIAN HURRICANE DESCENDS UPON GALVESTON

The frightful West Indian hurricane which descended upon the beautiful, prosperous and progressive but ill-fated city of Galveston on Saturday, September 8, 1900, causing the loss of many thousands of lives and the destruction of millions of dollars' worth of property, has had no parallel in history. The storm then ravaged Central and Western Texas, killing several hundred people and inflicting damage which cost millions to repair

When the gale approached the island upon which Galveston it situated, it lashed the waves of the Gulf of Mexico into a tremendous fury, causing them to rise to all but mountain height. Then, combining their forces, the wind and water pounced upon their prey.

In the short space of four hours the entire site of the city was covered by angry waters, while the gale blew at the rate of one hundred miles an hour. Business houses, public buildings, churches, residences, charitable institutions and all other structures gave way before the pressure of the wind and the fierce onslaught of the raging flood. Those which did not crumble altogether were so injured, in the majority of cases, that they were torn down.

Such a night of horror as the unfortunate inhabitants were compelled to pass has fallen to the lot of few since the records of history were first opened. In the early evening, when the water first began to invade Galveston Island, the people residing along the beach and near it fled in fear from their homes and sought the highest points in the city as places of refuge, taking nothing but the smaller articles in their houses with them. On and on crawled the flood, until darkness had set in, and then, as though possessed of a fiendish vindictiveness, hastened its speed and poured over the surface of the town, completely submerging it—covering the most elevated ground to a depth of five feet and the lower portions ten and twelve feet.

The hurricane was equally malignant, if not more fiendish and cruel as the flood, and tore great buildings and beautiful homes to pieces with evident delight, scattering the debris far and wide. Telegraph and telephone lines were thrown down, railway tracks and bridges—the latter connecting the island and city with the mainland—torn up, and the mighty, tangled mass of wires, bricks, sections of roofs, sidewalks, fences and other things hurled into the main thoroughfares and cross streets, rendering it impossible for pedestrians to make their way along for many days after the waters and gale had subsided.

Forty thousand men, women and children cowered in terror for eight long hours, the intense blackness of the night, the swishing and lapping of the waves, the demoniac howling and shrieking of the wind and the indescribable and awful crashing, tearing and rending as the houses, hundreds at a time, were wrecked and shattered, ever sounding in their ears. Often, too, the friendly shelter where families had taken refuge would be swept away, plunging scores and scores of helpless ones into the mad current which flowed through every street of the town. Fathers and mothers were compelled to undergo the agony of seeing their children drown, with no possibility of rescue; husbands lost their wives and wives their husbands, and the elements were only merciful when they destroyed an entire family at once.

All during that fearful night of Saturday until the gray and gloomy dawn of Sunday broke upon the sorrow-stricken city, the entire population of Galveston stood face to face with grim death in its most horrible shapes, as they realized that with every passing moment souls were being hurried into eternity.

Not one inhabitant of Galveston old enough to realize the situation had any idea other than that death was to be the fate of all before another day appeared. When this long and weary suspense, to which was added the chill of the night and the growing pangs of hunger, was at last broken by the first gleams of the light of the Sabbath morn, the latter was not entirely welcome, for the face of the sun was hidden by morose and ugly clouds, from which dripped, at dreary intervals, cold and gusty showers.

Thousands were swallowed up during the darkness and their bodies either mangled and mutilated by the wreckage which had been tossed everywhere, left to decompose in the slimy ooze deposited by the flood or forced to follow the waves in their sullen retirement to the waters of the Gulf.

Dejection and despondency succeeded fright. The majority of the businessmen of the city had suffered such losses that they were overcome by apathy. Nearly all the homes of the people were in ruins. The streets were impassable and the dead lay thickly on every side. All telegraph and telephone wires were down and, since miles and miles of railroad track had disappeared and the bridges carried away, there was absolutely no means of communication with the outer world, except by boat. The strange spectacle was then presented of the richest city of its size in the richest country in the world lying prostrate, helpless and hopeless—prey to ghouls, vultures, harpies, thieves, thugs and outlaws of every sort—its people starving, and the putrid bodies of its dead breeding pestilence.

## SKETCH OF THE CITY OF GALVESTON

The City of Galveston is situated on the extreme east end of the Island of Galveston. It is six square miles in area, its present limits being the limits of the original corporation and the boundaries of the land purchased from the Republic of Texas by Colonel Menard in 1838 for the sum of $50,000. Colonel Menard associated with himself several others, who formed a town site company with a capital of $1,000,000. The City of Galveston was platted on April 20, 1838, and seven days later the lots were put on the market. The streets of Galveston are numbered from one to fifty-seven across the island from north to south, and the avenues are known by the letters of the alphabet, extending east and west lengthwise of the island.

The founders of the city donated to the public every tenth block through the center of the city from east to west for public parks. They also gave three sites for public markets and set aside one entire block for a college, three blocks for a girls' seminary, and gave to every Christian denomination a valuable site for a church.

The growth of the city in population was slow until after the war of the rebellion against Mexico. It is a remarkable fact that in spite of its population, Galveston does double the amount of business of any city in America. The population in 1890 was 30,000, showing an increase of over 400 per cent in thirty years. At the time of the disaster the population was estimated at 40,000.

Galveston has over two miles of completed wharves along the bayfront and others under construction, all of which are equipped with modern appliances. The Galveston Wharf Company, which owns practically all the wharfage, has expended millions during the last five years for improvements in the way of elevators and facilities for handling grain and cotton. During the cotton season, Sept. 1 to March 31 inclusive, large oceangoing craft line the wharves, often thirty or more steamers and as many large sailing vessels being accommodated at one time, besides the numerous smaller vessels and sailing craft doing a coastwise trade.

Manufacturing is one of the chief supports of the city. In this branch of industry Galveston leads any city in the State of Texas by 50 per cent in number and more than 100 per cent in capital employed and product turned out. Of factories the city has 306, employing a capital aggregating $10,886,900, with an output of $12,000,000 a year.

The jetty construction forms one of the chief features of its commercial advantages. The construction began in 1885, progressing slowly for five years, when the desire of the citizens for a first-class harbor led to the formation of a permanent committee, which succeeded in getting a bill through Congress authorizing an expenditure of $6,200,000 on the harbor. The bill provided that there should be two parallel stone jetties extending nearly six miles out into the Gulf, one from the east point of Galveston Island, the other from the west point of Bolivar Peninsula. The jetties are fifty feet wide at the bottom and slope gradually to five feet above mean low tide, and are thirty five feet wide at the top, with a railroad track running their entire length, which railroad is the property of the Federal Government. The immediate effect of early construction of the jetties was to remove the inner bar, which formerly had thirteen feet of water over it, and which now has over twenty-one feet of water.

The principal business street of Galveston is the Strand, which is of made-land 150 feet from the water of the bay, in the extreme northern end of the city. Besides being the principal port of Texas, Galveston is the financial center of the State, and some of the largest business houses in Texas have their offices in the Strand. Among the business houses on this street are the following:

Sealy, Hutchins & Co., bankers; most modern banking building in Texas; four-story structure, in which is also located the office of the Mallory steamship line, and also the offices of Congressman R. B. Hawley, one of the Republican leaders in the State.

H. Kempner, cotton broker; four-story brick building.

First National Bank, J. Runge, President. Mr. Runge is also President of the Cotton Exchange, President of the Galveston Cotton mills, and President of the City Railway Company.

W. L. Moody & Co., bankers and cotton factors; four-story brick. Mr. Moody is an intimate friend of W. J. Bryan and periodically entertains him at Lake Surprise, a famous duck hunting ground fifteen miles inland from Galveston.

General offices of the Gulf, Colorado & Santa Fe Railway and the Galveston, Henderson & Houston Railway, the gulf terminus of the International & Great Northern Railway.

Adoue & Lobit, bankers; four-story brick.

Island City Savings Bank and Gulf City Trust Company, M. Lasker, President; four-story brick.

Texas Loan and Trust Company and Flint & Rogers, cotton factors; four-story brick building.

Mensing Bros., wholesale grocers; four-story brick.

Western Union Telegraph Company and Mexican Cable Company; four-story brick building.

Galveston Dry Goods Company; four-story brick.

Hullman, Owen & Co., wholesale grocers; four-story brick building.

Wallace, Landis & Co., wholesale grocers; five-story brick.

L. W. Levy & Co., wholesale liquor dealers; four-story brick.

Schneider Bros., wholesale liquor dealers; four-story brick.

Beers, Kennison & Co., general insurance agents in Texas for several large companies; four-story brick.

Concisely put and with no waste of words, the following facts comprise the history of the unfortunate city:

1. It is the richest city of its size in the United States.

2. Is the largest & most extensively commercial city of Texas.

3. Is the gateway of an enormous trade, situated as it is between the great West granaries and Europe.

4. Lies two miles from the northeast corner of the Island of Galveston.

5. Is a port of entry and the principal seaport of the State.

6. Its harbor is the best, not only on the coast line of Texas, but also on the entire gulf coast from the mouth of the Mississippi to the Rio Grande.

7. Is the nearest and most accessible first-class seaport for the States of Texas, Kansas, New Mexico and Colorado, the Indian Territory and the Territory of Arizona and parts of the States and Territories adjoining those just mentioned.

8. Is today the Gulf terminus of most of the great railway systems entering Texas.

9. Ranks third among the cotton ports of the U. S.

10. Its port charges are as low as or lower than any other port in the United States.

11. Is the only seaport on the gulf coast west of the Mississippi into which a vessel drawing more than 10 feet of water can enter.

12. Has steamship lines to Liverpool, New York, New Orleans and the ports of Texas as far as the Mexican boundary.

13. Has harbor areas of 24 feet depth and over 1,300 acres; of 30 feet depth and over 463 acres. The next largest harbor on the Texas coast has only 100 acres of 24 feet depth of water.

14. Lowest maximum temperature of any city in Texas.

15. Boasts the finest beach in America and is a famous summer and winter resort.

16. Public free school system unexcelled in the U. S.

17. Has never been visited by any epidemic disease since the yellow fever scourge of 1867.

18. Has forty miles of street railways in operation.

19. Has electric lights throughout the city (plant is owned by the city.)

20. It has millions invested in docks, warehouses, grain elevators, flouring mills, marine ways, manufactories and mercantile houses.

## "The Most Promising Town in the South"

"Galveston was the most promising town in the South, so far as shipping is concerned," said Thomas B. Bryan, the founder of North Galveston, the day after the disaster occurred. "There has been persistent opposition to it on the part of a railroad that wished the transportation of cotton and other produce farther east, but finally the geographical position of Galveston triumphed. Even Collis P. Huntington, the railroad magnate, succumbed, and later he inaugurated improvements in Galveston on the most colossal scale, involving an expenditure of many millions of dollars. One of the last announcements Mr. Huntington made before his death was that Galveston would become the greatest shipping port in America if money could accomplish it. At the time I was in Galveston, a few weeks ago, there was an army of workmen employed by the Southern Pacific Railroad constructing great docks and wharves, which were to eclipse any on the globe.

"Some conception of Galveston can be formed by supposing the business district of Chicago—say from Lake to Twenty-second Street—were to extend out into the lake on a pier for a distance of three miles and at a height above the water varying from three to seven, and possibly, in some places, nine feet. My own observation of Galveston induced my taking hold of the nearest eligible elevated locality for residences, which is North Galveston, sixteen miles from the city proper. It has an elevation above the water of fifteen to twenty feet more than Galveston, and is free from inundation. No news has reached me from North Galveston, and, though damage may have been done by wind, I am confident none can be done by water or waves."

## HOW THE HURRICANE ORIGINATED

Storms which move with the velocity of that which swept Galveston and which are common to the southern and southeastern coasts of the United States invariably originate, according to Weather Forecaster H. J. Cox of the United States Weather Bureau at Chicago, in "the doldrums," or that region in the ocean where calms abound. In this particular instance the place was south of the West Indies and north of the equator. The region of the doldrums varies in breadth from sixty to several hundred miles, and at different seasons shifts its extreme limits between 5 degrees south and 15 degrees north. It is always overhung by a belt of clouds which is gathered by opposing currents of the trade winds.

"The storm which swept Galveston and the surrounding country, I should say, originated at a considerable distance south of the West Indies, in this belt of calms," said Forecaster Cox the Monday night following the catastrophe.

"It was caused by two strong currents meeting at an angle, and this caused the whirling motion which finally spent its force on the coast of Texas. It is seldom that a storm originating in the doldrums moves so far inland as did this one, but it is not, however, unprecedented. The reason this storm reached so far as Galveston was that the northwesterly wind moved about twice as fast as it usually does before reaching land. Usually the force of these winds are spent on the coast of Florida and sometimes they reach as far north as North Carolina. When they strike the land at these points they are given a northeasterly direction.

"This storm missed the eastern coast of the United States, and consequently was deflected to the west. Thunderstorms are prevailing in Kansas and all of the districts just north of the course of the storm, which is the natural result after such commotion of the elements. The conditions of the land are such about Galveston that when the storm reached that far it had no possible means of escape, and hence the dire results. If there had been a chance for the wind to move further west along the coast it would in all probability have passed Galveston, giving the place no more than a severe shaking up. In this event the worst effect would in all probability have been felt on the eastern coast of Mexico."

It was an absolute impossibility for anyone to form an idea of the extent and magnitude of the disaster within a week of its occurrence. The morning of Sunday, when the wind and the waves had subsided, the streets of the city were found clogged with debris of all sorts. The people of Galveston could not fully realize for several days what had happened. Four thousand houses had been entirely demolished and hardly a building in the city was fit for habitation.

The people were apathetic. They wandered around the streets in an aimless sort of way, unable to do anything or make preparations to repair the great damage done. The Monday following the catastrophe, Galveston was practically in the hands of thieves, thugs, ghouls, vampires, and bandits (some of them women) who robbed the dead, mutilated the corpses which were lying everywhere, ransacked business houses and residences and created a reign of terror which lasted until the officers in command of the force of regulars stationed at the beach barracks sent a company of men to patrol the streets. The governor of the state ordered out all the regiments of the National Guard and various associations of businessmen also equipped men to assist the soldiers in doing patrol duty in the city and suburbs.

The depredations of the lawless element were of an inconceivably brutal character. Unprotected women, whether found upon the streets or in their houses, were subjected to outrage or assault and robbed of their clothing and jewelry. Pedestrians were held up on the public thoroughfare in broad daylight and compelled to give up all valuables in their possession. The bodies of the dead were despoiled of everything and, in their haste to secure valuables, the ghouls would mutilate the corpses, cutting off fingers to obtain the rings thereon and amputating the ears of the women to get the earrings worn therein.

The majority of the thieves and vampires were residents of the city of Galveston and were reinforced by desperadoes from outside towns like Houston, Austin, and New Orleans, who took advantage of the rush to the city immediately after the disaster, obtaining free transportation on the railroad and steamers upon a pretense that they were going to Galveston for the purpose of working with relief parties and the gangs assigned for burial of the dead. Their outrages became so flagrant and the people of the city became so terrified that the city authorities were unable to cope with them, most of the officers of the police department having been victims of the flood. So an appeal was made to the governor to send state troops and procure the preservation of order. Captain Rafferty, commanding Battery O of the First Regiment of Artillery, U. S. A., was also implored to lend his aid in putting down the lawless bands, and he accordingly sent all the men in his command who had not met death in the gale.

There was some delay in getting the state troops to Galveston because so many miles of railroad had been washed away. The Adjutant General was compelled to notify some companies of militia by courier, but Captain Rafferty ordered his men on duty at once, with instructions to promptly shoot all persons found despoiling the dead. Most of the vampires were negroes. Some of them, however, were white women, the latter being as savage and merciless in their treatment of the dead as the most abandoned of their male companions. The regulars were put on duty on Tuesday night and, before morning, had shot several of the thugs, who were executed on the spot when found in the act of robbery. In every instance the pockets of the harpies slain by the United States troops were found filled with jewelry and other valuables, and in some cases, notably that of one negro, rings were found in their possession which had been cut from the hands of the dead, the vampires being in such a hurry that they could not wait to tear the rings off. On Wednesday evening the government troops came across a gang of fifty desperadoes, who were despoiling the bodies of the dead found enmeshed in the debris of a large apartment house. With commendable promptness the regulars put the ghouls under arrest and, finding the proceeds of their robberies in their possession, lined them up against a brick wall and without ceremony shot every one of them. In cases where the villains were not killed at the first fire, the sergeant administered coup de grace. Many of the thugs begged piteously for mercy, but no attention was paid to their feelings and they suffered the same stern fate as the rest.

When the state troops arrived in the city they took the same severe measures and the result was that within forty-eight hours the city was as safe as it had ever been. The police arrested every suspicious character and the jail and cells at the police station were filled to overflowing. These people were deported as soon as possible and notified that if they returned they would be shot without warning. The temper of the citizens of Galveston was such that they would not tolerate those who were criminals or disinclined to work. Every able-bodied man in town was impressed for duty in relief and burial parties and whenever an individual refused to do the work required he was promptly shot. By Thursday morning all the men required had been obtained and relief and burial parties were filled to the quota deemed necessary. The work of disposing of the bodies of the dead, administering to the wants of the wounded and the clearing of the streets of the debris was proceeding satisfactorily.

The dead lay in the streets and vacant places in hundreds and the heat of the sun began to have its natural effect. Decomposition set in and the stench became unbearable. At first an effort was made to identify the corpses, but it was soon found to be an impractical task, as any delay in removing the dead imperilled the living. Fears entertained in regard to pestilence were speedily verified and the people of the city were taken ill by scores. It was difficult to obtain men to perform the duty of burying the bloated corpses of the victims of the catastrophe and consequently the city

authorities ordered that the dead be loaded on barges,
taken a few miles out to sea, weighted and thrown into the
water. The ground had become so watersoaked that it was
impossible to dig graves or trenches for the reception of
the bodies, although in many instances people buried relatives and friends in their yards and the ground surrounding
their residence. Along the beach hundreds of corpses were
buried in the sand, but the majority of the burials were at
sea. By Wednesday night 2,500 bodies had been cast into
the water, while about 500 had been interred within the city
limits. Precautions were taken, however, to mark the graves
and when the ground had dried sufficiently the bodies were
disinterred and taken to the various cemeteries where, after
burial, suitable memorials were erected to mark their last
resting place. No attempts were made at identification after
Wednesday, lists being simply made of the number of victims. The graves of those buried in the sand were marked by
head boards with the inscriptions, "White man, aged forty,"
"White woman, aged twenty-five," and "male" or "female"
child, as the case might be.

So accustomed did the burial parties become to the handling of the dead that they treated the bodies as though they
were merely carcasses of animals and not bodies of human
beings and they were dumped into the trenches prepared
for their reception without ceremony of any kind. The ex-
cavations were then filled up as hurriedly as possible, the
sand being packed down tightly. This might have seemed
inhuman, unfeeling, and brutal, but the exigencies of the
situation demanded that the corpses be put out of the way as
speedily as possible.

Great difficulty was experienced in securing men to transport bodies to the wharves where the barges lay, and it was
practically impossible to get anyone to touch the bodies of
the negro victims, decomposition having set in earlier than
in the cases of the whites. Had it not been that the members of
the fire department volunteered their services, the remains
of the negroes would have remained unburied for a longer

time than they were. Finally, however, patience ceased to be a virtue and orders were given the guards to shoot any man who refused to do his duty under the circumstances. The result of this was that beginning on Wednesday there was less delay in the matter of disposing of the dead. However, in spite of the activity of the burial parties, the work of clearing the streets of corpses was a most tedious one.

## FORECAST OFFICIALS REPORT ON THE STORM

The forecast official of the United States Weather Bureau at Galveston made the following report, September 14, on the storm:

"The local office of the United States weather bureau received the first message in regard to this storm at 4 p. m., September 4. It was then moving northward over Cuba. Each day thereafter, until the West India hurricane struck Galveston, bulletins were posted by the United States weather bureau officials giving the progressive movements of the disturbance.

"September 6 the tropical storm had moved up over southern Florida, thence it changed its course and moved westward in the gulf and was central off the Louisiana coast the morning of the 7th, when northwest storm warnings were ordered up for Galveston. The morning of the 8th the storm had increased in energy and was still moving westward, and at 10:10 a. m. the northwest storm warnings were changed to northeast. Then was when the entire island was in apparent danger. The telephone at the United States weather bureau office was busy until the wires went down; many could not get the use of the telephone on account of the line being busy. People came to the office in droves inquiring about the weather. About the same time the following information was given to all alike:

" 'The tropical storm is now in the gulf, south or southwest of us; the winds will shift to the northeast-east and probably to the southeast by morning, increasing in energy. If you reside in low parts of the city, move to higher grounds.'"

"Prepare for the worst, which is yet to come," were the only consoling words of the weather bureau officials at Galveston from morning until night of the 8th, when no information further could be given out.

The local forecast official and one observer stayed at the office throughout the entire storm, although the building was wrecked. The forecast official and one observer were out taking tide observations about 4 a. m., September 9. Another observer left after he had sent the last telegram which could be gotten off, filed at Houston over the telephone wires about 4 p. m. of the 8th. Over half the city was covered with tide water by 3 p. m. One of the observers left for home at about 4 p. m., after he had done all he could, as telephone wires were then going down. The entire city was then covered with water from one to five feet deep. On his way home he saw hundreds of people and he informed all he could that the worst was still to come, and to the people who could not hear his voice on account of the distance he motioned for them to go downtown.

The lowest barometer by observation was 28.53 inches at 8:10 p. m., September 8, but the barometer went slightly lower than this, according to the barograph. The tide at about 8 p. m. stood from six to fifteen feet deep throughout the city, with the wind blowing slightly over a hundred miles an hour. The highest wind velocity by the anemometer was ninety-six miles from the northeast at 5:15 p. m., and the extreme velocity was a hundred miles an hour at about that time. The anemometer blew down at this time and the wind was still higher later, when it shifted to the east and southeast, when the observer estimated that it blew a gale of between 110 and 120 miles. There was an apparent tidal wave of from four to six feet about 8 p. m., when the wind shifted to the east and southeast, that carried off many houses which had stood the tide up to that time.

The observer believed from the records he managed to save that the hurricane moved inland near Galveston, going up the Brazos Valley.

The warnings of the United States Weather Bureau were the means of thousands of lives being saved through the hurricane. It was so severe, however, that it was impossible to fully prepare for such destruction. The observer of the United States Weather Bureau at Galveston, to relieve apprehension, stated on September 14 that the barometer had gone up to about the normal, and there were no indications of another storm following.

# CHAPTER TWO:
## THE AFTERMATH

The surviving people of Galveston did not awaken from sleep on Sunday morning, for they had not slept the night before. For many weary hours they had stood face to face with death, and knew that thousands had yielded up their lives and that millions of dollars worth of property had been destroyed.

There was not a building in Galveston which was not either entirely destroyed or damaged, and the people of the city lived in the valley of the shadow of death, helpless and hopeless, deprived of all hope and ambition—merely waiting for the appearance of the official death roll.

Confusion and chaos reigned everywhere; death and desolation were on all sides; wreck and ruin were the only things visible wherever the eye might rest; and with business entirely suspended and no other occupation than the search for and burial of the dead it was strange that the thoroughfares and residence streets were not filled with insane victims of the hurricane's frightful visit.

For days prior to the storm's arrival, the people of Galveston knew there was danger ahead. They were warned repeatedly, but they laughed at all fears, business went on as usual, and when the blow came it found the city unprepared and without safeguards.

Owing to the stupefaction following the awful catastrophe, the people were in no condition, either physical or mental, to provide for themselves, and therefore depended upon the outside world for food and clothing.

The inhabitants of Galveston needed immediate relief, but how they were to get it was a mystery, for Galveston was not yet in touch with the outside world by rail or sea. The city was sorely stricken, and appealed to the country at large to send food, clothing and water. The waterworks were in ruins and the cisterns all blown away, so that the lack of water was one of the most serious of the troubles.

Never did a storm work more cruelly. All the electric light and telegraph poles were prostrated and the streets were littered with timbers, slate, glass and every conceivable character of debris. There was hardly a habitable house in the entire city, and nearly every business house was either wrecked entirely or badly damaged.

On Monday there were deaths from hunger and exposure, and the list swelled rapidly. People were living as best they could—in the ruins of their homes, in hotels, in schoolhouses, in railway stations, in churches, in the streets by the sides of their beloved dead.

So great was the desolation one could not imagine a more sorrowful place. Street cars were not running; no trains could reach the town. Only sad-eyed men and women walked about the streets. The dead and wounded monopolized the attention of those capable of doing anything whatsoever, and the city was at the mercy of thieves and ruffians.

All the fine churches were in ruins. From Tremont to P Street, thence to the beach, not a vestige of a residence was to be seen. In the business section of the city the water was from three to ten feet deep in stores, and stocks of all kinds, including foodstuffs, were total losses. It was a common spectacle—that of inhabitants of the fated city wandering around in a forsaken and forlorn way, indifferent to everything around them and paying no attention to inquiries of friends and relatives. God forbid that such scenes are enacted again in this country.

It was thought the vengeance of the fates had been visited in its most appalling shape upon the place which had unwittingly incurred its wrath. It was fortunate after all, however, that those compelled to endure such trials were temporarily deprived of their understanding. They were so stunned that they could not appreciate the enormity of the punishment.

The first loss of life reported was at Bietter's saloon, in the Strand, where three of the most prominent citizens of the town—Stanley G. Spencer, Charles Kellner and Richard

Lord—lost their lives and many others were maimed and imprisoned. These three were sitting at a table on the first floor Saturday night, making light of the danger, when the roof suddenly caved in and came down with a crash, killing them. Those in the lower part of the building escaped with their lives in a miraculous manner, as the falling roof and flooring caught on the bar, enabling the people standing near it to crawl under the debris. It required several hours of hard work to get them out. The negro waiter who was sent for a doctor was drowned at Strand and Twenty-first Streets, and his body was found a short time afterward.

Fully 700 people were congregated at the city hall, most of them more or less injured in various ways. One man from Lucas Terrace reported the loss of fifty lives in the building from which he escaped. He himself was severely injured about the head.

Passing along Tremont Street, out as far as Avenue P, climbing over the piles of lumber which had once been residences, four bodies were observed in one yard and seven in one room in another place, while as many as sixty corpses were seen lying singly and in groups in the space of one block. A majority of the drowned, however, were under the ruined houses. The body of Miss Sarah Summers was found near her home, corner of Tremont Street and Avenue F, her lips smiling, but her features set in death, her hands grasping her diamonds tightly. The remains of her sister, Mrs. Claude Fordtran, were never found.

The report from St. Mary's Infirmary showed that only eight persons escaped from that hospital. The number of patients and nurses was one hundred. Rosenberg Schoolhouse, chosen as a place of refuge by the people of that locality, collapsed. Few of those who had taken refuge there escaped—how many cannot be told, and will never be known.

Never before had the Sabbath sun risen upon such a sight and, as though unable to endure it, the god of the day soon veiled his face behind dull and leaden clouds, and refused to

shine. Surely it was enough to draw tears even from inani-
mate things.

At the Union Depot, Baggagemaster Harding picked up
the lifeless form of a baby girl within a few feet of the station.
Her parents were among the lost. The station building was
selected as a place of refuge by hundreds of people although
all the windows and a portion of the south wall at the top
were blown in. The occupants expected every moment to be
their last and escape was impossible, for about the building
the water was fully twelve feet deep. A couple of small shan-
ties were floating about, but there was no means of making
a raft or getting a boat.

Every available building in the city was used as a hospital.
As for the dead, they were being put away, anywhere. In one
large grocery store on Tremont Street, all the space that
could be cleared was occupied by the wounded.

It was nothing strange to see the dead and crippled everywhere, and the living were so fascinated by the dead they
could hardly be dragged away from the spots where the
corpses were piled. There were dead by the score, by the
hundreds and by the thousands. It was a city of the dead; a
vast battlefield, the slain being victims of flood and gale. The
dead were at rest, but the living had to suffer, for no aid was
at hand.

In the business portion of the town the damage could not
be even approximately estimated. The wholesale houses
along the Strand had about seven feet of water on their
ground floors, and all window panes and glass protectors of
all kinds were demolished. On Mechanic Street, the water
was almost as deep as on the Strand. All provisions in the
wholesale groceries and goods on the lower floors were
saturated and rendered valueless.

In clearing away the ruins of the Catholic Orphans' Home
heartrending evidence of the heroism and love of the Sisters
was discovered. Bodies of the little folks were found which
indicated by their position that heroic measures were taken
to keep them together so that all might be saved.

The Sisters had tied them together in bunches of eight and then tied the cords around their own waists. In this way, they probably hoped to quiet the children's fears and lead them to safety. The storm struck the Home with such terrific force that the structure fell, carrying the inmates with it and burying them under tons of debris. Two crowds of children, tied and attached to Sisters, have been found. In one heap the children were piled on the Sisters, and the arms of one little girl were clasped around a Sister's neck. In the wreck of the Home over ninety children and Sisters were killed. It was first believed that they had been washed out to sea, but the discovery of the little groups in the ruins indicates that all were killed and buried under the wreckage.

Sunday and Monday were days of the greatest suffering, although the population had hardly sufficiently recovered from the shock of the mighty calamity to realize that they were hungry and cold. On Monday all relief trains sent from other cities toward Galveston were forced to turn back, since the tracks had been washed away.

On Tuesday Mayor Jones of Galveston sent out the following appeal to the country:

> It is my opinion, based on personal information, that 5,000 people have lost their lives here. Approximately one-third of the residence portion of the city has been swept away. There are several thousand people who are homeless and destitute—how many there is no way of finding out. Arrangements are now being made to have the women and children sent to Houston and other places, but the means of transportation are limited. Thousands are still to be cared for here. We appeal to you for immediate aid.
>
> WALTER J. JONES,
> Mayor of Galveston

Some relief had been sent in with the railroad to Texas City, six miles away, having been repaired, boats taking the supplies from that point into Galveston.

Food and women's clothing were the things most needed just then. While the men could get along with the clothes they had on and what they had secured since Sunday, the women suffered considerably and there was much sickness among them in consequence. It was noticeable, however, that the women of the city had, by their example, been instrumental in reviving the drooping spirits of the men. There was a better feeling prevalent Tuesday among the inhabitants, as news had been received that within a few days the acute distress would be over, except in the matter of shelter. Every house standing was damp and unhealthy, and some of the wounded were not getting along as well as hoped. Many of the injured had been sent out of town to Texas City, Houston and other places, but hundreds still remained. It would have endangered their lives to move them.

Tuesday night ninety negro looters were shot in their tracks by citizen guards. One of them was searched and $700 found, together with four diamond rings and two water-soaked gold watches. The finger of a white woman with a gold band around it was clutched in his hands.

In the afternoon, at the suggestion of Colonel Hawley, a mounted squad of nineteen men, under Adjutant Brokridge, was detailed by Major Faylings to search a house where negro looters were known to have secreted plunder.

"Shoot them in their tracks, boys! We want no prisoners," said the Major. The plunderers changed their location before the arrival of the detachment, however, and the raiders came back empty-handed. Twenty cases of looting were reported between 3 and 6 in the evening.

At 6 o'clock a report reached Major Faylings that twenty negroes were robbing a house at Nineteenth and Beach Streets. "Plant them," commanded the young Major, as a half dozen citizen soldiers, led by a corporal, mustered before him for orders. "I want every one of those twenty negroes, dead or alive," said the Major. The squad left on the double quick. Half an hour later they reported ten of the plunderers killed.

The following order was posted on the streets at noon on Tuesday:

> To the Public: The city of Galveston being under martial law, and all good citizens being now enrolled in some branch of the public service, it becomes necessary, to preserve the peace, that all arms in this city be placed in the hands of the military. All good citizens are forbidden to carry arms, except by written permission from the Mayor or Chief of Police or the Major commanding. All good citizens are hereby commanded to deliver all arms and ammunition to the city and take Major Faylings' receipt.
>
> WALTER J. JONES,<br>Mayor of Galveston

### What a Relief Party Saw Sunday Morning

Starting as soon as the water began to recede Sunday morning, a relief party began the work of rescuing the wounded and dying from the ruins of their homes. The scenes presented were almost beyond description. Screaming women, bruised and bleeding, some of them bearing the lifeless forms of children in their arms; men, broken-hearted and sobbing, bewailing the loss of their wives and children. The streets filled with floating rubbish, among which there were many bodies of the victims of the storm, constituted part of the awful picture. In every direction, as far as the eye could reach, the scene of desolation and destruction continued.

It was certainly enough to cause the stoutest heart to quail and grow sick, and yet the searchers well knew they could not unveil even a fraction of the misery the destructive elements had brought about. They knew, also, that the full import and heaviness of the blow would not be realized for days to come.

Although those in the relief party were prepared to see the natural evidences following upon the heels of the mighty storm, they did not anticipate such frightful revelations. It was a butchery, without precedent, a gathering of victims that was so ghastly for any man to have imagined. As the party went on, the members met others who made reports of things that had come under their notice.

There were fifty killed or drowned in one section of town; one hundred in another; five hundred in another. The list grew larger with each report. It was a matter of wonder, and increasing wonder, too, that a single soul escaped to tell the tale.

No one seemed entirely sane, for there was madness in the very air. All moved in an atmosphere of gloom; it was difficult to move and breathe with so much death on all sides. Yet no one could keep his eyes off of those horrible, fascinating corpses. They riveted the gaze. Life and death were often so closely intermingled they could not be told apart. It was the apotheosis of the frightful.

Those who had escaped the hurricane and flood were searching for missing dear ones in such a listless way as to irresistibly convey the idea that they did not care whether they found them or not. It was the languor of hopelessness and despair. Some of those who had lost their all were even merry, but it was the glee of insanity.

As Sunday morning dawned the streets were lined with people, half-clad, crippled in every conceivable manner, hobbling as best they could to where they could receive attention of physicians for themselves and summon aid for friends and relatives who could not move.

Police Officer John Bowie, who had recently been awarded a prize as the most popular officer in the city, was in a pitiable condition; the toes on both of his feet were broken, two ribs caved in, and his head badly bruised, but his own condition, he said, was nothing. "My house, with wife and children, is in the gulf. I have not a thing on earth for which to live."

The houses of all prominent citizens which escaped destruction were turned into hospitals, as were also the leading hotels. There was scarcely one of the houses left standing which did not contain one or more of the dead as well as many injured.

The rain began to pour down in torrents and the relief party went back down Tremont Street toward the city. The misery of the poor people, all mangled and hurt, pressing to the city for medical attention, was greatly augmented by this rain. Stopping at a small grocery store to avoid the rain, the party found it packed with injured. The provisions in the store had been ruined and there was nothing for the numerous customers who came hungry and tired. The place was a hospital, no longer a store.

Further down the street a restaurant, which had been submerged by water, was serving out soggy crackers and cheese to the hungry crowd. That was all that was left. The food was soaked full of water, and the people who were fortunate enough to get those sandwiches were hungry and made no complaint.

It was hard to determine what section of the city suffered the greatest damage and loss of life. Information from both the extreme eastern and extreme western portions of the city was difficult to obtain at that time. In fact, it was nearly impossible, but the reports received indicated that those two sections had suffered the same fate as the rest of the city and to a greater degree.

Thus the relief party wended its way through streets which, but a few hours before, were teeming with life. Now they were the thoroughfares of death. It did not seem as if they could ever resound to the throb of quickened vitality again. It seemed as though it would take years to even remove the wreckage. As to rebuilding, it appeared as the work of ages. Annihilation was everywhere.

## GALVESTON PEOPLE REFUSED TO HEED THE WARNING WHEN DISASTER WAS PREDICTED

As marked out on the charts of the United States Weather Bureau at Washington the storm which struck Galveston had a peculiar course. It was first definitely located south by east of San Domingo, and the last day of August the center of the disturbance was approximately at a point fixed at 14 degrees north latitude and 68 degrees west longitude. From there it made a course almost due northeast, passing through Kingston, Jamaica, and if it had continued on this same line it would have struck Galveston just the same, but somewhat earlier than it did. The storm apparently was headed for Galveston all the time, but when it was almost due south of Cienfuegos, Cuba, it changed its course so as to go almost due north, across the Island of Cuba, through the toe of the Florida peninsula, and up the coast to the vicinity of Tampa. Here the storm made another sharp turn to the westward and headed again almost straight for Galveston.

It was this sharp turn to the westward which could not be anticipated, so the Weather Bureau sent out its hurricane signals both for the Atlantic and the gulf coast, well understanding that the prediction as to one of these coasts would certainly fail. As soon as the storm turned westward from below Tampa the Weather Bureau knew the Atlantic coast was safe, and turned its attention toward the gulf.

The people of Galveston had abundant warning of the coming of the hurricane, but, of course, could not anticipate the destructive energy it would gain on the way across the Gulf of Mexico.

The Weather Bureau was informed that the first sign of the disturbance was noticed on Aug. 30 near the Windward Islands. On Aug. 31 it still was in the same neighborhood. The storm did not develop any hurricane features during its slow passage through the Caribbean Sea and across Cuba, but was accompanied by tremendous rains. During the first twelve hours of Sept. 3, in Santiago, Cuba, 10.50 inches rain fell and 2.80 inches fell in the next twelve. On Sept. 4 the rainfall during twelve hours in Santiago was 4.44 inches, or a total fall in thirty-six hours of 17.20 inches. There were some high winds in Cuba the night of Sept. 4.

By the morning of the 6th the storm center was a short distance northwest of Key West, Fla., and the high winds had commenced over Southern Florida—forty-eight miles an hour from the east being reported from Jupiter and forty miles from the northeast from Key West. During the 6th, barometric conditions over the eastern portion of the United States changed as to prevent the movement of the storm along the Atlantic coast, and it, therefore, continued northwest over the Gulf of Mexico.

On the morning of the 7th it apparently was central-south of the Louisiana coast, about longitude 89, latitude 28. At this time storm signals were ordered up on the North Texas coast, and during the day were extended along the entire coast. On the morning of the 8th the storm was nearing the Texas coast and was apparently central at about latitude 28, longitude 94.

Galveston's disastrous storm was predicted with startling accuracy by the weather prophet, Prof. Andrew Jackson DeVoe. In the "Ladies' Birthday Almanac," issued from Chattanooga, Tenn., in January, 1900, Prof. DeVoe forecasts the weather for the following month of September as follows:

This will be a hot dry month over the Northern States, but plenty of rain over the Atlantic coast States. First and second days hot and sultry. Third and fourth heavy storms over the extreme Northwestern States, causing thunderstorms over the Missouri Valley and showery, rainy weather over the whole country from 5th to 8th. On the 9th a great cyclone will form over the Gulf of Mexico and move up the Atlantic coast, causing very heavy rains from Florida to Maine from 10th to 12th.

## GRUESOME SCENES AND HARROWING INCIDENTS

Gruesome scenes and soul-harrowing incidents of the time immediately following the great gale in Galveston were graphically portrayed in a letter from a young woman caught on the island in the awful storm. It was written by Miss Nellie Cary to her parents, who live at 5408 Lake Avenue, Chicago. Miss Cary had been home on a vacation for several weeks and left Chicago for Galveston the Tuesday evening before the hurricane, reaching the doomed city just in time to participate in the terrible experience. Her letter follows:

"Galveston, Wednesday, September 12—Dearest Parents: Have not had a minute to write and cannot collect my thoughts to tell you of the horrible disaster down here. Thousands of dead in the streets—the gulf and bay strewn with dead bodies. The whole island demolished. Not a drop of water—food scarce. If help does not reach us soon there will be great starvation for everybody.

"The dead are not being identified at all—they throw them on drays and take them to barges, where they are loaded like cordwood, and taken out to sea to be cast into the waves, now peaceful, which were so hungry for them in their anger.

"I was at the wharf this morning for a short time and saw three barges loaded with their gruesome freight. The bodies are frightful, every one nearly nude. God alone knows who they are.

"The bay is full of dead cattle and horses, together with human corpses, blistering in the hot sun. It will be impossible to remove the dead from the debris for weeks. The whole island is frightful. I saw thirty-eight bodies taken from one house. Everyone is striving to get the bodies buried for fear of the plague.

"I never expected to get out alive, but thank God, not one of us was killed. We were driven back to the stairs, and up, stair by stair, by the great waves. The wind was blowing over a hundred miles an hour, and the rain fell in torrents. Never shall I forget the sight as darkness settled upon us. I thought of you, papa and mamma, and prayed that you might be comforted. Our roof is now gone, the walls have fallen around us, but we still have a floor and—I can't tell you, it is too horrible.

"I was nearly drowned getting home from the office at 4 o'clock Saturday afternoon. Mrs. Whitman is almost crazy and is in a dangerous condition. I have lost everything; am now wearing clothes borrowed from those who were more fortunate. The stench is terrible.

"Thousands of horses and cattle without owners are in the most pitiable condition imaginable; not a drop of water for them to drink since Saturday morning. And the people—I wonder that everybody is not mad from the horrors. No account can exaggerate it. It is absolutely necessary that everybody in the United States do what they can.

"Nearly all our help at Clark & Courts are drowned—Mr. Hansinger, his whole family, our other bookkeeper and a number of the girls. The town is under martial law to protect it from the mob. Last night a negro was arrested with ten fingers in his pockets, with valuable rings on them. Mr. Fayling, at our house, is in command of the protective force. They have had to shoot many to keep the horrible ghouls in control. Eddie Rogers is next in command, and is doing noble work. I have done what I could to help the dying and wounded.

"We were on the highest point of ground in Galveston. That is all that saved us. For blocks and blocks, reaching into miles, not a house remains; not a building but is completely demolished—houses just torn board from board and piled up. I have climbed over wreckage forty feet high in the streets to get to places. I think we were more fortunate than any one else in town. I think not one was killed, though our escape was narrow. With the exception of Mrs. Whitman all were calm, though I reckon everybody quaked inside—I know I did.

"Thursday—Am well. Had something to eat this morning, and a little rainwater. Coffee is plenty, but water scarce.

Today the flesh slips off the bodies as they take hold to drag them from the ruins. They are piling them in great heaps now and burning them. The horrors multiply. I have seen men shot down in the streets by the soldiers. The stench is untold. Last night the awful smell kept us awake although we were utterly exhausted. It fills your throat and mouth, and makes your head ache so.

"The horrible experiences will take years to tell and more than a lifetime to forget. If you could be here you would feel that your anxiety was nothing. It is so pitiable to see husbands, with a look of despair in their eyes, searching for their wives and children; wives for their loved ones; and, most pitiable of all, the comparatively few children—although they are enough, God knows, to be left orphans and homeless—looking into everyone's face with frightened, appealing eyes. It is heartrending.

"Now I am much better off. I am safe, so please don't worry. I hope to hear from you soon. Best love and kisses to both from                                    —NELLIE"


## INHABITANTS DID NOT HEED PAST LESSONS

Although Galveston had been struck three times with floods and hurricanes even this experience was not enough to convince the residents that it might happen again. Only a few of the more cautious had any idea after the last disaster of taking steps to prevent its repetition. Asked if anything would be done to make future floods impossible they might probably quote the old saw: "Lightning never strikes in the same place twice," and seem to think that settled it. In the next sentence they would compare the damage done in the floods of 1875 and 1886 with this latest disaster.

"No," said E. M. Hartrick, assistant United States engineer, "the people of Galveston will go on living in fancied security just as they did before. The plan to put a dike around the city is perfectly feasible and so is a series of jetties. I think the good old Holland plan is the best. The city doesn't need to be raised. I was six years city engineer of Galveston, and following the storm of 1886 drew plans for a dike ten feet high and extending all around the island except on the north side. There the wharves were to be raised and form the dike.

"Galveston gave this plan consideration, and there is a map of the city in existence which shows it with a dike surrounding it. The legislature gave authority to bond the city, but it was some months after the flood when this had been secured, and the people said, 'Oh, we'll never get another one,' and they didn't build."

The construction by the government of two jetties, one eight miles long extending out southeast for the purpose of making a narrower and deeper channel for boats coming into Galveston harbor, made the necessity of remedial work more apparent, but nothing was done. In the last storm, the southwesterly one of the jetties pocketed the water and carried it up over the southeastern end of the island.

This was the place where whole blocks of buildings were literally washed away, leaving hardly enough of the foundations to indicate that buildings ever stood there. In that part of the city the water rose to a depth of fifteen feet in the streets. Had the houses demolished by waves and swept away by wind not formed into a great jam similar to a log jam, but extending along the south shore of the island for seven miles, this enormous body of water would have swept over the entire island and the number of dead would have been quadrupled.

"It formed a dike," said Engineer Hartrick, in calling attention to this feature of the flood, "and had it not been for that dike we might not any of us be here now."

According to Mr. Hartrick, Galveston had the wrong style of architecture for a gulf town. Its newer buildings were built on the northern plan with balloon frames, and poorly adapted to stand a blow.

"This storm was a hurricane," he said, "just such as they have in the West Indies every summer, but which we have here perhaps once in a hundred years. Still we never know when one may come again, and we should build our houses accordingly."

Colonel Davidson, a member of the relief committee, had given some time in the past to consideration of projects to prevent inundations. He favored the jetty system, but, like Engineer Hartrick, said nothing would ever be done.

"You never heard of a man wanting an umbrella when it wasn't raining, did you?" he asked. "What we want is not to keep all the water out. We want the waves to break their force before they rise on to the island. It was the force of the great waves which, wrecked the houses."

The work of extracting bodies from the mass of wreckage continued. Tuesday, September 18, over 400 bodies were taken out of the debris which lined the beach front. With all that had been done to recover bodies buried beneath or pinned to the immense drift, the work had scarcely started. There was no time to dig graves and the putrefying flesh, beaten and bruised beyond identification, was consigned to the flames. Volunteers for this gruesome work came in fast. Men who had avoided the dead under ordinary conditions were working with a vigorous will and energy in putting them away.

Under one pile of wreckage Tuesday afternoon twenty bodies were taken out and cremated. In another pile a man pulled out the remains of two children and for a moment gazed upon them, then mechanically cast them into the fire. They were his own flesh and blood. As they slowly burned he watched them until they were consumed, then resumed his work assisting others in removing other bodies.

A large force of men was still engaged in removing the dead from Kurd's Lane, located about four miles west of the city. At this point the water ran to a height of fourteen feet, and hung up in trees and fences were the bodies of men, women and children, which were being collected and cremated as fast as possible.

On the mainland the searching for and cremating of bodies that either perished or found lodgment there was being prosecuted vigorously.

The situation throughout the country extending from Bolivar to High island was possibly worse than in any other section of the mainland.

Clara Barton, president of the Red Cross Society, issued an appeal on September 18 to the American people for money and supplies for the sick and wounded. Her idea was to spend some of the money with local merchants wherever practicable.

Chairman Davidson of the relief committee stated that the greatest sufferers from the storm were the people of limited means who owned homes near the beach. There were hundreds of these people who owned mortgaged lots and had homes constructed by the loan companies and though their property was swept away the loan companies were protected by liens.

Mr. Davidson advised that a fund be raised for people who had suffered in this way, that they might be able to restore what took them years to accumulate and was taken from them in a single night.

The resources of the numerous sub-relief stations scattered throughout the city were taxed to their utmost capacity, and long lines of people awaited their turns for provisions and clothing.

At Texas City a force of deputy United States marshals under Marshal Grant was guarding the entrance to Galveston and keeping back all people who could show no good reason for desiring to go there. People were daily leaving the city, a majority being women and children. The city was still under martial law, and remained so for weeks. Idlers and sightseers who eluded the guards on the mainland upon their arrival were pressed into the street service. There was no place for a man who would not work. It was work or go to jail, and they generally went to jail.

## SAD SIGHTS AT VIRGINIA POINT

When the relief train reached Virginia Point, which is on the mainland, opposite Galveston, it was found that of those who survived the flood and hurricane the majority was severely injured. Most of them were bruised and maimed, presenting a pitiful sight, their limbs lacerated and bleeding. All bemoaned the fate of those dear to them.

Many of the dead—and the beach was strewn with corpses—had their faces and heads mutilated so that it was almost impossible to learn the names of those who found their last resting place in the crude graves hurriedly dug. A headboard was placed on the grave in every instance, giving as nearly as possible age and accurate description. It was found necessary in many instances to bury three and four in one grave.

Those who survived the wreck were homeless and had had nothing to eat since Saturday. As most of them were injured it was not possible for them to organize a movement on their part. Life sustenance was furnished these survivors in order that they might not swell the list of dead.

Most of the bodies found in and around the vicinity of Virginia Point were supposed to have been washed inland from Galveston.

## HOUSTON ACCEPTS GALVESTON REFUGEES

Houston was the great rendezvous for supplies sent to Galveston, and they poured in there by the carload, beginning on Tuesday. The response to the appeal for aid by the people of Galveston, on the part of the United States and, in fact, every country in the world, was prompt and generous.

That relief was an absolute necessity was made apparent from the appearance of the refugees who began to flock into Houston as soon as the boats began to run to Galveston after the catastrophe. In addition to these, thousands of strangers arrived also, and the Houston authorities were at a loss as to what to do with them. Some of these visitors were from points far distant, who had relatives in the storm-stricken district, and had come to learn the worst regarding them; others had come to volunteer their services in the relief work, but the greatest number consisted of curious sightseers, almost frantic in their efforts to get to the stricken city and feast their eyes on the sickening, repulsive and disease-breeding scenes. In addition there were hundreds of the sufferers themselves, who had been brought out of their misery to be cared for here.

The question of caring for these crowds came up at a mass meeting of the Houston general relief committee held Monday. Every incoming train brought scores more of people, and immediate action was necessary. It was decided finally to pitch tents in Emancipation Park, and there as many of the strangers as possible were cared for. The hotels could not accommodate one-tenth of them.

First attention, naturally, was given the survivors of the storm. Mayor Brashear sent word to Mayor Jones of Galveston that all persons, no matter who they were, rich or poor, ill or well, should be sent to Houston as soon as possible. They would be well provided for, he said. The urgency of his message for the depopulation of Galveston, he explained, was that until sanitation could be restored in the wrecked city everybody possible should be sent away.

It was estimated that nearly 1,000 of the unfortunate survivors were sent to Houston on Tuesday from Galveston in response to Mayor Brashear's request. Every building in Houston at all habitable was opened to them, and all the seriously ill comfortably housed. The others were made as comfortable as possible, but it was not only food and clothing that was wanted; the only relief some of them sought could not be furnished. They were grieving for lost ones left behind—fathers, mothers, sisters, wives and children. Nearly everybody had some relative missing, but few of them were certain whether they were dead or alive. All, however, were convinced that their loved ones were dead.

Men, bareheaded and barefooted, with sunken cheeks and hollow eyes; women and children with tattered clothing and bruised arms and faces, and mere infants with bare feet bruised and swollen were among the crowds seen on the streets of Houston. Women of wealth and refinement, with hatless heads and gowns of rich material torn into shreds, were among the refugees. At times a man and his wife, and sometimes with one or two children, could be seen together, but such sights were infrequent, for nearly all who went to Houston had suffered the loss of one or more of their loved ones.

But with all this suffering there was a marvelous amount of heroism shown. Just a week before, most of these people had happy homes and their families were around them. The Tuesday following the disaster they were homeless, penniless and with nothing to look forward to. Yet there was scarcely any whimpering or complaining. They walked about the streets as if in a trance; they accepted the assistance offered them with heartfelt thanks, and apparently were greatly relieved at being away from the scenes of sorrow and woe at home. They were all made to feel at home in Houston, and that they were welcome and that everything in the power of the people of Houston would be done for their comfort and welfare, and yet they seemed not to understand half that was said to them.

John J. Moody, a member of the committee sent from Houston to take charge of the relief station at Texas City, reported to the Mayor of Houston on Tuesday as follows:

> To the Mayor—Sir: On arriving at Lamarque this morning I was informed that the largest number of bodies was along the coast of Texas City. Fifty-six were buried yesterday and today within less than two miles, extending opposite this place and toward Virginia City. It is yet six miles farther to Virginia City, and the bodies are thicker where we are now than where they have been buried. A citizen inspecting in

the opposite direction reports dead bodies thick for twenty miles.

The residents of this place have lost all—not a habitable building left, and they have been too busy disposing of the dead to look after personal affairs. Those who have anything left are giving it to the others, and yet there is real suffering. I have given away nearly all the bread I bought for our own use to hungry children.

A number of helpless women and beggared children were landed here from Galveston this afternoon and no place to go and not a bite to eat. Tomorrow others are expected from the same place. Every ten feet along the wreck-lined coast tells of acts of vandalism; not a trunk, valise or tool chest but what has been rifled. We buried a woman this afternoon whose finger bore the mark of a recently removed ring.

The United States government furnished several thousand tents for the Houston camp, which was under the supervision of the United States Marine Hospital authorities.

## Twenty-Eight Regulars Drowned

General McKibbin, who was sent to Galveston by the War Department to investigate the conditions prevailing there, made the following official report on Wednesday, September 12:

Houston, Texas, September 12, 1900—Adjutant-General, Washington—Arrived at Galveston at 6 p.m., having been ferried across bay in a yawl boat. It is impossible to adequately describe the condition existing. The storm began about 9 a.m. Saturday and continued with constantly increasing violence until after midnight. The island was inundated; the height of the tide was from eleven to thirteen feet. The wind was a cyclone. With few exceptions, every building in the city is injured. Hundreds are entirely destroyed.

All the fortifications except the rapid-fire battery at San Jacinto are practically destroyed. At San Jacinto every building except the quarantine station has been swept away. Battery O, First Artillery, United States Army, lost twenty-eight men. The officers and their families were all saved. Three members of the hospital corps lost. Names will be sent as soon as possible. Loss of life on the island is possibly more than 1,000. All bridges are gone, waterworks destroyed and all telegraph lines are down.

Colonel Roberts was in the city and made every effort to get telegrams through. City under control of committee of citizens and perfectly quiet.

Every article of equipment or property pertaining to Battery O was lost. Not a record of any kind is left. The men saved had nothing but the clothing on their persons. Nearly all are without shoes or clothing other than their shirts and trousers. Clothing necessary has been purchased and temporary arrangements made for food and shelter. There are probably 5,000 citizens homeless and absolutely destitute, who must be clothed, sheltered and fed. Have ordered 20,000 rations and tents for 1,000 people from Sam Houston. Have wired Commissary-General to ship 30,000 rations by express. Lieutenant Perry will make his way back to Houston and send this telegram. McKIBBIN

CONDITION OF THE GOVERNMENT WORKS

Captain Charles S. Riche, U. S. A., corps of engineers, when seen after he had completed a tour of inspection of the government works around Galveston, made the following statement:

The jetties are sunk nearly to mean low tide level, but not seriously breached. The channel is as good as before, perhaps better, twenty-five feet certainly.

Fort Crockett, fifteen-pounder implacements, concrete all right, standing on filling; water underneath. Battery for eight mortars about like preceding, and mortars and carriages on hand unmounted and in good shape. Shoreline at Fort Crockett has moved back about 600 feet. At Fort San Jacinto the battery for eight twelve-inch mortars is badly wrecked, and magazines reported fallen in. The mortars are reported safe. No piling was under this battery. Some of the sand parapet is left. The battery for two ten-inch guns badly wrecked. Both gun platforms are down and guns leaning. The battery for two 4.7-inch rapid-fire guns, concrete standing upon piling, both guns apparently all right. The battery for two fifteen-pounder guns, concrete apparently all right, standing on piling.

Fort Travis, Bolivar Point—Battery for three fifteen-pounder guns, concrete intact, standing on piling. East gun down. Western gun probably all right. The shoreline has moved back about 1,000 feet on the line of the rear of these batteries.

Under the engineers' corps are the fortifications, built at a considerable expense; also the harbor improvements, upon which more than $8,000,000 had been expended.

## FEARED THE CITY WAS BEYOND REPAIR

"I fear Galveston is destroyed beyond its ability to recover," is the manner in which Quartermaster Baxter concluded his report, made September 12, to the War Department at Washington. He recommended the continuance of his office only long enough to recover the office safes and close up accounts, and declared all government works were wrecked so restoration was impossible.

This gloomy prophecy for the city's future was reflected in an official report to Governor Sayers of Texas, by ex-State Treasurer Wortham, who spent a day at Galveston, investigating the situation. His statement claimed that 75 per cent of the city was demolished and gives little hope for rebuilding.

Mr. Wortham, who acted as aid to Adjutant-General Scurry, Texas National Guard, during the inquiry, said in his report:

The situation at Galveston beggars description. I am convinced that the city is practically wrecked for all time to come.

Fully 75 per cent of the business of the town is irreparably wrecked, and the same per cent of damage is to be found in the residence district. Along the wharf front great ocean steamers have bodily bumped themselves on the big piers and lie there, great masses of iron and wood, that even fire cannot totally destroy. The great warehouses along the water front are smashed in on one side, unroofed and gutted throughout their length, their contents either piled in heaps on the wharves or along the streets. Small tugs and sailboats have jammed themselves half into the buildings, where they were landed by the incoming waves, and left by the receding waters. Houses are packed and jammed in great confusing masses in all of the streets.

Great piles of human bodies, dead animals, rotting vegetation, household furniture, and fragments of the houses themselves are piled in confused heaps right in the main streets of the city. Along the gulf front human bodies are floating around like cordwood. Intermingled with them are to be found the carcasses of horses, chickens, dogs, and rotting vegetable matter. Above all arises the foulest stench that ever emanated from any cesspool, absolutely sickening in its intensity and most dangerous to health in its effects.

Along the Strand adjacent to the gulf front, where are located all the big wholesale warehouses and stores, the situation is even worse. Great stores of fresh vegetation have been invaded by the incoming waters, and are now turned into garbage piles of most befouling odors. The gulf waters while on the land played at will with everything, smashing in doors of stores, depositing bodies of humans where they pleased, and then receded, leaving the wreckage to tell its own tale of how the work had been done. As a result, the great warehouses are tombs, wherein are to be found the dead bodies of human beings and carcasses, almost defying the efforts of relief parties.

In the pile of debris along the street, in the water, and scattered throughout the residence portion of the city, are to be found masses of wreckage, and in these great piles are to be found more human bodies and household furniture of every description.

Handsome pictures are seen lying alongside of the ice cream freezers and resting beside the nude figure of some man or woman. These great masses of debris are not confined to any one particular section of the city.

The waters of the gulf and the winds spared no one who was exposed. Whirling houses around in its grasp, the wind piled their shattered frames high in confusing masses and dumped their contents on top.

Men and women were thrown around like so many logs of wood and left to rot in the withering sun.

I believe that with the best exertions of the men it will require weeks to secure some semblance of physical order in the city, and it is doubtful even then if all the debris will be disposed of.

I never saw such a wreck in my life. From the gulf front to the center of the island, from the ocean back, the storm wave left death and destruction in its wake.

There is hardly a family on the island whose household is not short a member or more, and in some instances entire families have been washed away or killed. Hundreds who escaped from the waves did so only to become victims of a worse death by being crushed by falling buildings.

Down in the business portion of the city the foundations of great buildings have given way, carrying towering structures to their ruin. These ruins, falling across the streets, formed barricades on which gathered all the floating debris and many human bodies. Many of these bodies were stripped of their clothing by the force of the water and the wind, and there was nothing to protect them from the scorching sun, the millions of flies, and the rapid invasion of decomposition that set in.

Many of the bodies have decayed so rapidly that they could not be handled for burial.

Some of the most conservative men on the island place the loss of human beings at not less than 7,500 and possibly 10,000, while others say it will not exceed 5,000.

COAST CITIES NOT PROPERLY CONSTRUCTED

Chief Willis L. Moore, of the United States Weather Bureau at Washington, being asked his opinion of the idea of rebuilding Galveston on some other site, replied as follows:

Weather Bureau, U. S., Washington, D. C, September 13, 1900.

I should not advise the abandonment of the city of Galveston. It is true that tropical hurricanes sometimes move westward across the gulf and strike the Texas coast, but such movement is infrequent. Within the last thirty years no storm of like severity has touched any part of the coast of the United States. There are many points on both the Atlantic and gulf coasts, some of them occupied by cities the size of Galveston, that are equally exposed to the force of both wind and water, should a hurricane move in from the ocean or gulf and obtain the proper position relative to them. It would not be advisable to abandon these towns and cities merely because there is a remote probability that at some future time a hurricane may be the cause of great loss of life and property.

We have just passed through a summer that for sustained high temperature has no parallel within the

last thirty years. Records of low temperature, tor-
rential rains, and other meteorological phenomena
that have stood for twenty and thirty years are not
infrequently broken. There does not appear to be,
so far as we know, any law governing the occurrence
or recurrence of storms. The vortex of a hurricane is
comparatively narrow, at most not more than twenty
or thirty miles in width. It is only within the vortex
that such a great calamity as has befallen Galveston
can occur.

It would seem that, rather than abandon the city,
means should be adopted at Galveston and other
similarly exposed cities on the Atlantic and gulf
coasts to erect buildings only on heavy stone foundations that should have solid interiors of masonry
to a height of ten feet above mean sea level. Rigid
building regulations should allow no other structures erected for habitations in the future in any city
located at sea level and that is exposed to the direct
sweep of the sea.

But Galveston should take heart, as the chances are
that not once in a thousand years would she be so
terribly stricken, and high, solid foundations would
doubtless make her impregnable to loss of life by all
future storms.

WILLIS L. MOORE
Chief, U. S. Weather Bureau

## COURAGE OF GALVESTON'S BUSINESSMEN

The courage of Galveston's businessmen under the distress-ing conditions was shown by the utterances of Mr. Eustace Taylor, one of the best-known residents of that city, a cot-ton buyer known to the trade in all parts of the country. Mr. Taylor was asked on Thursday succeeding the flood for an opinion as to the future of Galveston. He said:

I think that what we have done here for the four days which have passed since the storm has been wonderful. It will take us two weeks before we can ascertain the actual commercial loss. But we are go-ing to straighten out everything. We are going to stay here and work it out. We will have a temporary wharf within thirty days, and with that we can resume busi-ness and handle the traffic through Galveston.

I think that within thirty or forty days business will be carried on in no less volume than before. I am go-ing to stand right up to Galveston.

If it costs me the last cent, I will stand up for Galves-ton. With our temporary wharf we shall put from 1,000 to 2,000 men at work loading vessels while we are waiting for the railroads to restore bridges and terminals on the island. We shall bring business by barges from Virginia Point and load in midstream. In this way we shall not only resume our commercial relations, but we shall be able to put the labor of the city at work.

This port holds the advantage over every other port of this country for accommodating 10,000,000 pro-ducers, and will accommodate millions of tons, and in inviting these millions, as we have, to continue their business through this port we must in our con-struction do it on the same lines employed by the communities of Boston, New York, Buffalo and Chicago, the stability of which was plainly illustrated in some structures recently erected in our community.

The port is all right. The ever-alert engineers in charge of the harbor here have already taken their soundings. The fullest depth of water remains. The jetties, with slight repair, are intact, and because of these conditions, which exist nowhere else for the territory and people it serves, the restoration will be more rapid than may be thought, and the flow of commerce will be as great, and for the courage and fortitude and foresight to look beyond the unhappy events of today, as prosperous and secure as in any part of our prosperous country.

## ELEVATORS & GRAIN NOT BADLY DAMAGED

J. C. Stewart, a well-known grain elevator builder, arrived at Galveston on Thursday, in response to a telegram from General Manager M. E. Bailey, of the Galveston Wharf Company. He at once made an inspection of the grain elevators and their contents, and then said not 2 per cent of the elevators had been damaged. The spouts were intact, and elevator "A" would be ready to deliver grain to ships the following Sunday.

The wheat in elevator "A" was loaded into vessels just as rapidly as they arrived at the elevator to take it. As soon as the elevator was emptied of its grain the wheat from elevator "Q" was transferred to it and loaded into ships. Very little of the wheat in elevator "B" had been injured, but the conveyors were swept away, and it was necessary to transfer the grain to elevator "A" in order to get it to the ships. Mr. Bailey put a large force of men to work clearing up such wharves, and the company was ready for new business along the line within eight days.

## BURNING BODIES BY THE HUNDREDS

Pestilence could only be avoided here by cremation. That was the order of the day. Human corpses, dead animals and all debris were therefore to be submitted to the flames. On Thursday upwards of 400 bodies, mostly women and children, were cremated, and the work went rapidly on. They were gathered in heaps of twenty and forty bodies, saturated with kerosene and the torch applied.

## CONFLICT OF AUTHORITY BREEDS TROUBLE

A conflict of authority, due to a misunderstanding, precipitated a temporary disorganization of the policing of the city of Galveston on Thursday. When General Scurry, Adjutant-General of the Texas National Guard, arrived at Galveston on Tuesday night, with about 200 militia from Houston, he at once conferred with the Chief of Police as to the plans for guarding property, protecting the lives of citizens and preserving law and order. An order was then issued by the Chief of Police to the effect that the soldiers should arrest all persons found carrying arms, unless they showed a written order, signed by the Chief of Police or Mayor of the city, giving them permission to go armed.

Sheriff Thomas had, meantime, appointed and sworn in 150 special deputy sheriffs. These deputies were supplied with a ribboned Badge of authority, but were not given any written or printed commission. Acting under the order issued by the Chief of Police, Major Hunt McCaleb of Galveston, who was appointed as aide to General Scurry, issued an order to the militia to arrest all persons carrying arms without the proper authority. The result was that about fifty citizens wearing deputy sheriff badges were taken into custody by the soldiers and taken to police headquarters. The soldiers had no way of knowing by what authority the men were acting with these badges and would listen to no excuses.

General Scurry and Sheriff Thomas, hearing of the wholesale arrests, called at police headquarters and consulted with Acting Chief Amundsen. The latter referred General Scurry to Mayor Jones. Then General Scurry and Sheriff Thomas held a conference at the City Hall. These two officers soon arrived at an understanding, and an agreement was decided upon to the effect that all persons deputized as deputy sheriffs and all persons appointed as special officers should be permitted to carry arms and pass in and out of the guard lines. General Scurry suggested that the deputy sheriffs and special police—and the regular police, for that matter—guard the city during the daytime and that the militia take charge of the city at night.

General Scurry was acting for and by authority granted by Mayor Jones, and promptly said he was there to work in harmony with the city and county authorities, and that there would be no conflict. When General Scurry and Sheriff Thomas called upon the Mayor, the Mayor said that he knew that if the Adjutant-General, the Chief of Police and the Sheriff would get together they could take care of the police work.

It was known that people were coming to Galveston by the score, that many of them had no business there, and that the city had enough to do to watch the lawless element of Galveston, without being burdened with the care of outsiders.

All deputy sheriffs wearing the badge issued by the Sheriff carried arms thereafter and made arrests, and were not interfered with in any way by the military guards.

## INADEQUATE TRANSPORTATION PREVENTS SUPPLIES FROM REACHING THE FAMINE-STRICKEN PEOPLE

On Thursday, September 13, trainload after trainload of provisions, clothing, disinfectants and medicines were lined up at Texas City, six miles from Galveston, all sent to the suffering survivors of the storm-swept city. Across the bay were thousands of people, friends of the dead and living, waiting for news of the missing ones and an opportunity to help, but only a meager amount of relief had at that time reached the stricken town. Two telegraph wires had been put up and partial communication restored to let the outside world know that conditions there were far more horrible than was at first supposed. That was about all. It was not that which was needed; it was just a more practicable connection with the mainland. True, more boats had been pressed into service to carry succor to the suffering and the suffering to succor, but they were few and small, and although working diligently night and day the service was inadequate in the extreme. And the people were still suffering—the sick dying for want of medicine and care; the well growing desperate and in many cases gradually losing their reason.

While there were many who could not be provided for because the necessary articles for them could not be carried in, there were hundreds who benefited. Those supplies which had arrived had been of great assistance, but they were far from ample to provide for even a small percentage of the sufferers, estimated at 30,000. Even the rich were hungry. An effort was being made on the part of the authorities to provide for those in the greatest need, but this was found to be difficult work, so many were there in sad condition. A rigid system of issuing supplies was established, and the regular soldiers and a number of citizens were sworn in as policemen. These attended to the issuing of rations as soon as the boats arrived.

Every effort was put forth to reach the dying first, but all sorts of obstacles were encountered, because many of them were so badly maimed and wounded that they were unable to apply to the relief committees, and the latter were so burdened by the great number of direct applications that they were unable to send out messengers.

The situation grew worse every minute; everything was needed for man and beast—disinfectants, prepared foods, hay, grain, and especially water and ice. Scores more of people died that day as a result of inattention and many more were on the verge of dissolution, for at best it was to be many days before a train could be run into the city, and the only hope was the arrival of more boats to transport the goods.

The relief committee held a meeting and decided that armed men were needed to assist in burying the dead and clearing the wreckage, and arrangements were made to fill this demand. There were plenty of volunteers for this work but an insufficiency of arms. The proposition of trying to pay for work was rejected by the committee, and it was decided to go ahead pressing men into service, issuing orders for rations only to those who worked or were unable to work.

Word was received that refugees would be carried from the city to Houston free of charge. An effort was made to induce all who are able to leave to go, because the danger of pestilence was frightfully apparent. There was any number willing to depart, and each outgoing boat, after having unloaded its provisions, was filled with people. The safety of the living was a paramount consideration, and the action of the railroads in offering to carry refugees free of charge greatly relieved the situation. The workers had their hands full in any event, and the nurses and physicians also. This unavoidable neglect often resulted in the death of many.

It was estimated $2,500,000 would be needed for the relief work. The banks of Galveston subscribed $10,000, but personal losses of the citizens of Galveston had been so large that very few were able to subscribe anything. The confiscation of all foodstuffs held by wholesale grocers and others was decided upon early in the day by the relief committee. Starvation would inevitably ensue unless the supply was dealt out with great care. All kerosene oil was gone, and the gas works and electric lights were destroyed. The committee asked for a shipload of kerosene oil, a shipload of drinking water and tons of disinfectants, such as lime and formaldehyde, for immediate use, and money and food next. Not a single tallow candle could be bought even with gold, or light of any kind procured.

No baker was making bread, and milk was remembered as a past luxury only. What was there to do with it? Everything was gone in the way of ovens and utensils. It was absolutely necessary to let the outside world know the true state of things. The city was unable to help itself. In fact, a great part of the mighty, noble state of Texas was prostrate. Even the country at large was paralyzed at the sense of the magnitude of the disaster, and was for the time being powerless to do anything. The entire world was thrilled with alarm, it being instinctively felt that the worst had not yet been made known.

Twenty-five thousand people had to be clothed and fed for many weeks, and many thousands supplied with household goods as well. Much money was required to make their residences even fit to live in. During the first few days after the disaster it was almost beyond possibility to make any estimate of the amount of money necessary to even temporarily relieve the sufferings of the unfortunate people.

As a means of enlightenment, Major K. G. Lowe, business manager of the *Galveston News*, was asked to send out a statement to the Associated Press, for dissemination throughout the globe, and he accordingly dispatched the following to Colonel Charles S. Diehl, General Manager of the Associated Press at the headquarters in Chicago:

> Galveston, Texas, Sept. 12— Charles S. Diehl, General Manager the Associated Press, Chicago
>
> A summary of the conditions prevailing at Galveston is more than human intellect can master. Briefly

stated, the damage to property is anywhere between
$15,000,000 and $20,000,000. The loss of life cannot be computed. No lists could be kept and all is
simply guesswork. Those thrown out to sea and
buried on the ground wherever found will reach the
horrible total of at least 3,000 souls.

My estimate of the loss on the island of the City of
Galveston and the immediate surrounding district
is between 4,000 and 5,000 deaths. I do not make
this statement in fright or excitement. The whole
story will never be told, because it cannot be told.
The necessities of those living are total. Not a single
individual escaped property loss. The property on
the island is wrecked; fully one-half totally swept out
of existence. What our needs are can be computed
by the world at large by the statement herewith submitted much better than I could possibly summarize
them. The help must be immediate.

R. G. LOWE
Manager, *Galveston News*

Thursday evening at the Tremont Hotel, in Galveston, occurred a wedding that was not attended with music and
flowers and a gathering of merrymaking friends and relatives.
On the contrary, it was peculiarly sad. Mrs. Brice Roberts
expected some day to marry Earnest Mayo; the storm which
desolated so many homes deprived her of almost everything
on earth—father, mother, sister and brother. She was left
destitute. Her sweetheart, too, was a sufferer. He lost many
of his possessions in Dickinson, but he stepped bravely forward and took his sweetheart to his home.

Galveston began, September 14, to emerge from the valley of the shadow of death into which she had been plunged
for nearly a week, and on that day, for the first time, actual
progress was made toward clearing up the city. The bodies
of those killed and drowned in the storm had for the most
part been disposed of. A large number was found when the

debris was removed from wrecked buildings, but on that date there were no corpses to be seen save those occasionally cast up by the sea. As far as sight, at least, was concerned, the city was cleared of its dead.

They had been burned, thrown into the water, buried—anything to get them quickly out of sight. The chief danger of pestilence was due almost entirely to the large number of unburied cattle lying upon the island, whose decomposing carcasses polluted the air to an almost unbearable extent. This, however, was not in the city proper, but was a condition prevailing on the outskirts of Galveston. One great trouble heretofore had been the inability to organize gangs of laborers for the purpose of clearing the streets.

## The Sad Situation
### Four Days After the Catastrophe

The situation in the stricken city on Wednesday, September 12, was horrible indeed. Men, women and children were dying for want of food and scores went insane from the terrible strain to which they had been subjected.

In his appeal to the country for aid, issued on Tuesday, September 11, Mayor Walter J. Jones said fully 5,000 people had lost their lives during the hurricane, this estimate being based upon personal information. Captain Charles Clarke, a vessel-owner of Galveston, and a reliable man, said the death list would be even greater than that, and he was backed in his opinion by several other conservative men who had no desire to exaggerate the losses, but felt that they are justified in letting the country know the full extent of the disaster in order that the necessary relief might be supplied.

It was the general opinion that to hide any of the facts would be criminal. Captain Clarke was not a sensationalist, but he well knew that the truth was what the people of the United States wanted at that time. If the people of the country at large felt they were being deceived in anything they would be apt to close their pocketbooks and refuse to give anything. If told the truth they would respond to the appeal for aid generously.

When relief finally began to pour in it was remarkable how soon the women of the city plucked up courage and went to work with the men. They had suffered frightfully, but they refused to give up hope. Many called upon the mayor and offered their services as nurses. Others prepared bandages for the wounded and aided the physicians in procuring medicines for the sick. They went among the men who were engaged in burying and otherwise disposing of the dead and cheered them with bright faces and soothing words. They were everywhere, and their presence was as rays of sunshine after the black clouds of the storm.

A regular fleet of steamers and barges was plying between Galveston and Texas City, only six miles distant and which had railway communication with all parts of the United States. As the railroad line to Texas City had been repaired, trains were sent in there as close together as possible, but this did not prevent many hundreds in Galveston from dying of starvation and lack of medical assistance.

## A City Official's Version of the Reign of Terror

A leading city official of Galveston gave the following version of the Reign of Terror, as the regime of the thugs and ghouls was called:

> Galveston suffered in every conceivable way since the catastrophe of Saturday. Hurricane and flood came first; then famine, and then vandalism. Scores of reckless criminals flocked to the city by the first boats that landed there, and were unchecked in their work of robbery of the helpless dead Monday and Tuesday.

Wednesday, however, Captain Rafferty, commanding the regulars at the beach barracks, sent seventy
men of an artillery company there to do guard duty
in the streets, and, being ordered to promptly shoot
all those found looting, carried out their instructions
to the letter.

Over 100 ghouls were shot Wednesday afternoon
and evening, and no mercy was shown vandals. If
they were not killed at the first volley the troops—
regulars of the United States Army and those of the
Texas National Guard—saw that the coup de grace
was administered.

Most of the robbers were negroes, and when executed were found loaded with spoil—jewelry wrenched
from the bodies of women, money and watches and
silverware and other articles taken from residences
and business houses.

Not only had these fiends robbed the dead, but they
mutilated the bodies as well. In many instances
fingers and ears of dead women were amputated to secure the jewelry. Some of the business organizations
of the city also furnished guards to assist in patrolling
the streets. Fully 1,000 men are now on duty.

Wednesday evening the regulars shot forty-nine
ghouls after they had been tried by court-martial,
which found them in possession of large quantities
of plunder. The vandals begged for mercy, but none
was shown them and they were speedily put out of
the way. The bandits, as a rule, obtained transportation to the city by representing themselves as having
been engaged to do relief work and to aid in burying the dead. Shortly after the first bunch of thieves
was executed another party of twenty was shot. The
outlaws were afterward put out of the way by twos
and threes, it being their habit to travel in gangs and

never alone. In every instance the pockets of these bandits were found filled with plunder.

More than 2,000 bodies had been thrown into the sea up to Wednesday night, this having been decided upon by the authorities as the only way of preventing a visitation of pestilence, which they felt should not be added to the horrors the city had already experienced. Tuesday evening, shortly before darkness set in, three barges, containing 700 bodies, were sent out to sea, the corpses being thrown into the water after being heavily weighted to prevent the possibility of their afterwards coming to the surface. As there were few volunteers for this ghastly work, troops and police officers were sent out to press men into the service. While these unwilling laborers, after being filled with liquor, agreed to handle the bodies of white men, women and children, nothing could induce them to touch the negro dead. Finally city firemen came forward and attended to the disposal of the corpses of the colored victims. These were badly decomposed, and it was absolutely necessary to get them out of the way to prevent infection.

No attempt had been made so far to gather up the dead at night because the gas and electric light plants were so badly damaged that they could furnish no illumination whatever. By Thursday night, however, some of the arc lights were ready for use. Since Wednesday morning no efforts at identification were made by the searchers after the dead, since it was imperative that the bodies be disposed of as soon as possible. While the barges containing the bodies were on their way out to sea lists were made, but that was the only care taken in regard to the victims, many of whom were among the most prominent people of the city. Of the hundreds buried at Virginia Point and other places along the coast not 10 per cent were identified, the stakes at the heads of the hastily dug graves simply being marked, "White woman, aged 30," "White man, aged 45," or "Male" or "Female child."

Ninety-six bodies were buried at Texas City, all but eight of which floated to that place from Galveston. Some were identified, but the great majority were not. State troops were stationed at Texas City and Virginia Point to prevent those who could not give a satisfactory account of themselves from boarding boats bound for Galveston. In burying the dead along the shore of the gulf no coffins were used, the supply being exhausted. There was no time to knock even an ordinary pine box together. Cases were known where people have buried their dead in their yards.

As soon as possible the work of cremating the bodies of the dead began. Vast funeral pyres were erected and the corpses placed thereon, the incineration carried out under the supervision of the fire department. Matters had come to such a pass that even the casting of bodies into the sea was not only dangerous to those who handled them, but there was the utmost danger in carrying the decomposed, putrefying masses of human flesh through the streets to the barges on the beach.

The cemeteries were not fit for burial purposes, and no attempt whatever was made to reach them until the ground was thoroughly dried out. Then the bodies of those buried in private grounds, yards and in the sands along the beach, not only on Galveston Island, but at Virginia Point and Texas City, were removed to the public places of interment, where suitable memorials were set up to mark their last resting places. It might have been deemed unfeeling and even brutal, but the fact was that the bodies of the unidentified victims received small consideration, were handled roughly by the workmen, and thrown into the temporary graves along the beach as though they were animals and not the remains of human beings. No prayers were uttered save in isolated instances, and the poor mangled bodies were consigned to the trench as hurriedly as possible. The burying parties had no time for sentiment, and so accustomed had the workers in the "dead gangs," as they were named, become to their gruesome task that they even laughed and joked when laying away the corpses.

Special attention was given the wounded. Physicians were on duty all the time, some of them not having been to bed since Friday night longer than an hour at a time. Victims not badly hurt were put aside for those suffering and actually requiring the services of surgeons. There were thousands of them. There were few in Galveston who did not bear the marks of wounds of some sort.

## TERRIBLE SCENES WITNESSED AT HOUSTON

The terrible scenes and happenings in Houston, the great amount of damage done and the intense suffering of the people there as a result of the recent storm were vividly portrayed in a letter from Walter Scott of that city to his sister in Chicago, received September 15.

"Much has been written about the damage done to Galveston," Mr. Scott wrote, "and I suppose things there are so terrible that little thought is given to other places. But right here in this city the damage is so great that one would not believe even time could repair it. Furthermore, the suffering here is indeed the greatest I ever heard of. Thousands of refugees are here from Galveston and other places and the city is being taxed to the limit to find places for all of them.

"Wednesday morning the first contingent arrived. There were about eight hundred, and a more forlorn, dejected and suffering lot of people never were brought together. The sick were cared for in hospitals and private homes, and the greater number of the others were assigned to places. But they apparently could not quiet themselves unless so fatigued and weak from loss of sleep and want of food that they practically fell down exhausted.

"They roamed the streets with scarcely any clothing on them, men, women and children; all were hollow-eyed and sunken-cheeked and on the verge of despair. It is terrible to realize how many families have been broken up.

"I have listened to harrowing tales until I am actually sick. The newspaper reports have not been exaggerated one iota. There is really nothing one can say which will express the situation. When I arrived at home from New Orleans at 10:30 o'clock Sunday night there wasn't a light in the city. Everything was in total darkness. It had been reported on the train that 7,000 lives had been lost at Galveston, but this we believed to be a gross exaggeration.

"But I have changed my mind. I think now it is a conservative figure. I groped my way through the darkness, stumbling over piles of debris, to my boarding place, and after no little difficulty succeeded in reaching my room. Upon lighting a match I found the place denuded of everything; the paper was stripped from the ceiling and was hanging in shreds from the walls. It was damp and cold. My landlady, hearing me, soon came in, and standing there in the darkness she gave me a harrowing account of what they passed through, the details of which the newspapers already have described. All the other people in the house had gone elsewhere, and she, her husband and myself were alone in the house.

"That night I slept in a fairly dry bed in a tolerably dry room, but all the windows in the house had been blown out, and the building was so damp and cold that we were almost afraid to sleep there. Some of the rooms in the lower part of the building were still flooded. There wasn't a room in the entire house that had not been damaged, and the servants' house in the yard was almost completely wrecked. The ruins were toppled over and leaning against our next-door neighbor's house.

"There is scarcely a structure in Houston which escaped the fury of the storm. With the exception of the First Presbyterian, every church lost its steeple, and all were damaged to some extent. The streets for two or three days and even longer afterward were filled with debris—telephone and telegraph poles and wires, huge piles of bricks and timber, tin roofs and all kinds of miscellaneous things, such as furniture, trees, etc.

"At Seabrook, a little seaside resort near here, only two homes were left standing."

Walter S. Keenan, general passenger agent of the Gulf, Colorado & Santa Fe Railroad, arrived in Chicago September 17 from Galveston. He was in the general office, which is connected with the Union station at Galveston, during the great storm and escaped without injury. He said the accounts of the Galveston disaster were in no way exaggerated. The debris, in some of the streets, he declared, was thirty feet high. He went to his office in the station Saturday morning and was compelled to remain there until Sunday afternoon without a bite to eat.

## HOW THE STORM AFFECTED TRADE

The following trade statement, issued from New York on Saturday, September 15, showed the effect of the great storm in commercial circles:

"The tropical storm that devastated the gulf coast, almost wiping out the city of Galveston and doing damage in other parts of the country, caused reduction in the volume of business at the South, and railroads in the gulf region have probably not shown their maximum losses of earnings as yet, but even after such, a catastrophe a recuperative power is shown.

"From many quarters of the West and Southeast a better distribution of merchandise is reported in jobbing and retail circles. The weather has continued favorable for the maturing corn crop, with cutting progressing and the crop generally beyond danger, but damage to cotton by the storm is still an unknown quantity. Prices of staple commodities are higher for the week, hoisted by the sharp rise in cotton, but in manufactured products there is little change, though steady increases of business at the current level is satisfactory.

"Cotton closed last week at the highest price in ten years, and a large short interest was awaiting reaction. Instead, there came news of the disaster in Texas and sensational reports that 1,000,000 bales had been destroyed. At the New York Exchange trading was far in excess of all previous records, and prices rose by bounds. Subsequently there were less exaggerated reports from the South, but the market failed to respond and middling uplands advanced 11 cents.

"The rise in the raw material caused sharp advances in cotton goods. In one week standard brown sheetings rose from 5.67 to 6 cents, wide bleached sheetings from 20 to 21 cents, standard brown drills from 5.67 to 5.87, and staple ginghams from 5 to 5.50 cents. Buyers who have been delaying for weeks are anxious to secure liberal supplies, both instant and distant."

## CLEAN UP

By the time Friday—practically the sixth day after the flood, although the waters did not subside nor the wind go down until about 2 o'clock on Sunday morning—had arrived many of the businessmen of the stricken city had recovered their courage and two or three banks and a few business houses were opened, although most of the streets were still choked with debris and practically impassable. On every corner was this sign:

```
. . . . . . . . . . . . . . . .
.                              .
.                              .
.         CLEAN UP             .
.                              .
.                              .
. . . . . . . . . . . . . . . .
```

Some women even ventured out shopping, picking their way over great masses of wreckage. Tremont Street was by that time opened from the bay to the beach, and Mechanic Street, the Strand and Winnie and Church Streets were being rapidly cleared. However, the stench from the putrefying bodies of the victims of the calamity still in the ruins of scores and hundreds of buildings was all but unbearable.

## "GALVESTON SHALL RISE AGAIN!"

"Galveston must rise again," said the *Galveston News* in an editorial on Thursday.

"At the first meeting of Galveston citizens Sunday afternoon after the great hurricane, for the purpose of bringing order out of chaos, the only sentiment expressed," the editorial says, "was that Galveston had received an awful blow. The loss of life and property is appalling—so great that it required several days to form anything like a correct estimate. With sad and aching hearts, but with resolute faces, the sentiment of the meeting was that out of the awful chaos of wrecked homes and wrecked business, Galveston must rise again.

"The sentiment was not that of bury the dead and give up the ship; but, rather, bury the dead, succor the needy, appeal for aid from a charitable world, and then start resolutely to work to mend the broken chains. In many cases the work of upbuilding must begin over. In other cases the destruction is only partial.

"The sentiment was Galveston will, Galveston must, survive, and fulfill her glorious destiny. Galveston shall rise again.

"If we have lost all else, we still have, life and the future, and it is toward the future that we must devote the energies of our lives. We can never forget what we have suffered; we cannot forget the thousands of our friends and loved ones who found in the angry billows that destroyed them a final resting place. But tears and grief must not make us forget our present duties. The blight and ruin which have destroyed Galveston are not beyond repair; we must not for a moment think Galveston is to be abandoned because of one disaster, however horrible that disaster has been.

"It is a time for courage of the highest order. It is a time when men and women show the stuff that is in them, and we can make no loftier acknowledgment of the material sympathy which the world is extending to us than to answer back that after we shall have buried our dead, relieved the sufferings of the sick and destitute, we will bravely undertake the vast work of restoration and recuperation which lies before us in a manner which shall convince the world that we have spirit to overcome misfortune and rebuild our homes. In this way we shall prove ourselves worthy of the boundless tenderness which is being showered upon us in the hour of desolation and sorrow."

This sentiment voiced the feeling of the people of the prostrate city pretty accurately, for they had begun to look around them and make plans for rebuilding, although it was many days after that before the streets were cleaned and the ground was dry enough to begin work.

## THE SITUATION A WEEK AFTERWARD

A newspaper correspondent who had unusual facilities for getting at the true state of affairs summed up the situation on Saturday, September 15, just a week after the awful visitation, as follows:

"The first week of Galveston's suffering has passed away, and the extent of the disaster which wind and flood brought to the city seems greater than it did even when the blow had just been struck.

"That 5,000 or more of the 40,000 men, women and children who made up the population of the city seven days ago are dead is almost certain. And the money value of the damage to the property of the citizens is so great that no one can attempt to estimate it within $5,000,000 of the real amount.

"In one thing the effects of the flood are irreparable. Water now covers 5,300,000 square feet of ground that was formerly a part of the city, but which now can never be reclaimed from the Gulf.

"A strip of land three miles long and from 350 to 400 feet wide along the south side of the city, where the finest residences stood, is now covered by the waves even at low tide. The Beach Hotel now has its foundations in the Gulf, although before the hurricane it had a fine beach 400 feet wide in front of it. This land is gone forever.

"Like men stunned and dazed, the survivors of the flood have worked and struggled to bury their dead and to make the city habitable for the living, but it may be doubted whether they even yet realize to the full extent what they have lost, or guess the suffering that is in store for them when their moments of leisure come and they begin to miss their friends and loved ones who are dead.

"It is certain now that, however much Galveston has suffered, the city will be rebuilt and be the scene of as great a business as before. But few of the men of the city can pay any attention yet to the work that is necessary for this restoration. Today they are busy with the roughest work of cleaning the city, of clearing away the debris, of burying the bodies which still are being discovered under ruins each day and of providing for their simplest necessities.

"The woman who a few days ago was the mistress of a splendid mansion, with every want provided for, now be seen half-clad making her way through the streets in search of a little food, and esteeming herself fortunate if her family is still intact to gather in the wreckage of the former home. The man who a few days ago was the owner of a great business and the master of many servants may today be seen working in the trying tasks of removing wreckage and hauling away to burial the decayed and unrecognizable bodies of the dead, under the direction of armed soldiers and deputy sheriffs, who are there to see that the work is not slighted.

"And around everyone is ruin. The broken and shattered houses, the scattered articles of furniture, above all the burning funeral pyres on which the bodies of many of the dead are being consumed, make the city a place of horror even to those whose personal wants are best provided for.

"The peril from the wind and waves was followed for those who survived by a peril of hunger and a peril of disease. There came also a peril to life and property from the great horde of robbers and inhuman outlaws who were attracted by the helpless condition of the city to seek their prey.

"The splendid response of the country to Galveston's appeal for help has removed all danger of further suffering from hunger, and the prompt action of Governor Sayers, through Adjutant General Scurry, and of Mayor Jones and the citizens' relief committee have reestablished order and made the horrible scenes of the stripping of corpses and the assaults on persons no longer possible. The city is still under martial law, and it will remain so, nominally at least, until normal conditions otherwise have been restored.

"The danger of pestilence is still great, however, and indeed the fear that other thousands may fall victims to a scourge of disease is gaining in strength and leading to an exodus of all the women and children and of many of the men of the city, who are crowding the boats to get away to the mainland.

"Added to the danger from the thousands of decomposing bodies both of men and of beasts, which still lie under ruined houses and along the gulf shore, is the danger from the unflushed sewers and closets in the city. Until yesterday it was practically impossible to flush the sewers in any part of the city on account of the lack of water, and although the condition is now much better there is much of evil still.

"Fevers and other diseases which may be bred under these conditions will not show themselves for ten days or longer, at the earliest. Some of the physicians in the city have issued statements today calculated to calm the apprehensions of the citizens in this matter. Among them is Dr. W. H. Blount, state health officer, who says that there is no great danger. He refers to the cyclone of 1867, which covered the city with slimy mud, and instead of breeding disease served practically to put an end to the yellow fever then prevalent.

"The work of clearing away the debris in the streets has been carried on with a fair degree of vigor, and it is expected that it will be pushed much faster from now on. The 2,000 laborers whom it has been decided to bring in from outside the city for the work will be able to take up the task without having to worry about the safety of the remnants of their own property which they may have left unprotected.

"The most important need is, however, for money to pay the men. Adjutant General Scurry said today: 'I have not a dollar to pay the men who are working in the streets all day long. I am not able to say to a single one of these men, "You shall be paid for your work." I have not the money to make good the promise and I hope and believe that the country will relieve the situation.

" 'We must have this city cleaned up at any cost, and with the greatest speed possible. If it is not done with all haste, and at the same time done well, there may be a pestilence, and if it once breaks out here it will not be Galveston alone that will suffer. Such things spread, and it is not only for the sake of this city, but for others outside of this place that I urge that above all things we want money.

" 'The nation has been most kind in its response to the appeal of Galveston, and from what I hear, food and disinfectants sufficient for temporary purposes at least, are here or on the way. The country does not understand, it cannot understand, unless it visit Galveston, the awful destitution prevailing here. Of all the poor people here, not one has anything. A majority of them could not furnish a single room in which to commence housekeeping even though they had the money to rebuild the room.

" 'These people have absolutely nothing except what is given them by the relief committee. They are in a condition of absolute want, they lack everything, and save for the splendid generosity of the nation they would be utterly without hope.'

"The gangs of men in the streets are still finding every now and then badly decomposed bodies. Few of these relics of human life can be recognized, and many of them are naked and without anything about them which would lead to identification. They are disposed of as rapidly as possible, but the work is very offensive and the men engaged in it cannot endure it steadily for any great length of time.

" 'Pull them out of the water as soon as seen and throw them into the flames as soon as taken from the water,' is the order, and it is effectually carried out.

"The best work in this direction was done along the shoreline of the gulf on the south side of the city. During the day bodies were found at frequent intervals, and just at sunset seven were found in the ruins of one house. It is expected that more will be found tomorrow, as the work gang that today found seven bodies will clear up the debris where it is known that fifteen people were killed.

"The soldiers from Dallas and Houston who have been here providing for order and helping in the work of cleaning up the city have become exhausted and it has been necessary to relieve them. The Craddock Light Infantry of Terrell arrived today to take up the work.

"The exodus to Houston and other neighboring cities is still going on. The sailboats across the bay are crowded to their fullest capacity, and they make as many round trips each day as they can."

## NOTHING LIKE IT IN THE HISTORY OF THE U. S.

"No calamity in the history of the United States approaches the horror of Galveston." Such was the declaration of Col. Walter Hudnall of the United States treasury department, Saturday, after filing a secret report to the government in which he outlined the damage sustained by the government and made confidential suggestions concerning the advisability of continuing the expenditures that have been made there annually.

"Galveston needs no more physicians or nurses," he continued. "Those who would rush to the aid of the stricken island should send quicklime, chloride of lime, carbolic acid and other disinfectants and stay away themselves. Today Galveston is a gigantic funeral pyre. From the wreckage ascend numerous pillars of smoke and the air is filled with the sickening odor of burning human flesh. But above all, making one forget even the presence of the uncounted dead, is the stench of decaying coffee, rice and other vegetable products that lie swelling with the heat and putrefying. Powerful chemicals and disinfectants are required to prevent what this is sure to produce—disease.

"In the face of these conditions Galveston is burying her dead, burning her wreckage, attempting to restore order and bring about a resumption of business.

"No words of complaint are heard. The woe which has come upon the island city is too great for tears and the afflictions of individuals in the loss of dear ones is entirely forgotten in the heroic fight that is being made for self-preservation for the community. Women of wealth steal through the streets without clothing, save for a bit of torn and grimy cloth wrapped about them. Men of means are in the same sorry plight and go about their gruesome task of cleaning up in so stolid a manner that it is obvious that Galveston has not awakened to the full horror of the situation. There has not been time to think.

"It is not uncommon to hear worn and haggard men refer to the loss of their families and their all with so little evidence of concern that it would attract wonder were not the senses of the visitor numbed by the terror of the situation. It is the reaction that is feared most by those who are leading the effort to make the city habitable. When this work is completed and there is time to think, a heartrending wail of woe will go up from the twenty-odd thousand mourning survivors and gloomy desperation is expected to succeed the energy that is now manifested.

"The spirit of the people is aptly illustrated by Capt. John Delaney, chief customs inspector of the port. Delaney, 60 years of age, lost his entire family, wife, son and daughters. The bodies of the son and daughters were recovered, but no trace of Mrs. Delaney has been found. Whether her body was cast into the sea from one of the dread funeral barges or buried may never be known. Terrible as was the blow, Delaney was at his post the day following the disaster, attired in a pair of overalls, all that he managed to save. Yesterday a butcher, fortunate in saving a portion of two suits, loaned Delaney a pair of trousers. Clad in them he boarded a big German tramp steamer that arrived in port, inspected her and sent her back to New Orleans, as she was unable to discharge her cargo at Galveston."

In his report to Washington Col. Hudnall placed the loss of life at from 6,500 to 8,000 and ridiculed the idea that any person could estimate the property loss at that time. He predicted that it would be impossible to estimate within $10,000,000 of the correct figures. His estimate was based upon what was said to be better information than that of any other visitor in Galveston, as he had made a thorough can-

vass of the city on horseback, visiting every locality where
it was possible to travel, instructions from the treasury department being to thoroughly investigate in every detail. No
one else had made such a canvass.

Vice-President and General Manager Trice of the International & Great Northern Railroad, after looking over the
situation in Galveston, said the railroad losses would aggregate $5,000,000 or $6,000,000 in that city alone.

At Galveston their wharves, warehouses, depots and
tracks were ruined. The costly bridges which connected the
island with the mainland were in ruins and must be entirely
rebuilt.

The International & Great Northern and Santa Fe had
considerable track washed out, while the Galveston, Houston and Northern suffered heavily.

All track between Seabrook and Virginia Point, with all of
the bridges, was washed away, and Section Foreman Scan-
lan and all his crew at Nadeau were lost.

## How the Insurance Companies Fared

Naturally the question of insurance carried on the lives and
property of people of Galveston was one much discussed after the first feeling of horror occasioned by the catastrophe
had worn away, and the fact was developed that while the life
insurance companies were somewhat badly hit—although
in not so great a degree as would naturally be supposed when
the heavy death list was taken into consideration—very little property insurance was carried by the businessmen and
property owners of the desolated city.

Although the loss of life was over 5,000, a large proportion of the victims was composed of women and children, a
class which rarely, if ever, carries insurance; again, the majority of the men drowned and crushed were residents of the
poorer districts of the town, the wealthier men having abandoned their homes at the first alarm and fled to the elevated

places. These victims were caught in their houses, together with their families, and husbands, wives and children died together.

As a matter of fact, the men who work for a living at trades and in the various branches of employment where skilled labor is not demanded, do not carry life insurance as a general thing, except in benevolent or fraternal societies of which they may be members, and this is the main reason why the "straight" life insurance companies, as they are called, did not suffer more than they did.

One of the most prominent insurance managers in the United States said three days after the catastrophe:

> Life insurance companies will feel the blow of the Galveston storm. How much insurance was carried by the victims of the storm is not known, but it must have been great in the aggregate. The large proportion of women and children among the dead will lighten the burden, as they do not often carry insurance.
>
> The rule requiring the body of the insured to be identified will have to be waived, because of the number of bodies buried at sea and otherwise without identification. Unless the rigor of this rule is relaxed by the insurers litigation will be boundless.
>
> Practically no property insurance was carried at Galveston.

Galveston and Houston representatives of the largest eastern insurance companies when seen concurred in the opinion that the insurance policies against storm losses carried by Galvestonians would not aggregate $10,000. They said there was absolutely no demand for such insurance at Galveston.

The head of one of the leading insurance firms in Galveston which represented many large eastern companies said: "We did not carry a dollar of storm insurance at Galveston, and while my information on that point is limited, I feel sure the storm insurance was very small. We never had a request for storm insurance policies. If there had been any demand at Galveston for insurance of this kind we would have heard of it.

"We held $50,000 storm insurance on two big oil mills at Houston and our loss will probably be $40,000 to $50,000 on these two structures. We held $25,000 storm insurance at Port Arthur and about $1,200 at Alvin. The insurance situation at Galveston is very quiet. There was no loss by fire, and I think the insurance against storms was trivial."

More than 4,000 houses were destroyed; millions of dollars' worth of property in dry goods, grocery and other business houses—wholesale and retail—was ruined; there was hardly a house in the city which did not suffer damage, the total property losses aggregating about $20,000,000; and yet, living in a section where storms were liable to occur at any time, little or no insurance was carried.

The first message by wire was sent out of Galveston Thursday at 4:16 p.m. over the wire of the Western Union Company. The company laid a cable across the channel, and through it they transmitted the message. The cable was brought from Chicago on a passenger train. The Postal Telegraph Company had several wires in good working order by Saturday night, as also had the Western Union Company.

The Mexican Cable Company secured both ends of its cable and established communication from Galveston with the outside world via the City of Mexico Friday evening.

## WOMAN REPORTER'S EXPERIENCE
## WITH THE AFTERMATH OF THE STORM

A woman—a newspaper correspondent, and the first of the fair sex from the outside to gain admittance to the Sealed City of Galveston—wrote a description of what she saw and heard there after the storm. She arrived in Galveston on Friday, and although she was on a relief train carrying doctors, nurses and medical supplies, she had hard work to get past the file of soldiers at the wharf, but she at last succeeded. Said she:

"The engineer who brought our train down from Houston spent the night before groping around in the wrecks on the beach looking for his wife and three children. He found them, dug a rude grave in the sand and set up a little board marked with his name.

"The man in front of me on the car had floated all Monday night with his wife and mother on a part of the roof of his little home. He told me that he kissed his wife goodbye at midnight and told her that he could not hold on any longer; but he did hold on, dazed and half-conscious, until the clay broke and showed him that he was alone on his piece of driftwood. He did not even know when the woman that he loved had died.

"Every man on the train—there were no women—there had lost someone that he loved in the terrible disaster and was going across the bay to try and find some trace of his family."

As the train neared Texas City, near Galveston, a great flame leaped up, and she said to one of four men near her, "What a terrible fire! Some of the large buildings must be burning." She then went on to say:

"A man who was passing on the deck behind my chair heard me. He stopped, put his hand on the bulwark and turned down and looked into my face, his face like the face of a dead man; but he laughed.

" 'Buildings!' he said. 'Don't you know what is burning over there? It is my wife and children—such little children!

Why, the tallest was not as high as this'—he laid his hand on
the bulwark— 'and the little one was just learning to talk.'

" 'She called my name the other day, and now they are
burning over there—they and the mother who bore them.
She was such a little, tender, delicate thing, always so easily
frightened, and now she's out there all alone with the two
babies, and they're burning.'

"The man laughed again and began again to walk up and
down the deck.

" 'That's right,' said the Marshal of the State of Texas, taking off his broad hat and letting the starlight shine on his
strong face. 'That's right. We had to do it. We've burned over
1,000 people today, and tomorrow we shall burn as many
more.

" 'Yesterday we stopped burying the bodies at sea; we had
to give the men on the barges whiskey to give them courage
to do the work. They carried out hundreds of the dead at one
time, men and women, negroes and white people, all piled
up as high as the barge could stand it, and the men did not
go out far enough to sea, and the bodies have begun drifting
back again.'

" 'Look!' said the man who was walking the deck, touching
my shoulder with his shaking hand. 'Look there!'

"Before I had time to think I had to look, and saw floating in the water the body of an old woman, whose hair was
shining in the starlight. A little farther on we saw a group of
strange driftwood.

"We looked closer and found it to be a mass of wooden
slabs, with names and dates cut upon them, and floating on
top of them were marble stones, two of them.

"The graveyard, which has held the sleeping citizens of
Galveston for many, many years, was giving up its dead. We
pulled up at a little wharf in the hush of the starlight; there
were no lights anywhere in the city except a few scattered
lamps shining from a few desolate, half-destroyed houses.
We picked our way up the street. The ground was slimy with
the debris of the sea.

"We climbed over wreckage, and picked our way through heaps of rubbish. The terrible, sickening odor almost overcame us, and it was all that I could do to shut my teeth and get through the streets somehow. The soldiers were camping on the wharf front, lying stretched out on the wet sand, the hideous, hideous sand, stained and streaked in the starlight with dark and cruel blotches. They challenged us, but the marshal took us through under his protection. At every street corner there was a guard, and every guard wore a six-shooter strapped around his waist.

"I went toward the heart of the city. I do not know what the names of the streets were or where I was going. I simply picked my way through masses of slime and rubbish which scar the beautiful wide streets of the once beautiful city.

"They won't bear looking at, those piles of rubbish. There are things there that gripe the heart to see—a baby's shoe, for instance, a little red shoe, with a jaunty tasseled lace—a bit of a woman's dress and letters.

"The stench, from these piles of rubbish is almost overpowering. Down in the very heart of the city most of the dead bodies have been removed, but it will not do to walk far out. Today I came upon a group of people in a by-street, a man and two women, colored. The man was big and muscular, one of the women was old and one was young.

"They were dipping in a heap of rubbish and when they heard my footsteps the man turned an evil, glowering face upon me and the young woman hid something in the folds of her dress. Human ghouls, these, prowling in search of prey.

"A moment later there was noise and excitement in the little narrow street, and I looked back and saw the negro running, with a crowd at his heels. The crowd caught him and would have killed him, but a policeman came up.

"They tied his hands and took him through the streets with a whooping rabble at his heels. It goes hard with a man in Galveston caught looting the dead in these days.

"A young man well known in the city shot and killed a negro who was cutting the ears from a living woman's head to get her earrings out. The negro lay in the street like a dead dog, and not even the members of his own race would give him the tribute of a kindly look.

"The abomination of desolation reigns on every side. The big houses are dismantled, their roofs gone, windows broken, and the high water mark showing inconceivably high on the paint. The little houses are gone—either completely gone as if they were made of cards and a giant hand which was tired of playing with them had swept them all off the board and put them away, or they are lying in heaps of kindling wood covering no one knows what horrors beneath.

"The main streets of the city are pitiful. Here and there a shop of some sort is left standing. South Fifth Street looks like an old man's jaw, with one or two straggling teeth protruding. The merchants are taking their little stores of goods that have been left them and are spreading them out in the bright sunshine, trying to make some little husbanding of their small capital. The water rushed through the stores as it did through the houses, in an irresistible avalanche that carried all before it. The wonder is not that so little of Galveston is left standing, but that there is any of it at all.

"Every street corner has its story, in its history of misery and human agony bravely endured. The eye-witnesses of a hundred deaths have talked to me and told me their heart-rending stories, and not one of them has told of a cowardly death.

"The women met their fate as did the men, bravely and for the most part with astonishing calmness. A woman told me that she and her husband went into the kitchen and climbed upon the kitchen table to get away from the waves, and that she knelt there and prayed.

"As she prayed, the storm came in and carried the whole house away, and her husband with it, and yesterday she went out to the place where her husband had been, and there was nothing there but a little hole in the ground.

"Her husband's body was found twisted in the branches of a tree, half a mile from the place where she last saw him.

She recognized him by a locket he had around his neck—the locket she gave him before they were married. It had her picture and a lock of the baby's hair in it. The woman told me all this without a tear or a trace of emotion. No one cries here.

"They will stand and tell the most hideous stories, stories that would turn the blood in the veins of a human machine cold with horror, without the quiver of an eyelid. A man sat in the telegraph office and told me how he had lost two Jersey cows and some chickens.

"He went into minute particulars, told how his house was built and what it cost, and how it was strengthened and made firm against the weather. He told me how the storm had come and swept it all away, and how he had climbed over a mass of wobbling roofs and found a friend lying in the curve of a big roof, in the stoutest part of the tide, and how they two had grasped each other and what they said.

"He told me just how much his cows cost and why he was so fond of them, and how hard he had tried to save them, but I said: 'You have saved yourself and your family; you ought not to complain.' The man stared at me with blank, unseeing eyes.

" 'Why, I did not save my family,' he said. 'They were all drowned. I thought you knew that; I don't talk very much about it.'

"The hideous horror of the whole thing has benumbed everyone who saw it."

# CHAPTER THREE:
## STORIES OF SURVIVAL

The experiences and adventures of those who were in the great and disastrous storm and escaped only after undergoing frightful anxiety make interesting reading. Those who emerged in safety from the fearful vortex were unusually fortunate, when it is considered that possibly 8,000 persons in Galveston lost their lives and hundreds fell victim to the fury of the hurricane in the territory adjacent to the ill-fated city.

Hon. John H. Poe, member of the Louisiana State Board of Education and resident of Lake Charles, was present when eighty-five passengers on the Gulf & Interstate train, which left Beaumont early Saturday morning from Bolivar Point, lost their lives. Mr. Poe was one of the passengers on this train and fortunately, together with a few others, sought safety in the lighthouse at Bolivar Point and was saved. The train reached Bolivar about noon and all preparations were made to run the train on the ferryboat preparatory to crossing the bay. But the wind blew so swiftly that the ferry could not make a landing and the conductor of the train, after allowing it to stand on the tracks for a few minutes, started to back it back toward Beaumont. The wind increased so rapidly, coming in from the open sea, that soon the water had reached a level with the bottom of the seats within the cars. It was then that some of the passengers sought safety in the nearby lighthouse, but in spite of all efforts eighty-five passengers were blown away or drowned. The train was entirely wrecked. Some of the victims were from New Orleans, as the train made direct connections with the Southern Pacific train which left New Orleans Friday night.

Those who were saved had to spend over fifty hours in the dismal lighthouse on almost no rations. The experience was one they will remember as one of the most terrible of their whole lives.

## COMMERCIAL TRAVELER'S EXPERIENCE IN GALVESTON

A graphic description of one man's experience was given by a commercial traveler—William Van Eaton. He reached Galveston Saturday morning. His narrative is especially interesting, because it shows with what suddenness the storm assumed a dangerous character.

"There was high wind and rain," said he, "but so little was thought of it, however, that myself and some acquaintances started down to the beach. The water came up so rapidly that we turned and hurried toward the Tremont Hotel. Before we reached it we had to wade in water waist deep.

"Within a few minutes," he went on to say, "women and children began to flock to the hotel for refuge. All were panic-stricken. I saw two women, one with a child, trying to get to the hotel. They were drowned not 800 yards from us."

Mr. Van Eaton was one of the first to cross from Galveston to the mainland after the storm subsided. He paid $15 to a boatman to make the crossing. When he reached the point he found an engine and a caboose chained together, with the water several feet deep around them. While he waited in the caboose for the water to go down, the bodies of two men and a boy floated against it and the trainmen tied them to one end of the car. Mr. Van Eaton counted fourteen bodies that had drifted in from the bay, all showing signs that they had been dashed against wreckage.

## ONLY ONE OUT OF FIFTY PEOPLE SAVED

Patrick Joyce, a railroad man who passed through the storm at Galveston in 1872, suffered such hardships in that city Saturday morning that he was convinced that the previous storm was only a "mild little blow" in comparison. He was one of the refugees picked up at Lamarque. He recounts:

"It began raining in Galveston early Saturday morning," About 9 o'clock work was discontinued by the company, and I left for home. I got there about 11 o'clock and found about three feet of water in the yard. It began to get worse and worse, the water getting higher and the wind stronger, until it was almost as bad as the Gulf itself with its raging torrents. Finally the house was taken off its foundation and demolished.

"There were nine families in the house, which was a large two-story frame, and of the fifty people residing there myself and niece were the only ones who could get away. I managed to find a raft of driftwood or wreckage and got on it, going with the tide. I had not got far before I was struck with some wreckage and my niece knocked out of my arms. I could not save her, and had to see her drown.

"I was carried on and on with the tide, sometimes on a raft, and again I was thrown from it by coming in contact with some pieces of timber, parts of houses, logs, cisterns and other things which were floating around in the Gulf and bay. Many and many a knock I got on my head and body, until I was black and blue all over. The wind was blowing at a terrific rate of speed and the waves were away up.

"I drifted and swam all night, not knowing where I was going or in what direction. About 3 o'clock in the morning I began to feel the hard ground, and then I knew I was on the mainland. I wandered around until I came to a house, and there a person gave me some clothes. I had lost most of mine soon after I started, and only wore a coat.

"I was in the water about seven hours, and this sensation, together with the feeling of all these bruises I have on my head and body, is not a pleasant one. I managed to save my own life through the hardest kind of a struggle, but I thought more than once I was done for, and I lost all I had in this world—relatives who were dear to me, home and all."

## HEROISM OF A HOTEL-KEEPER IN SAVING LIVES

James Black, a well-known merchant at Morgan's Point, saved nine lives during the storm. The story of his heroism was told by W. S. Wall of Houston, Tex., who has a summer home at Morgan's Point.

"My wife was taking supper at the Black Hotel," said Mr. Wall, "when Mr. Black rushed into the dining room and called upon all to fly for their lives. The tidal wave was on them in an instant, and almost before they could leave the hotel to go to a higher point where the Vincent residence stood, some five or six blocks away, the rushing waters were all about them more than three feet deep.

"Mr. Black, struggling against the elements, bore my wife in safety to the Vincent home, miraculously escaping being crushed by a heavy log which the rushing waters carried along the pathway of escape. Returning immediately to the hotel, Mr. Black in like manner brought safely to the Vincent home his aged father and mother, Mr. and Mrs. James Black, Sr. His next act of heroism was to rescue Mrs. Rushmore, her two daughters, two grandchildren and another woman whose name I cannot recall. The Vincent home withstood the storm, but the Black Hotel was wrecked.

"Louis Braquet, manager of the Black Hotel, was engulfed in the waves and gave up his life in the successful rescue of his wife and a colored servant girl."

## SPENT A MOST THRILLING NIGHT...

F. T. Woodward, who was a passenger on the first train to arrive at Dallas from Houston, the Monday night succeeding the catastrophe, spent a thrilling Saturday night in the Grand Central station in the latter city. One hundred and fifty other persons shared his memorable experiences.

"The depot, standing as it does isolated and alone," said Mr. Woodward, "was exposed to the full force of the hurricane, and the first strong gust at 8 o'clock was followed by a sound of shattering glass. Several of the windows of the general offices overhead had given way under the almost irresistible pressure. This was the beginning of seven hours of mortal dread.

"The storm continued to rage with unabated fury and the roar of the wind was accompanied by the sound of crashing glass, as one after another of the many windows was torn from its fastenings and shattered against the brick walls of the building or upon the sidewalk below. Women clasped their children in their arms, as though they expected to be torn asunder the next moment. Men began to scan the pillars and partition walls supporting the floor above and to take up such positions as seemed to be most conducive to safety in the event the huge building was razed by the storm.

"The crashing of glass was soon followed by a sound of ripping and tearing. Section after section of the tin roof was rolled up like sheets of parchment and hurled hundreds of feet away. To add to the terror and confusion, the electric lights suddenly went out and the building was left in darkness, except where the trainmen with their lanterns stood.

"Then many moved toward the main entrance of the building, with the evident intention of seeking other quarters, but they were checked at the door by the blinding sheet of water which was being driven by the wind with mighty force, and which lay between them and any place of refuge. They appeared to hesitate between a choice of being drenched by water and possibly struck by a flying section of roof and of remaining in the depot until the end.

"The question was soon settled. Even as they looked on, the roof of the Grand Central Hotel was torn off, many of its inmates rushing into the street. Almost simultaneously a wail went up from the people in the Lawlor Hotel as the big skylight on top was torn loose and fell crashing down the shaft, causing pandemonium. This seemed to satisfy those in the depot that no haven of safety could be found, and they determined to make the best of the situation.

"Just then, above the roar of the wind, the crashing of glass and the flapping and pounding and tearing of tin, a new sound was heard. It was that of falling brick. Everyone stood crouched, prepared to leap to either side as the occasion might require. Everyone realized the gravity of the situation, but, there was no shrieking, no fainting. Every woman stood the ordeal with such fortitude as to lend courage to even the faintest-hearted man. Even the babies were mute and clung to their mothers' necks in breathless despair.

"Nearer and nearer came that awful rumbling. A shower of brick and mortar fell in the rear of the women's waiting-room. Nothing remained of the tin-covered awning. Few if any doubted that the end had come and that in another moment all would be buried beneath the ruins.

"Suddenly the sound ceased. The brick had fallen and the lower story of the building remained intact. It was soon learned that the entire wall stood unbroken and that the fall of brick and mortar was but the collapse of several large chimneys surmounting the top of the building.

"As soon as this became known the effect upon the awestruck mass was electrical. Men lighted cigars, women cheered and laughed, and though more chimneys fell, more glass was shivered and the loosened tin on the roof continued to pound furiously until nearly 3 o'clock in the morning, there was no more panic, and all felt that the building would withstand the fury of the storm. And it did."

HOW HE GOT INTO AND OUT OF GALVESTON

A. V. Kellogg, civil engineer in the employ of the Houston & Texas Central Railroad, with headquarters at Houston, told an interesting story of how he got into and out of Galveston during and after the great storm, and of his observations in the stricken city. He went to Galveston Saturday morning, over the Galveston, Houston & Henderson Road, arriving a few hours after the storm began.

"When we crossed the bridge over Galveston Bay, going into Galveston," said Mr. Kellogg, "the water had reached an elevation equal to the bottom caps of the pile bents, or two feet below the level of the track. After crossing the bridge and reaching a point some two miles beyond, we were stopped by reason of a washout of the track ahead, and were compelled to wait one hour for a relief train to come over the Galveston, Houston & Henderson track. During this period of one hour the water rose a foot and a half, running over the rails of the track.

"The relief train signaled us to return half a mile to higher ground, where the passengers were transferred, the train crew leaving with the passengers and going on the relief train. The water had reached an elevation of eight or ten inches above the Galveston, Houston & Henderson track, and was flowing in a westward direction at a terrific speed. The train crew was compelled to wade ahead of the engine and dislodge driftwood from the track.

"At 1:15 we arrived at the Santa Fe Union Depot. By that portion of the day the wind was increasing and had then reached a velocity of about thirty-five miles an hour.

"After arriving at Galveston I immediately went to the Tremont Hotel, where I remained the balance of the day and during the night. At 5:30 the water had begun to creep into the rotunda of the hotel, and by 8 o'clock it was twenty-six inches above the floor of the hotel, or about six and one-half feet above the street level.

"The front windows of the hotel were blown out, the roof was torn off and the skylights over the rotunda fell crashing on the floor below. The refugees began to come into the hotel between 5:30 and 8 o'clock, until at least 800 or 1,000 persons had sought safety there. The floors were strewn with people all during the night.

"Manager George Korst did everything in his power to help the sufferers from the effects of the storm and to give them shelter. When the wind was blowing from the north-east it was at a velocity of about forty-five miles an hour, but at 8 o'clock it had reached the climax, the speed then being fully 100 miles. The vibration of the hotel was not unlike that of a box car in motion. I tried to sleep that night, but there was so much noise and confusion from the crashing of buildings that I could not get any rest.

"I arose early Sunday morning. The sights in the streets were simply appalling. The water on Tremont Street had lowered some eight feet from the high-water mark, leaving the pavement clear for two blocks north and seven blocks south of the Tremont Hotel. The streets were full of debris, the wires were all down and the buildings were in a very much damaged condition. Every building in the business district was damaged to some extent, with but one or two exceptions, noticeably the Levy Building and Union Depot, both of which remain intact and went through the storm without a scratch.

"The refugees came pouring into the heart of the city, many of them having but little clothing, and scores were almost naked. They were homeless and without food or drink, and many had lost their all and were really in destitute circumstances.

"Mayor Jones issued a call for a mass meeting, which was held Sunday morning at 9 o'clock, and was attended by a large number of prominent citizens. Steps were taken to furnish provisions and relieve the suffering of the refugees and bury the dead. A conservative estimate of the number of people killed or drowned is from 1,500 to 3,000.

Early in the morning it was learned that the water supply had been cut off for some unknown reason. I presume that it was caused by the English ship which was blown against the bridges, cutting the pipes. At any rate, the city was without water and something had to be done by the citizens of Houston to relieve the situation. People who had depended on cisterns had their resources swept away, and there were but few large reservoirs to be found in the business district.

"The scene on the docks was a terrible one. The small working fleet and the larger schooners were washed up over the docks and railroad tracks in frightful confusion. The Mallory docks were demolished. The elevators were torn in shreds. Three oceanliners were anchored off the docks and seemed to be in good condition. The damage to the shipping interests is something immense, the Huntington improvements being entirely swept away.

"I tried to get out of the town as quick as I could, and succeeded in securing passage on the first sloop which sailed, the *Annie E.*, under Captain Willoughby. We sailed from the Twenty-second slip at 11 o'clock, with seven people aboard. When we got outside of the harbor we found a terrible gale blowing and the sea running very high. Under three reefs and the peak down, we set our course for North Galveston.

"As we passed Pelican Flats we could see the English steamer anchored off over toward where the railroad bridge should be, and came to the conclusion that she had evidently broken the water mains and cut the supply off from the city. Another oceanliner could be seen off the shore of Texas City, in what would seem to have been about two feet of water in a normal tide.

"We passed within a few hundred yards of where the Half-Moon Lighthouse once stood, but could see no evidence of the lighthouse, it being completely washed away.

"The waters of the bay were strewn with hundreds of carcasses of dead animals. We had a very hazardous passage, running against a five-mile tide, but managed to reach North Galveston at 1:35 o'clock.

"At North Galveston we found that a tidal wave had crossed the peninsula, carrying destruction in its path. The factory building and the opera house were completely blown down and other buildings destroyed. While there were no deaths reported at North Galveston, there were many hardships endured during the battle with the elements."

## NEWSPAPER MAN'S GRAPHIC
## DESCRIPTION OF THE FLOOD

"It was one of the most awful tragedies of modern times which has visited Galveston. The city is in ruins and the dead will number probably 1,000."

So says Richard Spillane, a well-known Galveston newspaper man, the first of his profession to come from the stricken city after the hurricane, and who arrived at Houston, after a perilous trip. He continued:

"I am just from the city, having been commissioned by the Mayor and Citizens' Committee to get in touch with the outside world and appeal for help. Houston was the nearest point at which working telegraph instruments could be found, the wires, as well as nearly all the buildings, between here and the Gulf of Mexico being wrecked.

"When I left Galveston, shortly before noon yesterday, the people were organizing for the prompt burial of the dead, the distribution of food and all necessary work after a period of disaster.

"The wreck of Galveston was brought about by a tempest so terrible that no words can adequately describe its intensity, and by a flood which turned the city into a raging sea. The Weather Bureau records show that the wind attained a velocity of eighty-four miles an hour, when the measuring instruments blew away, so it is impossible to tell what was the maximum.

"The storm began at 2 o'clock Saturday morning. Previous to that a great storm had been raging in the gulf, and the tide was very high. The wind at first came from the north and was in direct opposition to the force from the gulf. While the storm in the Gulf piled the water upon the beach side of the city, the north wind piled the water from the bay onto the bay part of the city.

"About noon it became evident that the city was going to be visited with disaster. Hundreds of residences along the beachfront were hurriedly abandoned, the families fleeing to dwellings in higher portions of the city. Every home was opened to the refugees, black or white. The winds were rising constantly, and it rained in torrents. The wind was so fierce that the rain cut like a knife.

"By 5 o'clock the waters of the Gulf and bay met, and by dark the entire city was submerged. The flooding of the electric light plant and the gas plants left the city in darkness. To go upon the streets was to court death. The wind was then at cyclonic velocity. Roofs, cisterns, portions of buildings, telegraph poles and walls were falling, and the noise of the wind and the crashing of the buildings were terrifying in the extreme.

"The wind and waters rose steadily from dark until 1:45 o'clock Sunday morning. During all this time the people of Galveston were like rats in traps. The highest portion of the city was four to five feet under water, while in the great majority of cases the streets were submerged to a depth of ten feet. To leave a house was to drown. To remain was to court death in the wreckage. Such a night of agony has seldom been equaled.

"Without apparent reason, the waters suddenly began to subside at 1:45 a.m. Within twenty minutes they had gone down two feet, and before daylight the streets were practically freed of the flood waters. In the meantime the wind had veered to the southeast.

"Very few buildings escaped injury. There is hardly a habitable dry house in the city. When the people who had escaped death went out at daylight to view the work of the tempest and the floods they saw the most horrible sights imaginable.

"In the three blocks from Avenue N to Avenue P, in Tremont Street, I saw eight bodies. Four corpses were in one yard. The whole of the business front for three blocks in from the Gulf was stripped of every vestige of habitation, the dwellings, the great bathing establishments, the Olympia and every structure having been either carried out to sea or its ruins piled in a pyramid far into the town, according to the vagaries of the tempest.

"The first hurried glance over the city showed that the largest structures, supposed to be the most substantially built, suffered the greatest. The Orphans' Home, Twenty-first Street and Avenue M, fell like a house of cards. How many dead children and refugees are in the ruins could not be ascertained. Of the sick in St. Mary's Infirmary, together with the attendants, only eight are understood to have been saved.

"The Old Woman's Home, on Rosenberg Avenue, collapsed, and the Rosenberg Schoolhouse is a mass of wreckage. The Ball High School is but an empty shell, crushed and broken. Every church in the city, with possibly one or two exceptions, is in ruins.

"At the forts nearly all the soldiers are reported dead, they having been in temporary quarters, which gave them no protection against the tempest or the flood.

"The bayfront from end to end is in ruins. Nothing but pilings and the wreck of great warehouses remains. The elevators lost all their superworks and their stocks are damaged by water.

"The life-saving station at Fort Point was carried away, the crew being swept across the bay fourteen miles to Texas City. I saw Captain Haines yesterday and he told me that his wife and one of his crew were drowned.

"The shore at Texas City contains enough wreckage to rebuild a city. Eight persons who were swept across the bay during the storm were picked up there alive. Five corpses were also picked up. In addition to the living and the dead which the storm cast up at Texas City, caskets and coffins from one of the cemeteries at Galveston were fished out of the water there.

"The cotton mills, the bagging factory, the gas works, the electric light works and nearly all the industrial establishments of the city are either wrecked or crippled. The flood left a slime about one inch deep over the whole city, and unless fast progress is made in burying corpses and carcasses of animals there is danger of pestilence.

"Some of the stories of the escapes are miraculous. William Nisbett, a cotton man, was buried in the ruins of the Cotton Exchange saloon and, when dug out in the morning, had no further injury than a few bruised fingers.

"Dr. S. O. Young, secretary of the Cotton Exchange, was knocked senseless when his house collapsed, but was revived by the water and carried ten blocks by the hurricane.

"A woman who had just given birth to a child was carried from her home to a house a block distant, the men who were carrying her having to hold her high above their heads, as the water was five feet deep when she was moved.

"Many stories were current of houses falling and inmates escaping. Clarence N. Ousley, editor of the *Galveston Evening Tribune*, had his family and the families of two neighbors in his house when the lower half crumbled and the upper part slipped down into the water. Not one in the house was hurt.

"Of the Lavine family, six out of seven are reported dead. Of the Burnett family only one is known to have been saved. The family of Stanley G. Spencer, who met death in the Cotton Exchange saloon, is reported to be dead.

"The Mistrot House, in the west end, was turned into a hospital. All of the regular hospitals of the city were unavailable.

"Of the new Southern Pacific works little remains but the pilings. Half a million feet of lumber was carried away, and Engineer Boschke says, as far as the company is concerned, it might as well start over again.

"Eight ocean steamers were torn from their moorings and stranded in the bay. The Kendall Castle was carried over the flats from the Thirty-third Street wharf to Texas City and lies in the wreckage of the Inman pier. The Norwegian steamer *Gyller* is stranded between Texas City and Virginia Point. An oceanliner was swirled around through the West Bay, crashed through the bay bridges and is now lying in a few feet of water near, the wreckage of the railroad bridges. The steamship *Taunton* was carried across Pelican Point and is stranded about ten miles up toward East Bay. The Mallory

steamer *Alamo* was torn from her wharf and dashed upon
Pelican flats and the bow of the British steamer *Red Cross*,
which had previously been hurled there. The stern of the
*Alamo* is stove in and the bow of the *Red Cross* is crushed.

"Down the channel to the jetties two other ocean steamships lie grounded. Some schooners, barges and smaller
craft are strewn bottom side up along the slips of the piers.
The tug *Louise* of the Houston Direct Navigation Company
is also a wreck.

"It will take a week to tabulate the dead and the missing
and to get anything near an approximate idea of the mone-
tary loss. It is safe to assume that one-half of the property of
the city is wiped out and that one-half of the residents have
to face absolute poverty.

"At Texas City three of the residents were drowned. One
man stepped into a well by a mischance and his corpse was
found there. Two other men ventured along the bayfront
during the height of the storm and were killed. There are but
few buildings at Texas City that do not tell the story of the
storm. The hotel is a complete ruin.

"For ten miles inland from the shore it is a common sight
to see small craft, such as steam launches, schooners and
oyster sloops. The life boat of the life-saving station was
carried half a mile inland, while a vessel that was anchored
in Moses Bayou lies high and dry five miles up from Lamarque."

## WENT THROUGH THE STORM OF 1875

"The great storm which has just devastated Galveston re-
minds me of the terrible equinoctial storm that swept over
that city in September of 1875," said Dr. Henry Stanhope
Bunting of Room 500, 57 Washington Street, Chicago.

"At that time I was a resident of Galveston, and my experience was similar to that of many others who escaped. The
loss of life and property was great.

"The situation of Galveston exposes the city to the waves whenever there is a severe windstorm. The island is thirty miles long and quite narrow. It is really only a great sand bar, rising four to five feet above the surface of the Gulf. At their highest point the sand banks are not more than ten feet above the normal surface of the water.

"The city is built at the northern end of the island at the entrance to Galveston Bay. The opening to the bay between the end of the island and the mainland gives the water a free sweep over the jetties when a heavy wind is blowing. In this way waves running several feet high pour immense volumes of water into the bay, causing its waters to rise many feet and flood the lowlands. In the rush of the waters back toward the gulf the narrow channel entrance to the bay is not a sufficient outlet and the flood sweeps into the city.

"It is seldom that the equinoctial storms are so severe that the back flow of the water inundates the island. In very heavy storms, however, as in the latest hurricane, the great waves might sweep across the island from the gulf and add to the work of destruction in rushing back to the gulf from the bay.

"The houses have no cellars. They are built on pillars of brick several feet above the ground. When the water is high it washes up to the first floor and sometimes drives the occupants of the building to the second story.

"When the storm struck in 1875 we were at a house near the water's edge five miles down the island from Galveston. The waves lifted the house off its brick pillars and dropped it in the water and sand, tilted at an angle of 45 degrees. With other families, we took refuge at a house on much higher ground, but even there we were driven to the second story."

## RESCUERS' FAMILIES PERISHED

John Davis, having apartments in a huge flat building, who was searching for the body of his wife in the debris of the structure, said there were fifty-two families there when the house collapsed, and he was the only survivor.

Policeman Joseph Bird and John Rowan rescued about 100 people Saturday from the fury of the storm. They returned to the police station only when the high water floated the patrol wagon and threatened to drown their team. They had no idea that the waters of the Gulf had invaded the western portion of the city where they lived until they returned to the police station. They started immediately for their homes, but their families had been swept away. Policeman Bird lost his wife and five children and Rowan his wife and three children.

Many refugees were picked up at Hitchcock and taken to the Jacquard Hotel, where they were given every possible attention. Many of these refugees were suffering from injuries and had been in the water for some time. Most of these persons had floated in on drift and rafts, and one of the party came ashore on a piano.

One hundred ammunition boxes from Camp Hawley were found near Hitchcock, and a pile-driver from Huntington wharf was driven inland to within a few hundred yards of the town. The prairie was covered with drift of all kinds—dead cattle, watercraft of all sizes, buggies, wagons and such like. Searching parties found dozens of bodies in Hall's Bayou and buried them.

## SEES FAMILY SWEPT AWAY

One of the refugees who arrived at Houston on the first relief train from Texas City, who had a sad experience in the hurricane, was S. W. Clinton, an engineer at the fertilizing plant at the Galveston stock yards. Mr. Clinton's family consisted of his wife and six children. When his house was washed away he managed to get two of his little boys safely to a raft, and with them he drifted helplessly about. His raft collided with wreckage of every description and was split in two and he was forced to witness the drowning of his sons, unable to help them in any way. Mr. Clinton says parts of the city are seething masses of water.

## A Genuine Hell Upon Earth

Joseph Johnson, a prominent citizen of Austin, who was among the list of missing, arrived at home Wednesday evening, direct from Galveston, and was received with joy by his family. Mr. Johnson went to Galveston on Friday, the day before the disaster, and was there during all the terrible storm and until Tuesday night, where he aided in the work of rescue and saw some sorrowing sights. He said many of the survivors got through the flood almost by miracle. He saw young men who were black-haired on Saturday come out of the ordeal with hair turned completely white on Sunday.

"It would take 5,000 men one year," he says, "to clear the streets and town of Galveston, so complete is the ruin. The biggest liar in America could not do justice to the existing condition of affairs there. I was in the Tremont Hotel during the storm. The building was thronged with refugees; women were praying throughout the night, and above the roar of the wind could be heard crash of buildings and splash of the waves against the building. We expected the hotel to go down any minute. At daylight Sunday morning I and four others started out to view the ruins. We passed eight bodies within a block, and when we reached the beach, where the waters were still running high, we stayed some time, and while there about one body per minute passed us, floating with the tide. Homes that were formerly elegant are a mass of wreckage.

"When I left the city the stench from decaying human bodies was simply terrible and almost unbearable. It is with difficulty that they can be handled at all, and the only ones who can now do the work are negroes. The sight is sickening. It is impossible to make any effort at identification, except to keep a record of the jewels and valuables taken from them. All pretense at holding inquests was abandoned yesterday. The bodies are piled on drays and hauled to the wharf, where they are lowered into the water. They are piled one on the other like so many animals, it being impossible to give them any attention. The bodies of poor and rich alike are treated in this manner. Hundreds of men and women who are seeking friends or relatives who are among the missing surround the places where the bodies are handled, and their cries of distress are almost unbearable.

"There was not a living animal on the island so far as I could see. Thousands of head of cattle and horses were drowned and killed. No cats or dogs survived the storm and not a bird is to be seen. No one can make anything like a reliable estimate of the number of deaths. I had to walk for twelve miles from the place where I landed on the mainland before I got out of the wreckage. The water swept the coast for a distance of twenty miles inland, and dead bodies are to be seen all over this territory. I passed a large number on my walk to get a train. The stench in this storm-swept part of the mainland is awful. It is estimated that over 5,000 head of cattle were drowned by the gulf waters in that section."

## STRANGE DEATH OF A WEALTHY ENGLISHMAN

One of the most pathetic stories of suffering in Galveston was brought to light Friday morning when the Southern Pacific train arrived at New Orleans from Houston. Among the passengers were Mrs. Mary Quayle of Liverpool, England, and Mr. Jonathan Hale of Gloversville, N. Y. Mrs. Quayle came from New York to Galveston, arriving there on the Thursday before the storm, accompanied by her husband, Edward Quayle, a tabulator on the Liverpool Cotton Exchange. Mrs. Quale and her husband took apartments in the Lucas Terrace, a fashionable place in the eastern end of Galveston Island.

All day Saturday, the day of the storm, her husband was not feeling well and remained in his room most of the time, lying down on a couch. When the storm became very bad after 8 o'clock he arose and went to the window to look out in the darkness, hoping to see, by an occasional flash of lightning, whether or not there was danger of destruction, as was greatly feared.

Suddenly there came an unusually violent fit of wind and the window out of which Mr. Quayle was peering was literally sucked out as if by a mighty air-pump, and he was taken along with it. Mrs. Quayle, so far as she was able to explain, instead of being drawn along in the direction of the storm, was thrown in the opposite direction against the door of her room.

When she came to her senses she found she was not severely hurt, and began to call for her husband. There was no reply, and in her fright she fairly shrieked out his name. Mr. Hale, who occupied the adjoining room, came to her assistance and cared for her until dawn of Sunday morning. Then they went out together and searched the adjacent portion of the city for her missing husband. But not a trace of him was to be found. The search was kept up until Monday night, by which time all the wounded had been cared for in the best possible way and all the unburied dead had become putrid. Then Mr. Hale brought Mrs. Quayle via Houston to New Orleans and they immediately took the Louisville & Nashville's train to New York.

## UNNERVED BY WHAT HE SAW

Michael B. Hancock, 3452 Dearborn street, Chicago, unnerved by the scenes of horror he witnessed among the ruins of Galveston on Tuesday, hastened to leave the stricken city, and arrived in Chicago Thursday afternoon. Sights of the dead bodies constantly before him, according to his statements, had left him practically without sleep since he first set foot on the island.

Hancock, who is a Pullman car porter, had a run from Chicago to Austin, but when he reached the end of his trip Monday he heard of the disaster at Galveston and decided to go with a relief party leaving Austin that night. The relief train was able to proceed only as far as Houston, and from there the goods were transported to the coast and put aboard a small excursion steamer.

He was accompanied by his conductor, Frank Alphons. Though they were with the relief party, they were stopped several times by the pickets at the steamer landings. After much difficulty, they gained a view of the city and the dead.

While in the midst of their sightseeing they were accosted by United States soldiers and commanded to assist in the recovery and burning of the dead bodies. Feigning to acquiesce, they managed to draw away from the soldiers, and then made a run for the beach. A small boat carried them to the mainland, and they made a forced march of twelve miles before they were able to obtain a vehicle to take them to Houston. Reaching Houston late at night, they started at once for Austin and the north. Alphons stopped at St. Louis and Hancock came straight through.

When visited at his residence Thursday night Hancock said:

"The sights in the wrecked city of Galveston were the most horrible that I have ever witnessed. Dead bodies were everywhere. Part of the city had been blotted out. For a distance of two miles along the bay, houses had been washed away and only the foundations left. The water had not yet entirely receded, and where business blocks and fine residences had once stood were simply holes marking the foundations. These were filled with floating debris and bodies of the drowned.

"The sight was ghastly in the extreme, as the working parties would arrive at one of these holes and start to drag the bodies of the dead from the pools of dirty water. Everyone was expected to work at recovering the dead, and the soldiers corralled Alphons and me and told us that we would have to assist in the work. At that time we were standing watching a party of five men working under a guard. They were lassoing the bodies and pulling them out on the higher places, and then piling them on boards preparatory to burning them.

"Just as some of the regulars were guarding us a terrible outcry arose from the men engaged in the rescue work. Running quickly to the scene of trouble, we saw one of the workers was in the grasp of one of the soldiers. Another soldier was covering him with his rifle. The man, a Mexican, dressed in shabby clothes and wearing a drooping sombrero, was standing sullenly eying the crowd, with one hand in his pocket. His captor grasped his arm suddenly and dragged his hand from the pocket, and five mutilated fingers which he had hacked from corpses dropped to the ground. Each had one or more rings on it.

"With the sight of these evidences of crime before them the workers seemed to go mad, and with cries of 'Lynch him!' 'Burn him!' made for the unfortunate wretch. Before that he had been standing stolid and unmoved, but the approaching danger shook his courage, and he sunk to the ground pleading for mercy. But there was no mercy for the monster, and the men were only prevented from killing him then and there by the interference of the soldiers.

" 'Leave him to us,' said the corporal in charge of the party as he ranged his men around the prisoner. 'We will attend to his case,' and with that he had the Mexican marched over and placed against a post not more than fifteen feet from the bodies he had mutilated. Selecting four soldiers as a firing party, he lined them up ten feet from the doomed man, and with the word 'Fire!' four bullets pierced the ghoul's body and he fell dead. Such was a measure of the speedy justice which is being meted out to vandals in Galveston. Besides this case, I heard of several more where the guilty men were given the benefit of a short court-martial, then sentenced to death and shot.

"I told Alphons that I did not want any of that kind of work, and that I never could stand the notion of handling the bodies, and suggested that we escape. He agreed with me, and we gradually edged away from the soldiers and finally made a run and reached the beach. Here we hired a small boy to row us to the mainland, and from there we had to walk twelve miles before we could get a rig to take us back to Houston.

"It will be a long time before I will want to return to Galveston, or before I can forget the terrible scenes I witnessed there. Since I left there I have been seeing the dead bodies all day, lying stark and stiff, with looks of terror on their faces, as though they had realized that a sure death was before them, and at night I have dreamed of having to help handle them. I tell you such things wear on a man, and I will bless the time when I can forget that I was ever in Galveston.

"The ruins show that the tidal wave must have struck the city broadside, as the buildings are washed away in almost a straight line back from the shore. The wave swept away buildings as far as twelve blocks inland for a space of nearly two miles. This ruined part comprised all the best part of the city. All the city buildings and the entire business portion of the city were swept away, and nothing remains to mark the spots where business blocks stood except half-submerged foundations filled with boards and dead bodies.

"The inhabitants who were rendered homeless and were not able to leave the city are now living in tents furnished by the United States government. Several distributing stations had been established and forces of men were busy issuing food and clothing to the unfortunate people. There appeared to be no lack of provisions, but water is scarce and there is no ice. While we were there the heat was almost unendurable, and the stench from the bodies made the task of the relief party anything but pleasant. Water has to be hauled for several miles. The electric-light plant was destroyed and the city is without light, but the moon has shone brightly, and the work of finding the bodies has been carried on day and night.

"Conservative estimates of the number drowned made by persons familiar with the city place the loss of life at 5,000. No one knows just how many were killed, and it will be difficult for an accurate statement to be ever made, as the authorities are making no attempt at identifying the dead, but are bending all their efforts toward getting the city cleaned up in order to prevent a pestilence. At first relatives of those killed were allowed to accompany the searching parties, but this was found to be too slow a method, and now the pickets are instructed to prevent anyone not connected with relief parties from entering the city.

"For the first two days the bodies were carried out to sea in steamers and dumped overboard, but now the officials are piling up the slain in heaps with boards and pieces of timber among them, and, after saturating the pile with oil, set fire to them.

"It hardly seems probable that they will rebuild Galveston, at least not on its present location. The city stood but little above the sea level, and the soil is sandy, which accounts for the complete destruction of most of the buildings even to the foundations.

"Many refugees came north with us, and all seemed to be in a hurry to leave the scene of desolation. They acted as though dazed, and many were unable to talk intelligently regarding their escape. All along the line we were besieged with questions regarding the safety of different people, but of course were unable to give our questioners any reliable information.

"Smaller towns through Texas that were struck by the hurricane had buildings blown down and a few casualties resulting. However, Galveston was the only city to suffer from the tidal wave, and that accounts for the large loss of life. Most of the dead in Galveston were drowned, and but few were killed by falling timbers. In Houston several buildings were blown down and about ten persons killed."

## Untold Sufferings on Bolivar Island

After suffering untold privations for over a week on Bolivar peninsula, an isolated neck of land extending into Galveston bay a few miles from the east end of Galveston Island, the Rev. L. P. Davis, wife and five young children reached Houston September 17 famished, penniless and nearly naked, but overcome with amazement and joy at their miraculous delivery from what seemed to them certain death. Wind and water wrecked their home, annihilated their neighbors and destroyed every particle of food for miles around, yet they passed through the terrible days and nights raising their voices above the shriek of the wind in singing hymns and in prayer. And through it all not one member of the family was injured to the extent of even a scratch.

When the hurricane struck the Rev. Mr. Davis' home at Patton beach the water rose so fast that it was pouring into the windows before the members of the family realized their danger. Rushing out Mr. Davis hitched his team and placing his wife and children into a wagon started for a place of safety. Before they had left his yard another family of refugees drove up to ask assistance, only to be upset by the waves before his very eyes. With difficulty the party was saved from drowning, and when safe in the Davis wagon were half floated, half drawn by the team to a grove.

With clotheslines Mr. Davis lashed his 12 and 14 year old boys in a tree. One younger child he secured with the chain of his wagon, and lifting his wife into another tree he climbed beside her. While the hurricane raged above and a sea of water dashed wildly below, Mrs. Davis clung to her 6-month-old babe with one arm, while with the other she held fast to her precarious haven of refuge. The minister held a baby of 18 months in the same manner, and while the little one cried for food he prayed. In other trees the family he had rescued from drowning found a precarious footing.

When the night had passed and the water receded, wreckage, dead animals and the corpses of parishioners surrounded the devoted party. There was nothing to eat, and, nearly dead with exhaustion, the preacher and his little flock set out on foot to seek assistance. They were too weak to continue far and sank down on the plain, while Mr. Davis pushed on alone. Five miles away a farmhouse was found, partially intact, and securing a team Davis returned for his half-dead party.

For two days they, remained at the home of the hospitable farmer and then set out afoot to find a hamlet or make their way over the desert-like peninsula to Bolivar Point. In the heat of the burning sun they plodded on along the water front, subsisting upon a steer which they killed and devoured raw, until finally they came upon an abandoned and overturned sailboat high on the beach.

With a united effort they succeeded in launching the boat and with improvised distress signals displayed managed to sail to Galveston. There, because of red tape, they were unable to secure clothing, although they were given a little food and transportation to Houston. Clad in an old pair of trousers, a tattered shirt and torn shoes, with his family in even worse plight, the circuit rider of the Patton Beach, Johnston's Bethel, Bolivar Point and High Island Methodist churches rode into Houston, dirty, weak and half-starved. Here the family were sent to a hospital and cared for.

They were sent to Dickinson, Tex., where they had relatives, who aided them until the Methodist church came to their relief.

Bolivar reported that up to September 16, 220 bodies had been found and buried and many were still lying on the sands. Assistance was needed. It was a fact generally commented upon and merely emphasized by the clergyman's experience, that while succor was being rushed to Galveston other sufferers were neglected. The relief trains en route from Houston to Galveston traversed a storm-swept section where famishing and nearly naked survivors sat on the wrecks of their homes and hungrily watched tons of provisions whirling past them while there was little prospect of aid reaching them.

## MAN HAD HIS BROKEN NECK SET

One of the most difficult operations known to medical history, and a rarity, was performed by Drs. Johnson, Lucas and Ryon Monday morning, September 17, at a hospital in Houston.

P. H. Wigzell, of Alvin, a suburban town not far from Galveston, was blown half a mile in his house and suffered dislocation of the cervical vertebrae. His head fell forward on his chest and he had no power to raise it. It was a plain case of broken neck and the physicians operated successfully. They placed the neck in a plaster cast and the man will live for years to come.

## MOST TERRIBLE WEEK OF HIS LIFE

L. F. Menage of Chicago, who returned from Galveston the Friday night succeeding the disaster, reached the Tremont Hotel, Galveston, the Friday evening before the terrible storm began. He said it had been the most terrible week in his experience; the most awful two days a man could imagine were the Sunday and Monday succeeding the hurricane. "One man would ask another how his family had come out," said Mr. Menage, "and the answer would be indifferent and hard—almost offish: 'Oh, all gone.' 'All gone' was the phrase on all sides.

"The night before the disaster, when I reached the hotel, it was blowing rather hard, and the clerk said we were in for a storm, and I asked him if his roof was firmly fixed, and he said, 'Well, it won't be quite as bad as that,' but by the next night at the same time there was three feet of water in the rotunda and the skylight had fallen in and the servants' annex had been blown to pieces, and the place was crowded with refugees who arrived from all points of the city in boats. Saturday night there was little sleep, yet no one realized the extent of the disaster.

"On Sunday morning one could walk on the higher streets, so quickly had the water gone down. I took a walk along the beach, and the place was one great litter of overturned houses, debris of all kinds and corpses. I met one woman who burst into tears at sight of a small rocker, her property mixed in among the wreckage. She had lost all her family in the flood.

"People were for the most part bereft of their senses from the horror, and a single funeral would have seemed more terrible—more solemn—than a pile of cremated bodies.

"The tales of looting are only too true, and as I passed northward in a sailboat on Tuesday I heard the shots ring out which told some ghoul was paying the penalty. Galveston will rise again on the old site, and without as much difficulty as is at present anticipated. Most of the people will, however, try and live on the mainland. At least 5,000 persons perished."

## BOY FLOATS MILES ON TRUNK

The miracles of Galveston were many. Some of them will not be received with full credit by readers. In the infirmary at Houston was a boy whose name is Rutter. He was found on Monday morning lying behind a trunk on the land near the town of Hitchcock, which is twenty miles to the north-ward of Galveston. The boy was only 12 years old. His story was that his father, mother, and two children remained in the house. There was a crash. The house went to pieces. The boy said he caught hold of a trunk when he found himself in the water and floated off with it. He was sure the others were drowned. He had no idea of where it took him, but when daylight came he was across the bay and out upon the still partially submerged mainland.

## ESCAPED IN BATHING SUITS

The wife of Manager Bergman of the Houston Opera House saw more of the storm than fell to the lot of most women who live to tell of it. She had been spending the summer at a Rosenberg Avenue cottage only a short distance from the beach.

On Saturday morning the water had risen there three feet. Putting on a bathing suit, Mrs. Bergman went to the Olympia to talk over the long distance telephone with her husband in Houston. This was about 10 a.m. At the Olympia she had to wade waist deep in the water. At 2 o'clock Mrs. Bergman became alarmed, and with her sister she left the summer cottage and started toward the more thickly settled part of the city. Neighbors laughed at the fear of the women. Out of a family of fifteen in the next house only three were saved.

Mrs. Bergman and her sister waded and swam alternately several blocks until they reached the higher streets. Then they hired a negro with a dray and told him to take them to the telephone exchange. Within two blocks from where the start was made in this way the mule got into deep water and was drowned. The women reached the telephone building, but when the firemen began to bring in the dead bodies they left and went to Balton's livery stable. This was only 600 yards away, but Mrs. Bergman says it was the hardest part of the trip, with the air full of flying bits of glass, slate and wood. In the stable they remained all morning.

When the sun had risen the water had so far receded that they went out to the site of their cottage. A hitching post was all that served to locate the place. No houses were left standing for many blocks around. A dead baby lay in the yard. The two women returned downtown. Passing a store with plate glass windows and doors blown out, they went in and helped themselves to the black cloth from which they made the gowns they still wore when they reached Houston three days later. During the storm they wore their bathing suits.

## STRANGE INCIDENTS OF THE FLOOD

Many instances of devotion of husband to wife, of wife to husband, of child to parent and parent to child could be mentioned. One poor woman with her child and her father was cast out into the raging waters. They were separated. Both were in drift and both believed they went out in the gulf and returned. The mother was finally cast upon the drift and there she was pounded by the waves and debris until she was pulled into a house against which the drift had lodged, and during all that frightful ride she held to her eight month old boy and when she was on the drift pile she lay upon the infant and covered it with her body that it might escape the blows of the planks. She came out of the ordeal cut and maimed, but the infant had not a scratch.

## THREW $10,000 OF DIAMONDS INTO THE WATER

Edward Zeigler, Thomas Farley and Alexander McCarthy arrived at Mobile, Ala., Thursday evening from Galveston. They left Galveston that morning on the tug *Robinson* with 130 other refugees and were taken to Houston. Until they arrived at New Orleans they were clad in undergarments and were coatless.

They escaped at 10:30 on Sunday morning from a house on the exposed beach by clinging to a log and floating to high ground. Zeigler was struck by floating wreckage, but was assisted by his companions to safety. An old negress, who gave the sleeping men warning, was drowned.

Zeigler was naked and the other men were in their night garments when they reached the crowd gathered near the Tremont House, but their appearance was similar to that of hundreds, many women being rescued for whom clothing had to be at once obtained. At noon Sunday they had sufficient space to move around with comfort, although filled with anxiety and penned in on all sides by the rapidly rising water. Four hours later the few thoroughfares above water were congested with crowds of hysterical women, crying children and frantic men.

The separation of families produced pathetic scenes when mothers mourned their offspring and men lamented the loss of all dear to them. There was no confusion, only a clinging closer together without discrimination of class or sex as the waters advanced foot by foot.

At dark the misery deepened and the women occupied the hotel and approaches, the highest point in the city, and the water continuing to advance, buildings and stores were thrown wide open to provide refuge in the upper stories. The men gave the better positions to the women.

As midnight approached conditions became worse; several women became demented and one woman, a member of the demi-monde, threw $10,000 worth of diamonds into the flood.

In the hotel the women kissed each other and said goodbye. They prayed and sang hymns in turn. With each announcement that the waters were rising many men and women gave up to the terrible mental strain and fainted.

The survivors paid a high tribute to the bravery in the face of death of the women of Galveston, and stated that although abject melancholy had fallen over all, the spirit of fortitude displayed by the women nerved the men. The horrors of that night were equaled on the succeeding days as the water receded.

## DARED EVERYTHING FOR WIFE AND SON

Of all the heroism and dogged tenacity of purpose noted in connection with the Galveston storm none was greater than that of W. L. Love of Houston. Mr. Love was a compositor on the *Houston Post*, and his wife and little son were visiting Mrs. Love's mother in Galveston when the storm struck the city.

Early Sunday morning when the first news of the Galveston disaster began to drift in, Mr. Love announced to the foreman of the composing-room, under whom he was working, that he intended starting immediately for Galveston.

He went to one of the depots and fortunately found a train leaving toward Galveston. He boarded it, but the train was forced to stop eight miles before it reached Galveston

Bay. He walked eight miles, arriving at the bay in about two hours. There was no boat in sight, not even a skiff or canoe.

He found a large cypress railroad tie near the water's edge and, procuring a coal hook from a locomotive that had blown from the track, he got astride the tie after having placed it in the water, and set out on a difficult and perilous journey across the three miles of salt water. Thus he labored for six trying hours, the sun beating down on him and with his body half submerged in the brine of the bay. At last the goal was reached and he pulled himself out of the water and stepped on the once fair island.

After having passed on his way more than a hundred decaying bodies of the storm victims, the heroic young man set about finding his wife and little boy. This he did after a lengthy search. His wife had lost her mother, father, brothers and sisters, numbering eight in all.

The little boy had been utterly stripped of his clothing by the wind and both he and his mother had an experience that rarely comes to a mother and son.

## PITIFUL TALES OF SOME OF THE SURVIVORS

The story of Thomas Klee was indeed most pitiful. Klee lived near Eleventh and N Streets. When the storm burst he was alone in his home with his two infant children. He seized one under each arm and rushed from the frail structure in time to cheat death among the falling timbers of his home.

Once in the open, with his babies under his arms, he was swept into the bay among hundreds of others. He held to his precious burden and by skillful maneuvering managed to get close to a tree which was sweeping along with the tide. He saw a haven in the branches of the tree and raised his two-year-old daughter to place her in the branches. As he did so the little one was torn from his arm and carried away to her death.

The awful blow stunned but did not render him senseless. Klee retained his hold on the other child, aged four years, and was whirled along among the dying and dead victims of the storm's fury, hoping to effect a landing somewhere.

An hour in the water brought the desired end. He was thrown ashore, with wreckage and corpses, and, stumbling to a footing, lifted his son to a level with his face. The boy was dead.

Klee remembered nothing until Thursday night, when he was put ashore in Texas City. He had a slight recollection of helping to bury dead, clear away debris and obey the command of soldiers. His brain, however, did not execute its full functions until Friday morning.

George Boyer's experience was a sad one. He was thrown into the rushing waters, and while being carried with frightful velocity down the bay saw the dead face of his wife in the branches of a tree. The woman had been wedged firmly between two branches.

Margaret Lees' life was saved at the expense of her brother's. The woman was in her Twelfth Street home when the hurricane struck. Her brother seized her and brought her to St. Mary's University, a short distance away. He returned to search for his son, and was killed by a falling house.

THRILLING EXPERIENCE OF A DALLAS GIRL

One of the most thrilling descriptions of personal experience with the fearful flood ever written was that of Miss Maud Hall, of Dallas, Tex., who was spending her school vacation with friends at Galveston. She wrote an account of her adventures to her parents, Mr. and Mrs. Emory Hall:

"Dear Papa and Mamma: I suppose before this you will have received my telegram and know I am safe. This has been a terrible experience. I hope I will be spared any more such. I am just a nervous wreck—fever blisters over my mouth, eyes with hollows under them, and shaking all over. When I close my eyes I can't see anything but piles of naked dead and wild-eyed men and women. I suppose I had better begin at the beginning, but I don't know if I can write with any sense. Saturday at about 11 o'clock it began raining, and the wind rose a little. Sidney Spann and two young lady boarders could not get home to dinner. After the dinner the men left and we sat around in dressing sacks watching the storm. All at once Birdie Duff (Mrs. Spann's married daughter) said: 'Look at the water in the street; it must be the gulf!'

"There was water from curb to curb. It rose rapidly as we watched it, and Mrs. Spann sent us all to dress. It rose to the sidewalk, and the men began to come home. I put what I could find in my trunk and locked it. Tell mamma, the last thing I put in was her gray skirt, for I thought it might be injured.

"It took two men to each woman to get her across the street and down to the end of the block. Trees thicker than any in our yard were whirled down the street; pine logs, boxes and driftwood of all sorts swept past, and the water looked like a whirlpool. Birdie and I went across on the second trip. The wind and rain cut like a knife and the water was icy cold. It was like going down into the grave, and I was never so near death…I came near drowning with another girl. It was dark by this time, and the men put their arms around us and down into the water we went. Birdie was crying about her baby that she had to leave behind until the next trip, and I was begging' Mr. Mitchell and the other man not to turn me loose.

"Mrs. Spann came last. The water was over her chin. It was up to my shoulders when I went over. One man brought a bundle of clothing, such as he could find for us to put on, wrapped up in his mackintosh. He had to swim over. I spent the night, such a horrible one, wet from shoulder to my waist and from my knees down, and barefoot. Nobody had any shoes and stockings. Mrs. Spann did not have anything but a thin lawn dress and blanket wrapped around her from her waist down. Nellie had a lawn wrapper and blanket, and Fannie had a skirt and winter jacket. Mr. Mitchell had a pair of trousers and a light shirt and was barefooted. The house was packed with people just like us.

"The house had a basement and was of stone. The windows were blown out, and it rocked from top to bottom, and the water came into the first floor. Of course no one slept. About 3 o'clock in the morning the wind had changed and blew the water back to the gulf, and as we stood at the windows watching it fall we saw two men and two girls wading the street and heard Sidney calling for her mother. She and the young lady with her spent the night crowded into an office with nine men in total darkness, sitting on boxes, with their feet up off the floor. It was an immense brick building four stories high. They were on the second floor. The roof and one story was blown away and the water came up to the second floor. It was down toward the wharf.

"As soon as we could we waded home. Such a home! The water had risen three feet in the house and the roof being gone the rain poured in. I had not a dry rag but a dirty skirt which was hanging in the wardrobe and an underskirt with it. My trunk had floated and everything in it was stained except the gray skirt. We had not had anything to eat since noon the day before, and we lived on whiskey. Every time the men would see us they would poke a bottle of whiskey at us, and make us drink some. All we had all day Sunday was crackers at 50 cents a small box and whiskey.

"We were all so weak we knew we could not get any worse, so Miss Decker and I went down about 10 o'clock. It was awful. Dead animals everywhere, and the streets filled with fallen telegraph poles and brick stores blown over. Hundreds of women and children and men sitting on steps crying for lost ones, and nearly half of them were injured. Wild-eyed, ghastly-looking men hurried by and told of whole families killed.

"I could not stand anymore and made them bring me home, and fell on the bed with hysterics. They poured whiskey down me, but the only effect it had was to make my head ache worse. I had about got straightened out when a girl and a woman came to the house—relatives of Mrs. Spann—who had lost their mother and friends and house, and all they had. They had hysterics, and everybody cried, and I had another spell. All day wagon after wagon passed filled with dead—most of them without a thing on them—and men with stretchers with dead bodies with just a sheet thrown over them, some of them little children.

"We waited, every minute expecting to have the two bodies brought here. But they had not been found up to now, and all hope is lost. There is a little boy in the house that spent the night in the water clinging to a log, and his father and mother and four sisters were drowned. He is all alone. Last night Mr. Mitchell took Miss Decker and I to another boarding house to find a dry bed. We slept on a folding bed, with nothing under us but a rug and sheet, and I had to borrow something dry to sleep in. The husband of the lady who lost her mother has just come from Houston. He walked and swam all the way. He is nearly wild, and she is just screaming. I cannot write any more. Am coming home soon as I can."

## MIRACULOUS SURVIVAL

The Stubbs family, consisting of father, mother and two children, was in its home when it collapsed. They found refuge on a floating roof. This parted and father and one child were swept in one direction, while the mother and the other child drifted in another. One of the children was washed off, but Sunday evening all four were reunited.

Mrs. P. Watkins became a raving maniac as the result of her experiences. With her two children and her mother she was drifting on a roof, when her mother and one child were swept away. Mrs. Watkins mistakes attendants in the hospital for her lost relatives and clutches wildly for them.

Harry Steele, a cotton man, and his wife sought safety in three successive houses which were demolished. They eventually climbed on a floating door and were saved.

W. R. Jones, with fifteen other men, finding the building they were in about to fall, made their way to the water tower and, clasping hands, encircled the standpipe to keep from being washed or blown away.

Mrs. Chapman Bailey, wife of the southern manager of the Galveston Wharf Company, and Miss Blanche Kennedy floated in the waters ten to twenty feet deep all night and day by catching wreckage. Finally they got into a wooden bathtub and were driven into the gulf overnight. The incoming tide drove them back to Galveston and they were rescued the next day. They were fearfully bruised. All their relatives were drowned.

A pathetic incident in the search for the dead occurred Friday. A squad of men discovered in a wrecked building five bodies. Among these bodies was one which a member of the burial party recognized as his own brother. The bodies were all in an advanced state of decomposition. They were removed and a funeral pyre was built, at which the brother assisted and, with Spartan-like firmness, stood by and saw the bodies of the dead reduced to ashes.

On Monday a brakeman of the Galveston, Houston & Northern left Virginia Point and started to walk toward Texas City. He found a little child, which he picked up and carried for miles. On his way he discovered the bodies of nine women. These he covered with grass to protect them from the vultures until some arrangements could be made for their interment.

## STATUES ON ALTAR NOT HARMED

St. Joseph's Catholic Church presents a strange contrast, with the roof and rear wall back of the altar being carried away. The wall collapsed, but the altar was not damaged and the frail life-size statues of St. Joseph and the Virgin on the altar were not harmed or moved.

When their home went to pieces the members of the Stubbs family—husband, wife, and two children— climbed upon the roof of a house floating by. They felt tolerably secure. Without warning the roof parted in two pieces. Mr. and Mrs. Stubbs were separated. Each had a child. The parts of the raft went different ways in the darkness. One of the children fell off and disappeared. Not until some time Sunday was the family reunited. Even the child was saved, having caught a table and clung to it until it reached a place of safety.

Another man took his wife from one house to another by swimming until he had occupied three. Each fell in its turn and then he took to the waves and they were separated and each, as the persons above mentioned, believed they were carried to sea. After three hours in the water he heard her call and finally rescued her.

## WASHED UP IN A TRUNK

Mrs. William Henry Haldeman was one of the mothers and whose newborn babe was christened William Henry. The experiences of this mother were horrible. Only a chapter was learned by a reporter, as told by Mother Joseph. Mrs. Haldeman was thrown on the mercies of the storm when her home went down and was swept away. The family had separated when they started to abandon their home to the greed of the storm. When Mrs. Haldeman was carried away on the roof of the wrecked cottage she lost all trace of the other members of the family, but never lost faith and courage. The roof struck some obstruction and the next instant Mrs. Haldeman was hurled from her improvised raft and landed in a trunk which was rocked on the waves.

Cramped up in the trunk, the poor woman, suffering agonies, was protected to a limited extent and was afforded some warmth. On went the trunk, tossed high on the sea, bumping against driftwood until the crude bark was hurled against the Ursuline convent walls and was pulled into the building. The little babe was born a few hours later and, while the good sisters and some of the women in the building were attending to the mother and child, another chapter in this family's history was being enacted just without the convent walls. In a tree in the convent yard a young man, a brother of Mrs. Haldeman, battled with the wind and wa-

ters while clinging fast to the limb of the tree which swayed
and bowed to the wind.

He knew not where he was. He could but merely discern
the outlines of the academy building. While not knowing his
chance of life or death he heard the plaintive cry of a child
near by. Reaching out with one hand he caught the dress of
a little tot, who, child-like, cried out, "Me swimming." The
child had run the mill race buoyed by the force of the storm
and had not had time to realize her peril. The young man in
the tree was Mrs. Haldeman's brother, and the child which
had come to him on the waves was Mrs. Haldeman's little
girl. A few minutes afterward a rescuing party was sent out
from the convent in response to cries for help and found the
young man and his niece and brought him to the sheltering
institution. The reunion of at least a part of the family followed a few minutes later.


## SAVED AS IF BY A MIRACLE

Destitute save for a few personal effects carried in a small
valise, and with nerves shattered by a week of horror, Mr.
and Mrs. C. A. Prutsman, with their two daughters, 12 and
6 years old, reached Chicago Sunday morning, September
16, from the flood-swept district of Texas.

"Yes, we were fortunate," said Mrs. Prutsman, as she
leaned wearily back in a rocking chair and tenderly contem-
plated the two children at her side. "It seems to me just like
an awful dream, and when I think of the hundreds and hundreds of children who were killed right before our very eyes,
I feel as though I always ought to be satisfied no matter what
comes."

Mr. Prutsman said:

"The reports from Galveston are not half as appalling as
the situation really is. We left the fated city Wednesday afternoon, going by boat to Texas City, and by rail to Houston.
The condition of Galveston at that time, while showing an

improvement, was awful, and never shall I forget the terrible scenes that met our eyes as the boat on which we left steamed out of the harbor. There were bodies on all sides of us. In some places they were piled six and seven deep, and the stench was horrible.

"I resided with my family at 718 Nineteenth Street. This is fourteen blocks away from the beach, yet my house was swept away at 5 p.m. Saturday, and with it went everything we had in the world. Fifteen minutes before, I took my wife and children to the courthouse and we were saved, along with about 1,000 others who sought refuge there. When we went through the streets the water was up to our arms and we carried the children on our heads.

"I assisted for several days in the work of rescue. In one pile of debris we found a woman who seemed to have escaped the flood, but who was injured and pinned down so she could not escape. A guard came along and, after failing to rescue her, deliberately shot her to end her misery.

"The streets present a gruesome appearance. Every available wagon and vehicle in the city is being used to transport the dead, and it is no uncommon thing to see a load of bodies ten deep. The stench in the city is nauseating. Since the flood the only water that could be used for drinking purposes was in cisterns, and it has become tainted with the slime and filth that covers the city until it is little better than no water at all.

"Since the city was placed under martial law conditions have been much better and there is little lawlessness. The soldiers have shown no quarter and have orders to shoot on sight. This has had a wonderful effect on the disreputable characters who have flocked into the city.

"Everybody who remains in Galveston is made to work, and the punishment for a refusal is about the same as that meted out to ghouls. I saw four colored men shot in one day. There were confined in the hold of a steamer in the harbor six colored men who were found by the soldiers with a flour sack almost filled with fingers and ears on which were jew-

els. These men probably have been publicly executed before
this time.

"In the work of rescue we found whole families tied together with ropes, and in several instances mothers had
their babes clasped in their arms.

"Scores of unfortunates straggle into Houston every day
and their condition is pitiable. Several have lost their reason.
The citizens of Houston are doing all in their power to meet
the demands of the sufferers, and every available building in
the city has been converted into a hospital. When we arrived
in Houston we scarcely had clothes enough to cover us and
the citizens fitted us out and started us north. The fear of
fever or some awful plague drove us from Galveston.

"Already speculators are flocking into the city, and there is
some activity among them over tax-title real estate. In several instances whole families were wiped out of existence,
and the opportunities in this line seem to be great."


THEY READ THEIR OWN OBITUARIES


Reported dead several times, their obituaries printed in
Galveston and Houston papers, Peter Boss, wife and son,
formerly of Chicago, were found on the afternoon of September 18, after having passed through a most thrilling experience.

Mr. and Mrs. Boss were the persons in search of whom
Mrs. M. C. McDonald, No. 4501 Drexel Boulevard, Chicago, went to Houston.

Mrs. Boss' story of her experience in the disaster was a
thrilling one. With her husband and son she was seated
at supper in her home on Twelfth Street when the storm
broke. She seized a handkerchief containing $2,000 from a
bureau, and, placing it in her bosom, went with her husband
and son to the second story.

There they remained until the water reached them and
they leaped into the darkness and the storm. They lighted

on a wooden cistern upon which they rode the entire night, clinging with one hand to the top of the cistern. Several times Mrs. Boss lost her hold, and fell backward into the water only to be drawn up again by her son. Timbers crashed against their queer boat, people on all sides of them were crushed to death or drawn into the whirling waters, but with grim perseverance the Boss family held on and rode the night out.

Mrs. Boss was pushed off the cistern several times by her frantic husband, but young Boss' presence of mind always saved her. With her feet crushed and bleeding, her clothing torn from her body and nearly exhausted, the woman was finally taken from her perilous position several hours after the hurricane started.

Her companions were without clothing and were delirious. They were the only persons saved in the entire block in which they lived. They were taken to emergency hospitals, where they all tossed in delirium until Sunday. Mrs. Boss lost her money, and the family, wealthy a week before, was penniless. They had to appeal to the city authorities for aid, and got but little.

EYE-WITNESS TELLS OF THE STORM

A graphic description of the storm was that given by R. L. Johnson, a prominent citizen of Galveston. He said:

"I reached home after wading in water to my neck and made immediate preparations to take my wife and three children where I felt their safety would be assured. The water began to rise so rapidly that in fifteen minutes we were driven to the second floor, and it was then impossible to leave the house. At this time Neighbor Kell's house, adjoining mine, went down with husband, wife and children. Then down Avenue S came two small cottages, which struck a telegraph pole and stopped directly in front of my house. I heard children crying and women screaming. The words, 'O God, save me,' I can still hear ringing in my ears.

"Another cottage came sweeping by and carried away the gallery of my house. The Artigan, Henman and Pennings houses, carrying eighteen persons, floated by and I could see the struggling forms in the water.

"I was expecting it was our turn next. I kissed my wife and children goodbye, and as I did so my eldest boy, a lad of 15, said: 'Father, it is not our time to die.' Then came the piercing scream of a woman, followed by a crash, and another house turned over on its side and was driven past by the wind and flood.

"The current was running like a mill race. The water was already on our second floor, and the waves kept knocking us about until we were completely exhausted. Then the wind went, and the water began to fall. I looked about and could not see a house for two blocks; there was nothing but flood of water in every direction. In the morning we found our house had been moved about ten feet and deposited upon the sand."

## INSANITY BEFALLS GALVESTON SURVIVORS

Hundreds of people became insane during the week succeeding the flood. They had bravely borne the loss of relatives, the hunger and fatigue, had apparently been unmindful of the horrors of the catastrophe, and had, as a rule, given no indications of mental aberration while the disaster was on, but when the danger was passed and relief from the great strain came, the overburdened mind gave way.

J. A. Fernandez, a prominent citizen of Galveston, who was connected with the relief work, told of many cases which came under his observation.

The second Sunday following the storm, September 16, he said, in recounting his experiences:

"There are at least 500 persons there whose minds have become unbalanced, and some have lost every vestige of their mental faculties. There are some raving maniacs among them, one of whom came under my personal observation. His name is Charles Thompson, a gardener. He occupied a room above me at the hotel, and during the night he kept raving and pacing the floor and kept calling on God to witness his action, continually invoking the mercy of the Deity. He has lost his family and home, and by a miracle saved himself.

"As soon as he was out of personal danger on that awful night he commenced rescuing women and children and saved seventy people, according to a gentleman who knew the circumstances. He then lost his mind. He created so much excitement at the hotel that two policemen were detailed to capture him. He heard them approaching and leaped out of a three-story window to an adjoining building. His fall was somewhat broken, but his body struck a bay window in my room. He was badly injured, but continued his mad flight. He baffled his pursuers and escaped. This occurred at 5 o'clock this morning. This is only one illustration of the conditions that prevail there.

"A man whose wife was drowned in the flood had been searching in vain for her remains for several days, and yesterday located the body in the water near Thirty-third Street and Avenue G. Soldiers had also seen the body, and they took it in charge. He protested and rushed to take possession of the body. The soldiers were stern and had to discharge their duty, and the husband, practically demented, was bound while the body was thrown in the flames and soon burned to a crisp. The man made frantic efforts to get away from the soldiers, but to no avail.

"In the course of my rounds I saw a family of six half-naked, and they appeared crazy, and would look into the face of every stranger with a vacant stare that was pitiable in the extreme. They were hurrying in the direction of the places where provisions were being distributed. They had lost their homes, and had only the clothing on their backs. There were thousands in a similar condition."

I. Thompson, a young man who was very active in saving lives during the night of the storm, became insane because of the awful scenes he witnessed. Thompson's friends first noticed his condition when he told them that one of the persons he rescued had deposited $10,000 in one of the Galveston banks to his credit and that he was going to live in luxury the rest of his life.

Thompson retired to his room on the third floor of the Washington hotel Saturday night seemingly sane. Soon afterward he became violent. The person engaged to watch him was compelled to leave the room for a short time, and when he returned found Thompson had wrenched the shutters off his window and leaped out upon an awning and thence to the street. He was seen running toward the bay, and in all probability threw himself in and was drowned.

Another case was that of a young woman who was caught in the storm, and with two other women and about fifty men and boys found refuge in an office. As the storm gradually subsided the young woman started for her home quite reassured. She found a wild waste of waters sweeping over the site of her home. Among the first victims carried into the temporary morgue were the young woman's mother, brother and two children. These were quickly followed by her brother's wife and her two sisters. The shock overthrew the girl's reason, and she became a nervous wreck, without a relative in the world.

## STORM REFUGEES PRECIPITATE PANIC IN A CONVENT

The Ursuline convent and academy, in charge of the Sisters of St. Angelo, proved a haven of refuge for nearly 1,000 homeless and storm-driven unfortunates. No one was refused admittance to the sheltering institution. Negroes and whites were taken in without question and the asylum was thrown open to all who sought its protecting wings.

In the midst of the storm the hundreds or more negroes grew wild and shouted and sang in true camp-meeting style until the nerves of the other refugees were shattered and a panic seemed imminent. It was then that Mother Superioress Joseph rang the chancel bell and caused a hush of the pandemonium. When quiet had been restored the mother addressed the negroes and told them that it was no time nor place for such scenes; that if they wanted to pray they should do so from their hearts, and the Creator of all things would hear their offerings above the roar of the hurricane, which raged with increased fury as she spoke to the awe-stricken assemblage.

The negroes listened attentively and when the mother told them that all those who wished to be baptized and re-sign themselves to God could do so nearly everyone asked that the sacrament be administered. The panic had been precipitated by the falling of the north wall of that section of the building in which the negroes had sought refuge. Order and silent prayer were brought about by the nun's determi-nation and presence of mind.

Families that had been separated by the conflict of ele-ments were united by the waters of the gulf tossing them into this haven of refuge. Heart-moving scenes were presented by these unions as the half-dead, mangled and bruised un-fortunates were rescued and dragged from the waters by the more fortunate members of their families.

The academy was to have opened for the fall session on Tuesday and forty-two boarding scholars from all parts of the State had arrived at the convent, preparatory to re-suming their studies on that date. The community of nuns comprised forty sisters, and they, too, were there adminis-tering cheer and mercy to the sufferers, many of whom were more dead than alive when brought into the shelter. Within this religious home and in the cells of the nuns four babies came into this world during that dark night.

Mother Joseph, in speaking of the incidents of the night within the convent walls, said that she believed it was the first time in the history of the world that a baby had been born in the nuns' cell of a convent. They were christened, for no one expected to live to see the light of day, and it was voted that these babes should not leave the world they had just entered without baptism, and, regardless of the religious belief of the parents, the little ones were baptized.

## THE FLOOD HORRORS DROVE THEM CRAZY

Three-fourths of the people who applied for relief were mentally dull. The physicians said with proper care most of them might be cured.

A young girl was brought into the general relief station in Galveston on Friday night. The relief corps found her huddled up in an empty freight car, laughing and singing to amuse herself. The doctors said food and care were all she needed to restore her to reason.

It was over a week after the flood before those from the outside really began to find out what the awful calamity was to the people in the desolated city.

The first shock was wearing off, the long lists of dead and missing were getting to be an old story, and the sick and suffering were crawling into places of refuge. Some of them had been sleeping on the open prairies ever since the storm—most of them, in fact—men with broken arms and legs, sick women and ailing children.

They would crawl out of the wreck of their homes and lie down on the bare ground to die.

Relief parties found such people as these every day and brought them into the hospitals as fast as possible. One relief party found 5,000 people in the vicinity of Galveston homeless, helpless, hopeless and tearless. It was a sight to cause a stone statue to weep.

Monday, September 17, a man rode up to a hospital at Houston, and told the doctors he had just come from the Brazos bottoms. Said he: "The folks there are starving. There is not a pound of flour left and the children are crying for milk. There are so many sick people there that we don't know what to do. Can you send someone down?"

The physician in charge said he would go at once. The man on horseback leaned over his saddle and tried to speak.

Something in his face frightened me. I called to two doctors. They ran out and caught him. He was in a dead faint. When we had brought him to he laughed sheepishly.

"I don't know what's the matter with me," he said. "Ain't never been taken this way before."

The doctors looked at each other and smiled, but the nurses' eyes were full of tears. The man had not tasted food for thirty-six hours, and he had ridden fifty miles in the broiling Texas sun.

More troops were called for on September 17 by Governor Sayers of Texas to relieve those on duty at Galveston who were worn out by their hard work. The response was prompt and hearty.

ILLINOIS GIRL HAS TRYING TIME IN THE RUINED CITY

Miss Alice Pixley, of Elgin, Ill., arrived at her home on Sunday, September 16, from Galveston, where she had a most trying time during the storm. She told her story in a wonderfully graphic way.

"I had been in Galveston for about six weeks, visiting Miss Lulu George, who lives on Thirty-fifth Street between N and N 1/2 streets. It was not until after the noon hour of Saturday that we were frightened. Buildings had gone down as mere egg shells before that death-dealing wind.

"About 1:30 p.m. I told Miss George that we must make our way to another building about half a block away. The water had risen over five feet in two hours, and as I hurried to the front door the wind tore down my hair and I was blinded for a time.

"I turned my eyes to the west and for three long miles there was not a building standing, everything had been swept away. How we ever reached the two-story building a hundred yards away I do not know. We waded through the water and every few minutes we were carried off our feet and dashed against the floating debris.

"The building we were trying to reach was a store and the foundation kept out the water. We hurried to the cellar and stayed there for several hours. At last the windswept waves found an opening and broke through the foundation and we had a mad run to escape the rushing, swirling waters.

"We reached the first floor and I shrank into a corner, expecting every second to be carried out to my death. How it happened I can never tell, but this and one other building were the only ones left for blocks around. As it was, several people were killed in the building we occupied and the other house that was left standing.

"After a time I felt faint from hunger and, though too weak to seek food, I told Miss George that I could go into another room. I staggered along the floor until I reached a window, and fell, half fainting, through it. As I leaned there I witnessed sights that I pray God will never make another see.

"Whirling by me, bodies, more than I could dare count, were crushed and mangled between a jumble of timbers and debris. Men, women and children went by, sinking, floating, dashing on I know not where. I wanted to close my eyes, but I could not. I cried aloud and made an attempt to go to my friends, but I was exhausted and all I could do was to watch the terrible scenes.

"Babies, oh, such pretty little ones, too, were carried on and on, gowned in dainty clothing, their eyes open, staring in mute terror above. Thank Providence they were dead.

"I was partly blinded by tears, but I could still see through the mist. Little arms seemed to stretch toward me asking assistance and there I lay, half prostrated, too weak to lend assistance.

"How it all ended I know not. I must have fainted for I awakened with 'We are saved, Alice,' ringing in my ears.

"When I found we could get out of the city I declared I would go at all costs. I thought of home and my parents and I wanted to telegraph, just like thousands of others, that I was safe.

"It was days before we could get away, however, and then

it was in a most terrible confusion. Eighty-eight persons crowded on a small boat and started for Houston.

"The day we left the militia was out in all its force. I could hear the sharp report of a rifle and the wail of some soul as he paid the penalty for his thieving operations.

"Later I saw the soldiers with their glistening rifles leveled at scores of men and saw them topple forward dead. Oh, they had to shoot those terrible beasts, for they were robbing the dead. They groveled in blood, it seemed.

"I saw with my own eyes the fingers of women cut off by regular demons in the search for jewels. The soldiers came and killed them and it was well.

"As we made our way toward the boat that was to take us from the City of Death I saw great clouds of smoke rising in the air. Upon the top of flaming boards thousands of bodies were being reduced to ashes.

"It was best, for the odor that arose from the dead bodies was awful. Still it made one's heart ache with a sorrow never to be equaled as one witnessed little children tossed into the midst of the hissing flames. Do you wonder I cry?

"Before me, no matter which way I turned, I could see dead bodies, their cold eyes gazing at me with staring intentness. I closed my eyes and stumbled forward, hoping I might escape for a moment the sight of dead bodies, but no; the moment I would open them again, right at my feet I would find the form of some poor creature.

"Coming to Chicago on the train I read the papers. They are mistaken, away wrong. They only say 5,000 dead. It will be more than 10,000.

"I know I am right; everyone in Galveston talks of 12,000, 15,000 and 18,000 dead, but it will be 10,000 at the very least.

"I believe the worst sight I witnessed was the 2,800 bodies being carried out to sea and buried in the gulf. Huge barges were tied at the wharves and loaded with the unknown dead. As fast as one barge was filled it made its way out from the shore, and weighting the bodies, men cast them into the water.

"Oh, those eyes," she cried, "that I might put them from my mind. I can see those little children, mere babies go floating by my place of refuge, dead, dead! God alone knows the suffering I went through. Thousands, yes thousands of poor souls were carried over the brink of death in the twinkling of an eye, and I saw it all."

# CHAPTER FOUR:
## RELIEF POURS IN

Mayor Jones, of Galveston, issued his appeal to the United States for help on the 11th of September, and the response was prompt and liberal.

The Mayor was not afraid the people of the United States and the world would call him sensational, for no one was better qualified to judge of the situation than he. He had spent almost every hour after the flood in working for the good of the city and had accomplished wonders. He organized the citizens, giving of his own money, induced others—more unwilling than he—to open their hearts and pocketbooks, and, in fact, took no rest for days after the calamity.

As he had been around the city several times before the appeal was issued, he knew the condition of things thoroughly. Therefore, the general public had confidence in what he said. The same day the General Relief Committee of Galveston issued the following:

Galveston, Tex., Sept. 11—To the Public of America:

A conservative estimate of the loss of life is that it will reach 3,000; at least 5,000 families are shelterless and wholly destitute. The entire remainder of the population is suffering in greater or less degree.

Not a single church, school or charitable institution, of which Galveston had so many, is left intact. Not a building escaped damage and half the whole number were entirely obliterated.

There is immediate need for food, clothing and household goods of all kinds. If nearby cities will open asylums for women and children the situation will be greatly relieved.

Coast cities should send us water as well as provisions, including kerosene oil, gasoline and candles.

The Secretary of the Treasury at Washington received a joint telegram from Postmaster Griffen and Special Deputy Collector Rosenthal, at Galveston. This described the destruction caused by the storm and said:

> Thousands homeless and destitute. Five hundred sheltered in custom house, which is practically roofless. Old custom house roofless and windows blown out. Need tents and 30,000 rations. Citizens' relief committee doing all in their power, but stock of undamaged provisions exhausted. With all the people housed, need extra force of six men to keep building in sanitary condition. Relief urgently requested.

The Secretary sent the government revenue cutter *Onondaga* from Norfolk to Mobile, Ala., to carry supplies to Galveston. The day the appeal was made Acting Secretary of War Meiklejohn at Washington authorized the chartering of a special train from St. Louis to carry Quartermasters' and commissary supplies to the relief of the destitute at Galveston.

Orders were also issued by the War Department for the immediate shipment to Galveston of 855 tents and 50,000 rations. These stores and supplies were divided between St. Louis and San Antonio.

On September 12, Governor Sayers issued the following statement:

> Austin, Tex, Sept. 12—Conditions at Galveston are fully as bad as reported. Communication, however, has been reestablished between the island and the mainland, and hereafter transportation of supplies will be less difficult.
>
> The work of clearing the city is progressing fairly well, and Adjutant-General Scurry, under direction of the mayor, is patrolling the city for the purpose of preventing depredations.

The most conservative estimate as to the number of deaths places them at 2,000.

Contributions from citizens of this state, and also from other states, are coming in rapidly and liberally, and it is confidently expected that within the next ten days the work of restoration by the people of Galveston will have begun in good earnest and with energy and success.

Of course, the destruction of property has been very great, not less than $10,000,000, but it is hoped and believed that even this great loss will be overcome through the energy and self-reliance of the people.

JOSEPH D. SAYERS,<br>Governor

On the same day, the Galveston General Relief Committee sent out this statement of the condition of affairs:

We are receiving numerous telegrams of condolence and offers of assistance. Nearby cities are supplying and will supply sufficient food, clothing, etc., for immediate needs. Cities farther away can serve us best by sending money. Checks should be made payable to John Sealy, Chairman of the Finance Committee. All supplies should come to, W. A. McVitie, Chairman Relief Committee.

We have 25,000 people to clothe and feed for many weeks and to furnish with household goods. Most of these are homeless, and the others will require money to make their wrecked residences habitable. From this the world may understand how much money we will need. This committee will from time to time report our needs with more particularity. We refer to dispatch of this date of Major B. G. Lowe, which the committee fully endorses. All communicants will please accept this answer in lieu of direct response

and be assured of the heartfelt gratitude of the entire
population.

W. C. JONES, Mayor
M. LASKER
J. D. SKINNER
C. H. McMASTER
R. G. LOWE
CLARENCE OUSLEY

Colonel Amos S. Kimball, Assistant Quartermaster
General, stationed at New York, was informed by army contractors on Tuesday, the day the appeal was sent out, that
Miss Helen Gould had purchased 50,000 army rations for
the Galveston sufferers. The rations were started from the
Pennsylvania railroad station in Jersey City at 3 p.m. the
same day. Miss Gould went directly to the contractors who
supply the army with provisions and ordered rations identi-
cal with those furnished for soldiers, consisting of bacon,
canned meats, beans, hard bread and coffee.

Chicago sent $25,000 to the Governor of Texas; Andrew
Carnegie gave $20,000 in cash; Sir Thomas Lipton cabled
from London to his manager at New York to send $1,000
at once, which was done; Davenport, La., sent $1,600 im-
mediately; Philadelphia wired Governor Sayers $5,000
without delay; the American Steel Hoop Company, American Tin Plate Company and American Sheet Steel Company gave $10,000 each, and the Southern Pacific Railway
Company, $5,000; Chicago started a trainload of supplies
southward, as also did the State of California; the railroads
hauling the cars free of charge; several newspapers in Chicago, New York and Kansas City either gave money or started
relief trains with doctors, nurses and medical supplies, with
orders to beat the best record time to Galveston; Cincinnati
began with $1,000 and subscribed that amount daily for
many days; Cleveland telegraphed $2,500, and then made it
$15,000; 30,000 rations and 900 United States army tents
were sent from St. Louis from the office of the United States

Quartermaster; the mayor of Colorado Springs, Colo., was told by the citizens to send $2,000 at once and he did so; nearly all the theatres of the United States gave benefits; the State of Kansas, having $500 left in its Indian Famine Relief Fund, sent that; people of the State of Texas sent $15,000 to the Governor at Austin; Houston raised $2,000 in cash; the Governors of nearly all the States issued proclamations calling upon their people to subscribe to the relief fund, the mayors of most of the cities doing the same—the consequence being that Governor Sayers had about $250,000 in hand in cash that very (Tuesday) night, with several hundreds of thousands more in sight and within call.

By Thursday he had $900,000 in hand and on Saturday had $1,500,000, in addition to which were several thousand cars loaded with supplies of all sorts—provisions, medicines, disinfectants, fruits, clothing, wines for the sick, tents, bandages, stoves, oil—everything that could possibly be needed.

It was estimated that fully $2,500,000 would be necessary to carry the sufferers through the fall and winter and into the following spring, for thousands of them were ill and unable to provide in any way for themselves. There were fully 50,000 men, women and children in Galveston and Central and Southern Texas who were dependent upon charity.

On Friday night Governor Sayers decided upon two important plans of action. The first was that he would allow all food and clothing shipped from the east and west to be concentrated in Galveston for the use of that city and that he would also grant that city the use of 30,000 laborers for a period of thirty days, the same to be paid $1.50 per man per day for that time out of the relief fund. In addition thereto all requests for money from the Galveston Relief Committee were to be granted.

His second decision was that he personally would look after the needs of the 30,000 destitute along the gulf coast on the mainland, provide them with flour and bacon and keep them going until they get on their feet again. Chairman

Sealy of the Galveston committee was to keep track of the Galveston situation, while the Governor looked out for the outside points.

That night a local committee from Galveston was sent to Houston and Virginia Point to take charge of the receiving and distribution of supplies that arrived there for the Galveston people. A serious matter confronting the authorities not only at the coast points, but in the cities near Galveston, was the rapid gathering of toughs, gamblers and rough characters generally, which after the flood were forced to leave Galveston island as they would not work. Others drifted into the mainland opposite Galveston and on to the neighboring towns by the hundreds in the hope of pickpocketing and the like among the crowds.

All this gathering of disorderly characters made the peace officers rather uneasy as to the future. The police and troops in Galveston and the special officers on the mainland were constantly on the alert to keep down trouble and prevent all possible thieving and they did not get the upper hand of this element until they had shot a score or more. These fellows would steal the provisions and supplies sent by the generous people from the outside, and whenever caught were shot without delay.

The following was sent out from Galveston on Saturday, Sept. 15, which showed how serious the situation was:

Galveston, Texas, Sept. 14—Hon. Joseph D. Sayers

Governor: After the fullest possible investigation here we feel justified in saying to you and through you to the American people that no such disaster has ever overtaken any community or section in the history of our country. The loss of life is appalling and can never be accurately determined. It is estimated at 5,000 to 8,000 people.

There is not a home in Galveston that has not been injured, while thousands have been destroyed. The property loss represents accumulations of sixty years and more millions than can be safely stated. Under these conditions, with ten thousand people homeless and destitute, with the entire population under a stress and strain difficult to realize, we appeal directly in the hour of our great emergency to the sympathy and aid of mankind.

> WALTER JONES, Mayor
> R. B. HAWLEY, Congressman
> McKIBBIN,
> Commander Department of Texas

General McKibbin, when he looked over the city three days before, had wired the War Department at Washington that perhaps 1,000 people had perished. He was a conservative man, as army officers usually are, and when he signed a statement saying probably 8,000 persons had lost their lives his signature carried weight with it.

Not only did the people of the United States sympathize deeply with the Texas sufferers, but those of other nations as well. President Loubet, of France, sent the following kind message to President McKinley at Washington:

> Rambouillet Presidence, Sept. 12—To His Excellency, the President of the United States of America:
>
> The news of the disaster which has just devastated the State of Texas has deeply moved me. The sentiments of traditional friendship which unite the two republics can leave no doubt in your mind concerning the very sincere share that the President, the government of the republic, and the whole nation take in the calamity that has proved such a cruel ordeal for so many families in the United States.
>
> It is natural that France should participate in the sadness, as well as in the joy, of the American people. I take it to heart to tender to your excellency our most heartfelt condolences, and to send to the families of the victims the expression of our afflicted sympathy.
>
> EMILE LOUBET

President McKinley sent this answer the next day:

Executive Mansion, Washington DC, Sept 13—His Excellency, Emile Loubet, President of the French Republic, Rambouillet, France:

I hasten to express, in the name of the thousands who have suffered by the disaster in Texas, as well as in behalf of the whole American people, heartfelt thanks for your touching message of sympathy and condolence.        WILLIAM McKINLEY

## SCHOOL CHILDREN GAVE THEIR PENNIES

Even the school children of the country helped the sufferers with their pennies. Miss Ethel Donelson, a pupil at the Grant School, Chicago, wrote a letter to a Chicago daily paper suggesting that the school children give some of their pennies to the victims of the great hurricane. The idea was carried out and several thousand dollars was raised in this way in Chicago. The plan was adopted also in several other cities.

When the suggestion was first made United States Postoffice Inspector Walter S. Mayor wrote as follows:

"I was reared in Galveston; lived there from my infancy until appointed to the government service nineteen years ago, and my mother and brother still live there.

"When Chicago had its great fire in 1871 the people of Galveston sent a generous subscription, and with it was one made up by the boys of the school I attended. Our teacher, E. E. Crawford, gave us a holiday for the purpose, and the fifty-odd boys organized themselves into a number of soliciting committees. I was on the committee with Charles Fowler, now one of Galveston's leading businessmen, and we two succeeded in collecting $8. In all, for our day's work we got together $200, which was turned into the general fund raised by the Citizens' Committee.

"In the twenty-nine years that have followed since then Chicago has pulled itself out of the ashes and risen to a high place among the world cities. Many forces have been brought to bear to accomplish this great end, but possibly the most potent one was the helping hand of the neighbor when help was needed. Among those who helped with their little mite may the school children of Galveston now be remembered.

"I most heartily second Miss Donelson's suggestion that the school children of Chicago be given an opportunity to aid their little brothers and sisters in Galveston, many of whom are naked and orphaned by the terrible disaster that has come to them.

WALTER S. MAYER,
Postoffice Inspector

NATIONAL AND EUROPEAN RELIEF

On Thursday, Sept. 13, American residents and visitors in Paris, France, together with Frenchmen whose sympathies were aroused by the storm disaster in Texas contributed 50,000 francs in twenty minutes for the relief of the sufferers. The Americans held a meeting in the Chamber of Commerce, which was largely attended. United States Ambassador Porter was a leader among those who proposed to organize for the work of aiding in the relief. The Americans perfected an organization and elected General Porter president, George Munroe, the banker, Treasurer, and Francis Kimball, secretary. The subscription list was then opened and the 50,000 francs raised. The Mayor of Galveston was informed by cable of the result.

The same day P. P. W. Houston, Member of Parliament for the West Toxteth division of Liverpool, England, and head of the Houston line of steamers, cabled £1,000 to Galveston for the relief of the sufferers.

Members of the American colony in Berlin, Germany, held a meeting Sunday, September 10, at the United States Embassy and raised $5,000.

Americans in London subscribed $10,000 and many London theatres gave benefits.

The Marquis of Salisbury, Premier of England, the Emperor William of Germany, the Emperor of Austria, the King of Italy, the Czar of Russia—in fact, nearly all the heads of state in the world cabled condolences, and the legislative bodies of foreign nations then in session passed resolutions of sympathy.

By Saturday New York had raised $174,000; Chicago, $91,000, together with many carloads of supplies which were sent as special trains, and the following cities had contributed the amounts named:

St. Louis $61,300

Boston $32,140

Philadelphia $29,358

New Orleans $26,000

Cincinnati $7,314

Cleveland $9,358

Colorado Springs $7,100

Minneapolis $13,430

Denver $12,180

Pittsburgh $26,123

Kansas City $15,321

Portland, Oregon $1,000

Peoria, Illinois $1,800

Memphis $8,426

San Francisco $16,000

Louisville $12,585

Baltimore $12,138

Milwaukee $13,431

Springfield, Illinois $2,314

St. Paul $6,904

Topeka, Kansas $5,110

Charleston, SC $6,008

Los Angeles $5,400
Detroit $4,936
Indianapolis $3,800
Helena, Montana $3,400
Johnstown, Pennsylvania $3,000

As stated before, the total contributed for the four and a half days ensuing from the time the appeal was issued was $1,500,000, while an additional $1,000,000 was not long in following. Both Chicago and New York increased their subscriptions largely.

In no case did the railroads charge for carrying the cars over their lines.

## THEIR PENALTIES WERE REMITTED

Navigation and other laws were set at naught by the United States authorities in order to help the Galveston and other flood sufferers. On Friday, September 14, the following telegram was referred to General Spaulding by President McKinley:

Galveston, Tex., Sept. 12—
To President of the United States:

In consequence of calamity and fear of sickness numerous people wish to leave the city. All our rail communication is cut off. The revenue cutter of this district is disabled and no American steamer immediately available. We therefore respectfully request you to instruct the proper authorities to allow British steamers *Caledonia*, and *Whitehall* and any other foreign vessels now here, but compelled to proceed to New Orleans for cargo, to carry passengers from Galveston to New Orleans.    W. C. JONES, Mayor
CLARENCE OUSLEY
J. D. SKINNER
C. H. McMASTER
R. G. LOWE,
"Committee"

General Spaulding at once sent the following telegram:

W. C. Jones, Mayor, Galveston, Tex.: Replying to your telegram of the 12th inst. addressed to President: If British steamships *Caledonia, Whitehall,* or other foreign vessels now in your port carry passengers in distress from Galveston to New Orleans or other American ports during present conditions this department will consider favorably applications for remission of penalties which may be incurred under the law. Advise masters.

O. L. SPAULDING,
Acting Secretary

On Friday night Governor Sayers stated that the work of relieving the flood sufferers was making excellent progress. He said:

Most generous contributions are coining in from all parts of the country sufficiently large to relieve the immediate wants as to food and clothing, and in the meantime the people of Galveston are recovering themselves, and I have no hesitancy in expressing the firm conviction that a strong reaction from an almost mortal blow to the city has already set in, and that in a short while the city will be in a condition to resume its normal and progressive position in commercial life. After a full conference today with an authorized committee from Galveston, I am more than convinced that the people there will be able, with the assistance already given, to handle the situation successfully.

## HOW GALVESTON'S BUSINESSMEN WERE HELPED

As a rule there is no sentiment in business, but the retail merchants of Galveston whose business and fortunes were swept away were not forgotten in the hour of need by the wholesale houses of Chicago, which announced just after the disaster that stocks of goods would be shipped promptly and willingly, any time and terms being accorded to the business of the gulf city. The regular way of determining credits was ignored, as was the credit man also. His cold judgment was not asked for, but instead sympathy and compassion for the unfortunate position of the merchants of the stricken city determined largely the stand the wholesalers announced they would take.

In doing this the houses of Chicago had the precedent established by the outside world in its treatment of them in the days following the great Chicago fire. Chicago men said they will do as they were done by, and the Galveston merchant had but to ask for the help he needed. Many Chicago houses wrote their Galveston customers at once advising them that they could have credit, time, and terms to suit themselves. This favor was also given to all businessmen who had lost all but names and prestige, whether they had been customers or not.

Firms that never had had any business with Galveston or Texas firms stated that they stood ready to ship goods on the same terms. No businessman in the damaged district, they said, whose misfortunes were due to the catastrophe could come to Chicago for supplies and go away without them even if he had not a dollar's worth of assets in the world, as long as he could show a former good business standing and repute.

"We will take any and all risks," said one after another of the representatives of Chicago wholesale houses. "In the present emergency credits cannot be measured by the regular business standards. Humanity must dictate the terms on which the merchants of Galveston who have bought from us, or who may want to buy from us, are to have goods and supplies."

Firm after firm of the wholesale district, whether or not they now have trade in the afflicted territory, made the same statement.

"We already have written to 200 former customers who are scattered along the coast, asking them how they came out of the disaster and offering them any terms of settlement their losses may warrant," said the credit man of one of the largest houses in the West, on the Friday following the flood. "We will view the facts in their cases not from a business but from a sympathetic standpoint."

"We are making our former customers time, terms and credits of their own asking," said the Vice-President of a great wholesale dry goods house. "We will make the same terms to new customers who have been good businessmen."

"We have advised former customers that their orders will be filled promptly for complete stocks," said the manager of a music and musical instrument house. "We have told them to make their own time and terms. We charge no interest."

"We are looking at the men of Galveston and not at their present assets," said the managing partner of a wholesale clothing house having a large Texas trade.

"We have sent word to fifty of our customers in Galveston to draw on us for new stocks without asking them if they have saved a penny from the catastrophe," said the President of one of the largest cigar and tobacco concerns in the city.

"The conditions are so distressing as to shame a Chicagoan asking what any Galveston businessman has today," said the manager of a grocery house. "We have never reached into Texas after trade, but shall do so immediately. Any businessman wanting our goods can have them on his own terms."

"Our customers in Galveston can send in their orders for new stocks and have them filled as quickly as if they forwarded double prices," said a furnishing goods wholesaler. "We are not asking them what their assets are."

## ADMINISTERING RELIEF EFFORTS

The situation at Galveston on Saturday night, just a week after the calamity, was thus described by a competent authority who arrived in the city the day after the flood: "It must be possible by this time to give some idea of the magnitude which relief must assume. There were 38,000 persons in the city when the census was taken a few weeks ago. After the storm 32,000 remained. This latter statement is made after careful inquiry from the best sources of information. About 8,000 have left the island, most of them women and children, to go to friends temporarily. Of the 29,000 remaining how many must be helped and how long?

"The question is a hard one. The men who knew most of the situation, who have labored day and night since Sunday, hesitate to answer.

"Mr. McVitie, the executive head of the relief work, said it was possible there were 3,500 persons in the city who did not require any assistance whatever. Mr. Lowe of the *Galveston News*, a most careful and conservative man, said he believed fully two-thirds of the surviving and remaining population were dependent today. Others familiar with the situation were asked for their opinions, and they estimated variously the number that must be helped temporarily at from two-thirds to three-fourths.

"The conclusion is forced that there are today in Galveston 20,000 persons who must be fed and clothed. The proportion of those who were in fair circumstances and lost all is astonishing. Relief cannot be limited to those who formed the poor class before the storm.

"An intelligent man left Galveston today, taking his wife and children to relatives. He said: 'A week ago, I had a good home and a business which paid me between $400 and $500 a month. Today I have nothing. My house was swept away and my business is gone. I see no way of reestablishing in the near future.'

"This man had a real estate and house-renting agency.

"At the military headquarters one of the principal officials doing temporary service for the city, said: 'Before the storm I had a good home and good income. I felt rich. My house is gone and my business. The fact is I don't even own the clothes I stand before you in. I borrowed them.'

"Now these are not exceptional cases. They are fairly typical. Men who worked for salaries, who related or owned good houses and considered themselves fairly well provided for, as the world goes, are today, by thousands, not only penniless, but without food, without clothes, and without employment.

"There must be fed and clothed these 20,000 until they can work out their temporal salvation. And then something ought to be done to help the worthy get on their feet and make a fresh start. Some people will leave Galveston. It is plain, however, that nothing like the number expected will go. Galveston is still home to the great majority. It was a city of fine local pride. It was one of the most beautiful of American cities, and with its surrounding of gulf and bay was a pleasant place to live in, even in summer. Those who can stay and live here will do so.

"If the country responds to the needs in anything like the measure given to Johnstown, Chicago, Charleston and other stricken cities and sections, Galveston as a community will not only be restored but will enter upon a greater future than was expected before the storm.

"This seems rather an extraordinary thing to say. It has been the experience, wherefore it is expected here. Since Tuesday there has been no doubt of Galveston's restoration. If in the future this city celebrates a flood anniversary the day upon which the community's courage was reborn ought to be remembered.

"From a central organization, the relief work has been divided by wards. A depot and a subcommittee were established in each ward of the city. 'They who will not work should not eat' was the principle adopted when the organization was perfected. Few idle mouths are now being fed in Galveston. There are fatherless, and there are widows, and there are sick who must have charity.

"But the able-bodied are working in parties under the direction of bosses. They are paid in food and clothing. In this way the relief committee is, within the first week, meeting the needs of the survivors and at the same time gradually clearing the streets and burning the ruins and refuse.

"A single report made by a ward committeeman to Mr. McVitie will serve to show on what scale this plan is being carried out. 'In my ward,' said the committeeman, 'I have 600 men employed and I am feeding 3,700 persons.'

"The system of the Galveston relief organization is admirable. Perhaps never before was economy practiced so rigidly in the distribution of the nation's largess. 'Our aim,' Mr. McVitie said, 'is to distribute no money at this time, but to employ with relief funds all of the labor in the clearing of the city and the cremation of the dead until we have removed to that extent the ravages of the storm.

" 'We employ all who can work and we give food and clothing as remuneration. We scrutinize most carefully applications for charity and grant none if the applicant is able to render service. We adopted this plan in the beginning and we are going to continue it. Most of our people responded to the rule and went to work. To those who were unwilling to work we applied the authority of martial law.

" 'All Galveston is now at work and the contributions which we are receiving from the sympathizing nation are going to pay for the most urgent work the storm imposed on us.'

"Six days have wrought surprising changes in conditions at Galveston. Each day has been a chapter in itself. Sunday was paralysis. On Monday came the beginning of realization. Tuesday might be called the crisis period. And the crisis was passed safely. What has been accomplished since the turning point on Tuesday is amazing. It is almost as incredible as some of the effects of this visitation are without precedent.

"On Sunday the people did little but go about dazed and bewildered, gathering a few hundred of the bodies which were in their way. On Monday the born leaders who are usually not discovered in a community until some great emergency arises began to forge in front. They were not men from one rank in point of wealth or intelligence. They came from all classes. For example there was Hughes, the longshoreman.

"Bodies which lay exposed in the streets and which were necessary to remove somewhere lest they be stepped on were carried into a temporary morgue until 500 lay in rows on the floor. Then a problem in mortality, such as no other American community ever faced, was presented. Pestilence, which stalked forth by Monday, seemed about to take possession of what the storm had left. Immediate disposition of those bodies was absolutely necessary to save the living. Then it was that Lowe and McVitie and Sealy and the others, who by common impulse had come together to deal with the problem, found Hughes.

"The longshoreman took up the most gruesome task ever seen away from a battlefield. He had to have helpers. Some volunteered, others were pressed into the service at the point of the bayonet. Whiskey by the bucketful was carried to these men and they were drenched with it. The stimulant was kept at hand and applied continuously. Only in this way was it possible for the stoutest-hearted to work in such surroundings. Under the direction of Hughes these hundreds of bodies already collected and others brought from the central part of the city—those which were quickest found— were loaded on to an ocean barge and taken far off into the gulf to be cast into the sea."

## CLARA BARTON'S VIEW OF THE SITUATION

Miss Clara Barton, head of the Red Cross Society, wrote of the situation at Galveston on September 18:

"It would be difficult to exaggerate the awful scene that meets the visitors everywhere. The situation could not be exaggerated. Probably the loss of life will exceed any estimate that has been made.

"In those parts of the city where destruction was the greatest there still must be hundreds of bodies under the debris. At the end of the island first struck by the storm, and which was swept clean of every vestige of the splendid residences that covered it, the ruin is enclosed by a towering wall of debris, under which many bodies are buried. The removal of this has scarcely even begun.

"The story that will be told when this mountain of ruins is removed may multiply the horrors of the fearful situation. As usual in great calamities, the people are dazed and speak of their losses with an unnatural calmness that would astonish those who do not understand it.

"I do believe there is danger of an epidemic. But the nervous strain upon the people, as they come to realize their condition, may be nearly as fatal. They talk of friends that are gone with tearless eyes, making no allusion to the loss of property.

"A professional gentleman who called upon me this afternoon, a gentleman of splendid human sympathies and refinement, wore a soiled black flannel shirt, without a coat, and in apologizing for his appearance said in the most casual, light-hearted way: 'Excuse my appearance; I have just come in from burying the dead.'

"But these people will break down under this strain, and the Red Cross is glad of the force of strong, competent workers which it has brought to their relief.

"Portions of the business part of the city escaped the greatest severity of the storm and are left partially intact. Thus it is possible to purchase here nearly all the supplies that may be wanting. Still, the Galveston merchants should be given the benefit of home demands.

"Mayor Jones has offered to the Red Cross as headquarters the best building at his disposal.

"Relief is coming as rapidly as the crippled transportation facilities will admit. No one need fear, after seeing the brave and manly way in which these people are helping themselves, that too much outside aid will be given.

"In reply to the question, 'What is most needed?' I would say: The most immediate needs are surgical dressings, the ordinary medical remedies, and delicacies for the sick."

## SWELLING THE RELIEF FUND

On September 18 Chicago had raised over $100,000 for the Galveston sufferers; New York nearly $300,000; St. Louis nearly $70,000, and other cities the following amounts:

Boston $32,700
Philadelphia $28,320
Pittsburgh $27,108
New Orleans $26,100
San Francisco $18,000
Kansas City $17,000
Louisville $14,000
Milwaukee $14,046
Baltimore $15,000
Denver $13,000
Minneapolis $12,000
Newark NJ $12,000
Cleveland $9,345
Memphis $9,123
Cincinnati $9,000
Colorado Springs $7,200
St. Paul $7,000
Topeka KS $5,438
Charleston SC $6,000
Omaha, Nebraska $6,212

Los Angeles $5,184
Detroit $5,190
Indianapolis $4,000
Helena, Montana $4,108
Johnstown, Pa., $3,000
Columbus, Ohio $3,100
South Bend, Indiana $1,985
Springfield, Ill., $2,000
Portland, Ore., $2,100
Lexington, Ky., $2,098

The United States embassy at Berlin, Germany, cabled $500 to Governor Sayers on September 17.

General J. B. Vinet, president of the Red Cross Society, State of Louisiana, New Orleans, received on Tuesday morning, September 18, a telegram from Miss Clara Barton, who was at Galveston, as follows:

Find greatest immediate needs here are surgical dressings, usual medicines and delicacies for the sick. No epidemic, but many people are worn out with suffering and exertion who need tender care and proper food.          —CLARA BARTON

Building material was needed at Galveston but its delivery was necessarily slow, owing to the lack of rail communication with the mainland.

There were still many pitiable cases of destitution. Many half-demented persons positively refused to leave their wrecked homes and as persistently refused to accept offers of relief extended them. In several instances parents who had lost children still occupied ruins of their former home and the surroundings had brought them to a state of mental and physical collapse.

The number who had gone insane as a result of their experiences will probably never be known. In every lot of refugees sent out of the stricken city there were many insane men and women. The victims first made light of their losses, and laughed immoderately when telling of the death of relatives in the flood. It was a very short step from this to uncontrollable madness.

The state militia companies did splendid work in patrolling the city after the storm, and many of the men were of the belief that they should be allowed to return to their homes and troops sent from other parts of the state to fill their places.

The fears of an epidemic were allayed by the presence and the distribution of medicines and disinfectants and therefore a feature which would undoubtedly have had the effect of causing many to seek succor elsewhere, was eliminated from the situation.

## GOVERNOR SAYERS SENDS HIS THANKS

Governor Sayers, of Texas, sent out the following expression of thanks on behalf of the sufferers in Galveston and as the representative of the people of his state:

"In behalf of the people of Texas I desire to express my acknowledgment to the people of the United States for the ready and generous response they have made in coming to the aid of our afflicted people. The number of deaths, the amount of destitution, and the loss of property is far greater than had been anticipated.

"The Secretary of the Navy has placed the revenue cutter *Galveston* at my disposal, and I have in turn placed it at the disposal of the mayor of Galveston. The addition of this cutter to the boats already loaned by the Federal government will give us five boats at Galveston to handle supplies and passengers to and from the mainland, and I anticipate that their presence there will relieve the situation materially.

"The city authorities at Galveston are in full control, and every effort is being made to bury the dead, to remove the debris, and to sanitate the city. Contributions of the most liberal character are reaching me, and I shall see that the money is used to the best advantage for the sufferers and that there shall be no waste of the magnificent contributions coming from the free hands and generous hearts of a sympathetic people."

No idea could possibly be formed as to the frightful crush of railroad trains bearing relief supplies in and around Houston and Texas City, the latter being but six miles from Galveston, but separated from it by a stretch of water. Owing to the small number of vessels plying between Texas City and Galveston the shipment of supplies to the latter was necessarily aggravatingly slow.

## TWO APPEALS WHICH BROUGHT MUCH MONEY

Two appeals for aid which brought in much money were the following, the first one being by the G. A. R. and Women's Relief Corps, Department of Texas:

"The appalling calamity that has befallen Galveston and the coast country has smitten hundreds of our comrades in the city, villages and on farms. In many instances, portions of whole families are lost; in a hundred others, houses are wrecked, livestock killed and crops destroyed.

"George B. McClellan Post of this city is doing what it can, but its efforts are all inadequate. Systematic organized assistance alone can avert distress, and we therefore appeal to the members of this department in behalf of these comrades. They had made their last stand and effort to secure for themselves and families homes on the coast country of Texas. Their all is involved. Far along in the evening of their life they cannot recuperate.

"If there was time to make another crop they have nothing with which to make it. Unless we help them they must abandon their homes, their all. If the principles of our order—fraternity, charity and loyalty—are of any avail, it is time to show it. Fraternity means organization—charity means everything and is the 'greatest of all.' Loyalty means standing by our comrades as well as the flag. They were our brothers in arms, they are our kindred in adversity.

"We confidently expect every post, every member of every corps to contribute something. Remittances and supplies from the G. A. R. should be made to Colonel E. G. Rust, assistant quartermaster general, and from the Women's Relief Corps to Mrs. Mina Metcalf, both of Houston, Texas.

CHARLES B. PECK,
Department Commander

ANNETTE VAN HORN,
Department Commander

The other was by President Michaux of the Travelers' Protective Association, addressed to the members of the organization throughout the United States:

"Whereas, A great calamity has befallen the city of Galveston, thousands of dead, dying and wounded to be cared for by our united and benevolent people; and

"Whereas, Numbers of traveling men are reported seriously wounded; therefore, to care for immediate wants, I deem it necessary to call on the traveling men to contribute as much as in their power to help, aid and assist our stricken companions.

"Our association is able and will take care of all its unfortunate members, and I appeal to you in the name of charity and love to assist us in caring for them not so fortunate. Remit what you can afford by post office, express money order to James E. Ludlow, San Antonio, Texas. Secretaries of all local T. P. A. posts will receive and remit your subscriptions. I trust that this appeal to the traveling men will be met by a quick response.

Sincerely and fraternally,

D. W. MICHAUX, President
Texas T.P.A. of America,
Houston, Texas


## HELP IN GETTING SUPPLIES TO THE NEEDY

Arrangements were completed by the Santa Fe road September 17 whereby it established a barge line to Galveston from Virginia Point. This helped somewhat in getting relief supplies from the mainland.

Clara Barton, head of the Red Cross league, arrived at Galveston that day. Captain W. A. Hutchins, superintendent of the Galveston life-saving station, returned from a trip along the island and reported that he saw a great many bodies. He said the life-saving crew at San Luis had taken from the beach 181 bodies and buried them at different points along the island.

# 20,000 FED DAILY

Twenty thousand people were fed and cared for daily in Galveston for many days with the supplies which poured in from all parts of the country. This number was cut at least one-half about October 1.

The estimated cost of the aid extended after the first week of suffering was $40,000 a day. The great bulk of the aid went to the 4,000 men at work cleaning up the wreckage, digging for bodies and cleaning the streets. Through them it went to their families. No able-bodied laboring man was allowed to escape the work, whether he needed aid or not, though most of them did. The businessmen in position to resume were allowed to attend to their stores, and their clerical forces were not interfered with.

On Tuesday, September 18, the debris hunting and street-cleaning work was put upon a cash basis, the wages being $1.50. Time had been kept from the beginning, though the records were not complete. All were paid for the full time they worked. This applied to those who had to be made to work at the point of a bayonet as well as those who volunteered their services.

This aid was given in the form of orders for tools for mechanics, lumber for those who had homes they wished to repair, etc. Heretofore practically every able-bodied man had been made to work, and unless he worked he got no supplies. The first few days' wages consisted entirely of rations, which were given according to the number and needs of the laborer's family, regardless of the amount of work he accomplished. Since other supplies began coming in they had been added.

The work of distribution was conducted systematically and with an apparent minimum of imposition and fraud. There was a central committee, of which W. A. McVitie, a prominent businessman, was chairman. Then there was a committee for each one of the twelve wards. As fast as goods or provisions arrived from the mainland they were placed in the central warehouse, from which the different ward chairmen requisitioned them, and they were taken to supply depots in the different wards. All day long there was a motley crowd around every one of these depots, negroes predominating at least two to one. Every applicant passed in review before the ward chairman.

"Ah want a dress foh ma sistah," said a big negress.

"You're 'Manda Jones, and you haven't any sister living here," replied the chairman.

"Foh de Lord, ah has; ah ain't 'Mandy Jones at all; we done live on Avenue N before de storm, and we los' everything."

"Go out with this woman and find out if she has a sister who needs a dress," ordered the chairman to a committeeman. In this way check was kept on all the applicants for aid.

At the Fifth Ward distributing station clothing was given away the evening of the 17th. A negro woman, who had been refused a supply, went outside and by way of revenge pointed out different ones of her friends and neighbors whom she alleged were similarly unentitled.

"Dat woman done los' nuthin' at all," she shrieked. "Ah did not los' nuthin' mahself and doan wan' nuthin'."

"What's the trouble?" asked a bystander.

An old negress who was lined up waiting her turn replied. "Oh, she's mad 'cause de white folks won't give her nuthin'."

So far no woman had been required to work, but a strong feeling developed to compel negro women to work cleaning up the houses. There were plenty of people who were willing to hire them, but as long as free food and clothing could be secured it was hard to get colored women to go in and clean up the partially ruined homes.

"Our supply of foodstuffs is adequate," said Chairman McVitie, "but just now we are a little short of clothing. We have no idea of the contents of the cars on the road to us. Frequently we don't know anything is coming until the cars reach Texas City. With the money which has been coming in we have been augmenting our supplies by purchasing of local merchants in lines where there was a shortage. What do we need most? Money. If we have money we can order just what we need and probably get better value than the people who are buying it. Many people have made the mistake of sending money to Houston and Dallas and asking committees there to buy for us. They do not know just what we need, and if we had the money we could do better for ourselves. Money should be sent to us."

One of the most remarkable things attending the Galveston disaster was the fortitude of the people. Their loss in relatives, friends and property had been so overwhelming that it seemed too much to be expressed with outward grief.

Two men who had not seen each other since the disaster met in the street.

"How many did you lose?" they asked by common impulse.

"I lost all my property, but my wife and I came through all right."

"I was not so fortunate. My wife and my little boy were both drowned." There was an expression of sympathy from the other, but nothing approaching a tear from either.

"They are making good progress cleaning up," remarked the one whose losses were heaviest, with a pleasant smile. The other one made a light answer and they passed on.

The people of Galveston had seen so much death that they were temporarily hardened to it. The announcement of the loss of another friend meant little to a man who had seen the dead bodies of his neighbors and townspeople hauled to the wharf by the drayload.

No services were attempted for the dead until nearly a month had passed. Neither were there memorial services.

The Rev. J. M. K. Kerwin, priest in charge of St. Mary's Catholic cathedral, said: "It was impossible. Priest and layman had to join in the work of cleaning the city of dead bodies. I don't expect there will be memorial services for a month."

Father Kerwin's church was among the few which was comparatively little damaged. He set the value of Catholic property destroyed in the city at $300,000. Included in this loss was the Ursula convent and academy, which was badly damaged. It covered four blocks between Twenty-fifth and Twenty-seventh Streets and Avenues N and O. It was the finest in the South.

The city rapidly improved in its sanitary conditions. The smell from the ooze and mud with which most of the streets were filled was stronger ten days after the tragedy than that which came from the debris heaps containing undiscovered bodies. When these heaps were being burned and the wind carried the smoke over the city the odor was very similar to that which afflicts Chicago at night when refuse is being burned at the stockyards, and no worse. Soon even the odor of the slime was gone. Every dumpcart in the city was at work.

Every Galveston businessman talked confidently of the future of the city, though many of the clerks announced their intention of going away as soon as they can accumulate money enough.

"I am not afraid of another storm," said a clerk in one of the principal stores. "But I'm sick and tired of the whole business."

The Southwestern Telephone and Telegraph Company, which is a branch of the Erie system, early began to rebuild its telephone system there.

"This will take us three months, and in the meantime we will give no service save long-distance," said D. McReynolds, superintendent of construction. "We will install a central emergency system the same as that in Chicago and put all wires under ground. We will employ 500 men if necessary to do the work in ninety days. The company's losses in Texas are $200,000—$300,000 here, $60,000 at Houston and the rest at other points."

Residents were greatly pleased at this announcement, as it showed the confidence of a foreign company in the future of Galveston.

## WORLD NOT SO HEARTLESS AS SUPPOSED

Perhaps the world is not so bad as it has been painted, or so heartless and indifferent as some pessimists would have us believe. Ordinarily men and women have enough to do in attending to their own affairs, expecting others, of course, to do the same, and consequently they pay small attention to what is going on around them; but when their hearts are really touched they drop everything and rush to the rescue of the afflicted.

So it was in the case of Galveston.

The catastrophe at Galveston served to bring conspicuously into notice the best and worst sides of human nature, which is always the common result of all appalling disasters.

The people of that afflicted city were suddenly overwhelmed by the almost unprecedented fury of the elements. Thousands were killed and injured. Thousands more lost their homes and places of business. They were suffering with hunger and menaced with pestilence. All were brought to a common level by dangers of every description, death in its most awful forms, and an outlook of terrible uncertainty.

And yet in the midst of all this ruin and suffering they were harassed by thugs and thieves and ghouls in human shape, who looted property, assaulted citizens who resisted them, and despoiled and disfigured the dead in a shockingly savage manner to secure rings and other jewels. Devoid of any feeling of sympathy or pity, they seized upon this awful disaster as an opportunity to enrich themselves. As soon, however, as the authorities could recover from the first shock of the disaster the city was placed under martial law, and the troops patrolling the island did not hesitate to kill every one of the vandals caught in the commission of his infamous work. Public opinion sustained this prompt style of punishment. It was a species of Southern lynching to which no objection was ever raised.

The disaster also brought into prominence the greed and mercenary passion of human nature. A clique of ravenous wretches, taking advantage of the fact that the city of Galveston was cut off from bridge communication with the mainland, conspired to secure control of the transportation facilities by water, and charged extortionate prices even to those who were seeking to carry relief to the suffering people. Never was a more inhuman trust organized.

Again, all the fresh provisions in the city were ruined, leaving only a few canned and dried articles which were available for food. The owners of these, bent upon making personal profit out of the necessities of their fellow citizens, pushed up the prices, raising bread to 60 cents a loaf and bacon to 50 cents a pound.

The mayor of Galveston, however, proved himself equal to the emergency, confiscated the food supply, reduced the prices to a reasonable rate, and compelled the owners of schooners and small craft to put down their prices also.

This was the dark side of human nature, but the picture had its bright side also. The news of the awful disaster had hardly appeared in the public prints before tens of thousands of helping hands were busy collecting relief. The Chief Executive of the nation, the Governors of States, and the mayors of cities issued their appeals to the people, whose sympathies were already aroused and whose hearts and hands were enlisted generously and enthusiastically in the work of relief.

Far-off countries sent their offerings; every city and town in the world where Americans live contributed; and crowned heads hastened to cable sympathy, together with more substantial evidences of their kindly feeling.

Without delay of any kind, instantly and spontaneously, the machinery of charity began its work. The people of the North might differ radically from the people of the South in many ways, but in the presence of such a dreadful visitation of nature, involving suffering and death, the brotherhood of man asserted itself and all things else were forgotten. Only the higher and nobler attributes of human nature assert themselves.

Private individuals, business houses, great corporations, municipal, state and national government vied with each other, as they did when fire swept over Chicago and the flood overwhelmed Johnstown, in expediting relief to the storm-ruined people of Texas.

Day by day trains sped to Galveston from every part of the country, loaded with supplies, and the telegraph wires carried orders for money, testifying to the unanimity of the great work of relief, and to the higher and nobler instincts of human nature when it is appealed to by the claims of humanity.

The ghouls of Galveston were comparatively few in number. Its generous sympathizers were to be counted by scores of millions.

The convicts in the Texas state penitentiary at Rusk were moved by the sufferings of the Galveston victims to contribute $40 to the relief fund. Are men who go to prison totally bad?

The scope and rapidity of the Galveston relief work all over the country afforded a spectacle at once gratifying and noteworthy. Trains laden with food and comforts for the sufferers were rushed towards the stricken city from every quarter of the United States.

From Boston to San Francisco nearly every city, regardless of size, contributed its quota to the generous cause. Even from across the Atlantic the Liverpool and Paris funds came, being on the list for $10,000 each. Within a week after the disaster Galveston was in possession of a magnificent relief fund that went far toward alleviating the physical sufferings of its homeless thousands.

Here is a social phenomenon that may well give pause to all critics who are wont to inveigh against our commercial and industrial age. These exhibitions of liberality are not rare in the United States. A long series of them might be compiled within the period between the Chicago fire and the Puerto Rican hurricane.

Singly and in the aggregate they are a striking negative to the charge of sordid commercialism in our individual and national life. The modern American is making more money than ever before, but he has a heart as well as a business head, and he is giving larger sums to noble causes than were ever given before.

Probably the increased willingness of the people to help stricken communities like Galveston is due more to the railroads and telegraph lines than to anything else. Modern charity is the child of modern conditions. These indispensable adjuncts to commercial enterprise alone make widespread relief work possible.

If the telegraph and the newspaper had not placed the sad picture of Galveston's misfortunes at once before the eyes of Americans from ocean to ocean there could have been no such national impulse of generosity.

About ninety years ago an earthquake in Southern Missouri brought calamity to many settlers, but it was a month before the news reached the East, and another month would have had to elapse before relief could have been carried to the sufferers. The impulse to give cannot thrive under such circumstances.

There have been tender hearts in all ages, but only in our time have the means of quick communication made human sympathy effective across continents. The railroad, the telegraph and the newspaper have lengthened the arm of charity quite as much as that of business.

The Galveston incident is also a fine example of the way in which these agencies bind all sections of the nation together in increasing solidarity.

# CHAPTER FIVE:
## TALLYING THE DAMAGES

Galveston's property loss by the hurricane was hardly less than $20,000,000; outside of that city, in Houston and other points in Central and Southern Texas, together with the agricultural and stock-raising districts, the property damage was nearly half that amount, or in the neighborhood of $10,000,000.

Probably seventy-five villages and towns were swept by the storm, and in most of these places there was loss of life.

It was reliably estimated from reports received at Austin, the capital city of Texas, from these places that the loss of life, exclusive of the death list of Galveston Island and City of Galveston, would aggregate 1,000 people. In many towns the percentage of killed or drowned exceeded that in the City of Galveston. Several towns were swept completely out of existence.

The scene of desolation in the devastated district was terrible to witness. The storm was over 200 miles wide and extended as far inland as Temple, a distance of over 200 miles from the gulf. The cotton crop in the lower counties was completely ruined. The same was true of the rice crop. The distress was keenly felt by the planters and small farmers throughout the storm-swept region.

In Houston the damage was not figured at over $400,00; at Alvin, $200,000, the town being virtually destroyed and 6,000 people in that section deprived not only of shelter and food for the time being but all prospect for crops in the year to come.

On the 15th of September, R. W. King sent out the following statement and appeal from Houston after a thorough investigation of the situation in and around Alvin:

"I arrived in Alvin from Dallas and was astonished and bewildered by the sight of devastation on every side. Ninety-five per cent of the houses in this vicinity are in ruins, leaving

6,000 people without adequate shelter and destitute of the necessaries of life, and with no means whatever to procure them. Everything in the way of crops is destroyed, and unless there is speedy relief there will be exceedingly great suffering.

"The people need and must have assistance. Need money to rebuild their homes and buy stock and implements. They need food—flour, bacon, corn. They must have seeds for their gardens so as to be able to do something for themselves very soon. Clothing is badly needed. Hundreds of women and children are without a change and are already suffering. Some better idea may be had of the distress when it is known that box cars are being improvised as houses and hay as bedding. Only fourteen houses in the Town of Alvin are standing, and they are badly damaged."

The damage at Hitchcock was not less than $100,000, but the news from there was disheartening. A bulletin from a reliable source, dated September 15, said:

"Country districts are strewn with corpses. The prairies around Hitchcock are dotted with the bodies of the dead. Scores are unburied, as the bodies are too badly decomposed to handle and the water too deep to admit of burial.

"A pestilence is feared from the decomposing animal matter lying everywhere. The stench is something awful. Disinfecting material is badly needed."

Other outside losses were:

| | |
|---|---|
| Richmond $75,000 | Belleville $5,000 |
| Fort Bend Co $300,000 | Hempstead $25,000 |
| Wharton $30,000 | Brookshire $35,000 |
| Wharton Co $100,000 | Waller Co $100,000 |
| Colorado Co $250,000 | Arcola $5,000 |
| Angleton $75,000 | Sartaria $50,000 |
| Velasco $50,000 | Dickinson $30,000 |
| Brazoria Co $80,000 | Texas City $150,000 |
| Sabine $50,000 | Columbia $10,000 |
| Paton $10,000 | Sandy Point $10,000 |
| Rollover $10,000 | Near Brazoria $35,000 |
| Winnie $10,000 | Other points $100,000 |

Damage to railroads outside of Galveston, $500,000.

Damage to telegraph and telephone wires outside of Galveston, $50,000.

Damage to cotton crop, estimated on average crop of counties affected, 50,000 bales at $60 a bale, $3,000,000.

Damage to stock was great, thousands of horses and cattle having perished during the storm. In Brazoria and other counties of that section there was hardly a plantation building left standing. All fences were also gone and the devastation was complete. Many large and expensive sugar refineries were wrecked. The negro cabins were blown down and many negroes killed. On one plantation, a short distance from the ill-fated town of Angleton, three families of negroes were killed.

The villages of Needville and Beasley in Fort Bend County were completely destroyed. Over twenty people were killed, most of the bodies having been recovered. Every house in that part of the country was destroyed and there was great suffering among the homeless people.

There was much destitution among the people of Richmond in the same county. Richmond was one of the most prosperous towns in south Texas. It was wholly destroyed and the homeless ones were without shelter. Their food supplies were provided by their more fortunate neighbors until other assistance could be had.

The State authorities heard from the Sartaria plantation, where several hundred State convicts were employed. Every building on the plantation was blown down and the loss to property aggregated $35,000. Fifteen convicts were caught under the timbers of a falling building and all killed. Over a score of others were injured. In addition to the loss on buildings the entire cane crop was destroyed on this as well as other plantations in that section.

Seven people were killed in the Town of Angleton, which was almost completely destroyed. In the neighborhood of Angleton five more persons were killed and their bodies have been recovered. The loss of life in that immediate section far exceeded the estimates given in the earlier reports.

The search for victims of the flood at Seabrook resulted in fifty bodies being recovered. Seabrook was a favorite summer resort with many Texas people, and its hotels were filled with guests. Many were out on pleasure jaunts when the storm came upon them. There were many guests in the private houses which were swept away. The casualties at Texas City were five.

Velasco, situated near the mouth of the Brazos River asked for help. Over one-half of the town was destroyed and eleven people lost their lives. Reports from the adjacent country showed that many negroes were killed.

Eleven negro convicts employed on a plantation in Matagorda County were killed by the collapse of a building in which they had sought refuge from the storm. The town of Matagorda, situated on the coast, was in the brunt of the storm. Several people were killed in the towns of Caney and Elliott, in the same county. The new buildings on the Clemmons convict farm, owned and operated by the State, were destroyed and several convicts injured. The crops were also ruined.

Over fifty negroes were killed in Wharton County, ten being killed on one plantation near the Town of Wharton. Bay City suffered a loss of nearly all of its buildings and three were killed there. There were many homeless people in Missouri City, every house in the town but two being destroyed. The destitute people were living out of doors and camping on the wet ground.

Outside of the cities of Galveston and Houston, the greatest suffering was between Houston and East Lake, inland, and on the coast to the Brazos River. There was no damage at Corpus Christi, Rockport, or in that immediate section of the coast.

People in immediate need of relief were those of the Colorado and Brazos river bottoms. The planters in that section had everything swept away last year, and the flood this year devastated their crops, leaving the tenants in a state bordering on starvation. An enormous acreage was planted in rice and the crop was ready for harvesting when the furious winds laid everything low.

At Wharton, Sugarland, Quintana, Waller, Prairie View and many other smaller places barely a house was left standing. Many of the farm hands had been brought into that section to assist at cotton picking and other farming. The people were huddled in small cabins when the first signs of a storm began brewing. But few escaped. Their clothing and everything was gone. They were absolutely devoid of even the necessities with which to sustain life.

To begin over again the owners of plantations had to rebuild houses, purchase new machinery and new draft animals. The loss of horses and mules in the stricken district was a severe blow. Livestock interests were also greatly harmed.

In the opinion of railway men, several years must elapse before the farming districts can be restored to their former conditions. The advanced prices of building material was a hard blow for the smaller farmers, who in most instances were owners of farms. Appeals for relief were received from everywhere in the storm center. The season had given promise of producing the best harvest in the previous fifteen years.

Five Houston people were drowned at Morgan's Point: Mrs. C. H. Lucy and her two children, Haven McIlhenny and the five-year-old son of David Rice. Mr. Michael McIlhenny was rescued alive, exhausted and in a state of terrible nervousness.

McIlhenny said the water came up so rapidly that he and his family sought safety upon the roof. He had Haven in his arms and the other children were strapped together. A heavy piece of timber struck Haven, killing him. McIlhenny then took up young Rice, and while he had him in his arms he was twice washed off the roof and in this way young Rice was drowned.

Mrs. Lucy's oldest child was next killed by a piece of timber and the younger one was drowned, and next Mrs. Lucy was washed off and drowned, thus leaving Mr. and Mrs. McIlhenny the only occupants on the roof. Finally the roof blew off the house and as it fell into the water it was broken in twain, Mrs. McIlhenny remaining on one half and McIlhenny on the other. The portion of the roof to which Mrs. McIlhenny clung turned over and this was the last seen of her. McIlhenny held to his side of the roof so distracted in mind as to care little where or how it drifted. He finally landed about 2 p.m. Sunday.

At Surfside, a summer resort opposite Quintana, there were seventy-five persons in the hotel. The water was about it, and the danger was from the heavy logs floating from above. Only a few men worked in the village, so a number of women went into the water to their waists, and assisted in keeping the logs away from the hotel, and no one was lost.

At Belleville every house in the place was damaged, and several were demolished, including two churches. One girl was killed near there. Not a house was left at Patterson in a habitable condition.

Two boarding cars were blown out on the main line and whirled along by the wind sixteen miles to Sandy Point, where they collided with a number of other boarding cars, killing two and injuring thirteen occupants.

A dead child, the destruction of all houses except one and the destitution of some fifty families is the record of the work of the hurricane at Arcadia. From fifty other towns came reports that buildings were wrecked or demolished. Most of them reported several dead and injured.

J. D. Dillon, commercial agent of the Santa Fe Railway Company, made a trip over the line of his road from Hitchcock to Virginia Point on foot, September 13, and gave a graphic account of his journey, which was made under many difficulties.

"Twelve miles of track and bridges are gone south of Hitchcock," said he. "I walked, waded and swam from

Hitchcock to Virginia Point, and nothing could be seen in all of that country but death and desolation. The prairies are covered with water, and I do not think I exaggerate when I say that not less than 5,000 horses and cattle are to be seen along the line of the tracks south of Hitchcock.

"The little towns along the railway are all swept away, and the sight is the most terrible that I have ever witnessed. When I reached a point about two miles north of Virginia Point I saw some bodies floating on the prairie, and from that point until Virginia Point was reached dead bodies could be seen from the railroad track, floating about the prairie.

"At Virginia Point nothing is left. About 100 cars of loaded merchandise that reached Virginia Point on the International & Great Northern and the Missouri, Kansas & Texas on the night of the storm are scattered over the prairie, and their contents will no doubt prove a total loss."

On Friday, September 14, from early morning until far into the afternoon Governor Sayers was in conference with relief committees from various points along the storm-swept coast. Among the first committees to arrive was one from Galveston. These men consulted at length with the Governor, and as a result of this conference it was decided that the State Adjutant General, General Scurry, should be left in command of the city, which was to be considered under military rule, and that he was to have the exclusive control not only of the patrolling of the city, but of the sanitary forces engaged in cleaning the city.

It was decided also that instead of looking to the laboring people of Galveston for work in the emergency an importation of outside laborers to the number of 2,000 should be made to conduct the sanitary work while the people of Galveston were given an opportunity of looking after their own losses and rebuilding their own property without giving any time to the city at large.

It was believed that with the work of these 2,000 outside laborers it would require about four weeks to clean the city of debris, and in the meantime the citizens could be working on their own property and repairing damage there.

Another relief committee from Velasco reported that 2,000 persons were in destitute circumstances, without food, clothing, or homes. Crops had been totally destroyed, all farming implements were washed away, and the people had nothing at hand with which to work the fields.

A relief committee from the Columbia precinct reported 2,500 destitute. Other sections sent in committees during the day, and as a result of all Governor Sayers ordered post-haste shipments of supplies.

The text of the message of sympathy received by President McKinley from the Emperor of Germany was as follows:

Stettin, Sept. 13, 1900
President of the United States of America,
Washington

I wish to convey to your excellency the expression of my deep-felt sympathy with the misfortune that has befallen the town and harbor of Galveston and many other ports of the coast, and I mourn with you and the people of the United States over the terrible loss of life and property caused by the hurricane, but the magnitude of the disaster is equaled by the indomitable spirit of the citizens of the new world, who, in their long and continued struggle with the adverse forces of nature, have proved themselves to be victorious. I sincerely hope that Galveston will rise again to new prosperity.          WILLIAM, I. R.

The President replied:

Executive Mansion, Sept. 14, 1900
His Imperial & Royal Majesty Wilhelm II
Stettin, Germany

Your majesty's message of condolence and sympathy is very grateful to the American government and people, and in their name, as well as on behalf of the many thousands who have suffered bereavement and irreparable loss in the Galveston disaster, I thank you most earnestly.

WILLIAM McKINLEY

# 1,500 NEGROES PERISHED AT GALVESTON

William Guest, a Pullman car porter, returned to Chicago from the storm-stricken district Monday, September 17. He said:
"I left Harrisburg night before last, and things then in the neighborhood were in a dreadful state. Galveston is about twenty miles distant, and the refugees were pouring in the direction of Houston in great numbers. Many well-to-do colored people have lost all they had. The Rev. W. H. Cain, a colored Episcopal minister, and his entire family were killed, and it was reported to me that Mrs. Cuney, the widow of Wright Cuney, was also lost, as well as a number of colored teachers employed in the public schools. At Houston relief committees have been organized."

The Rev. Mr. Cain was well known in Chicago, having preached several times from the pulpit of the St. Thomas Episcopal church on Dearborn near Thirtieth Street.

Cyrus Field Adams, publisher of the *Appeal*, Chicago, received a letter from Galveston from W. H. Noble, Jr., saying that about 1,500 Afro-Americans lost their lives in the storm, and that fully 10,000 were homeless.

Cooped up in a house that collapsed after being carried along by a deluge of water, John Elford, brother of A. B. Elford, No. 260 South Lincoln Street, Chicago, his wife and little grandson, met death in the flood during the Galveston storm. Milton, son of John Elford, was in the building with the family at the time, and was the only one of the many occupants including fifteen women known to have escaped.

A. B. Elford, bookkeeper for A. M. Foster & Co., No. 120 Lake Street, was dumfounded when he received the first information of the disaster, for he had no idea of his brother being in Texas. John Elford was a retired farmer and merchant of Langdon, N. D. He had taken his family on a trip to old and New Mexico.

On September 17 Mr. Elford received the following letter from Langdon, N. D.:

"We have just received a letter from Milton. Father, mother, Dwight and Milton went to Galveston from Mineral Springs, Tex., where they had previously been stopping. They were so delighted with Galveston on reaching there that they sold their return tickets and decided to remain about two months. They were at first in a house near the beach, but moved farther away and to a larger and stronger house when the water began to rise.

"All at once the water came down the street bringing houses and debris. They started to build a raft, but before it could be got together the house started to float. It had gone but a short distance when it went to pieces. Milton was struck with something and knocked out into the water. He came up, caught a timber and climbed to a roof, and thus managed to make his escape. He saw no one escape from the building as it collapsed. We do not believe the bodies have yet been recovered.

"We have wired for more definite news regarding the bodies, but have heard nothing more. —EDGAR ELFORD"

Dwight Elford, one of the drowned, was only five years old. He was the son of George Elford of Langdon.

## TOTAL DEAD AND MISSING

It was given out from Galveston on Tuesday, September 20, that so far as could be ascertained on that date, the loss of life in the great catastrophe was as follows:

Identified.............................4,754
Unidentified (recovered).........300
Missing...............................2,000

Total....................................7,054
Dead in Central &
Southern Texas....................1,044
High Island...........................563

Total....................................1,607

This makes the grand total of dead 8,661. The horrifying news reached Dallas late on the afternoon of September 18 that High Island, a seaside resort thirty miles northeast of Galveston, near the gulf shore and in the southwestern corner of Jefferson County, Tex., was entirely destroyed by the hurricane of the 8th. The place had about 1,000 residents, many of them visitors.

Not a house was left standing and more than 400 dead bodies were found by relief and exploring parties. General Manager Spangler, of the Gulf & Interstate Railway, also received information on that date that more than thirty miles of that road had been entirely destroyed between Bolivar Point and High Island.

After looking over the situation carefully, the decision was arrived at, ten days succeeding the tragedy, that to put Galveston on her feet would require $5,000,000. Such was the opinion of Congressman Hawley, one of the city's representative businessmen. This did not mean that the sum mentioned would come anywhere near restoring the city to the condition before the storm. Far from it. Mr. Hawley did not so intend to be understood. He was asked:

"What measure of relief will burn your dead, clean and purify your streets and public places, feed and clothe the living, and place your people where they can be self-sustaining and on the way to regain what has been lost?"

His reply was: "It will take $5,000,000 to relieve Galveston from the distress of the storm. At least that sum will be needed to dispose of the dead, to remove the ruins, and to do what is right for the living. I think that we should not only feed and clothe, but that we ought to have some means to help people who have lost everything to make a start toward the restoration of their homes. To do this will require every dollar of $5,000,000."

There were then on the scene more nurses and physicians than required. The injured were recovering rapidly from their hurts, which were largely superficial. Many men and women were suffering from severe nervous shock and found it impossible to sleep. Food was coming in by boatload and carload faster than it could be handled, in such generous quantities that no further doubts were entertained about supplies.

Estimates of the number dependent upon the relief committees varied. Mayor Jones made it about 8,000, while other authorities put the number as high as 15,000. In the business center the streets had been cleaned and opened. All buildings still showed marks of wind and water, but goods were displayed and business was being transacted.

The city was gradually assuming the bustling ante flood appearance. The principal streets were electrically lighted. Stenches no longer assailed the nostrils, except in the outside circle of destruction, where much debris still remained untouched. Cremation of the dead was being pushed, but it was many days before the working parties got out the last of the bodies.

The whole twenty-two miles' length of the island was submerged. The horrors of the western portion beyond the city limits were just being learned at San Luis. One hundred and eighty-one bodies were buried on September 17. Between twenty and thirty bodies were counted among the piles of the railroad bridge between the island and Virginia Point. In Kinkead's addition about 100 were lost, eighteen in one house.

The farther the men worked in the Denver reservoir section the more numerous were the dead. Fires were burning every 300 feet on the beach and along many of the streets.

Mayor Walter C. Jones made a statement on that day of conditions and needs of Galveston people, basing his conclusions on the most reliable information which has come to him.

Mayor Jones' statement was as follows:

"It is almost impossible to speak definitely as yet of the needs of our people. We are broke, the majority of us. Galveston must have suffered, in my estimation, based upon all of the reports I have, $20,000,000. We now need money more than anything.

"From the advice I have received I believe the shipments of disinfectants and food supplies now on the way will be sufficient to meet the immediate wants. By the time these are used we shall have regained our transportation facilities and stocks of everything, so that we can use money more advantageously.

"It is impossible to state just how much money has reached us. We have received from the Governor, at Austin, $100,000 in cash. That is from the general fund. Special contributions have come through the Chamber of Commerce, the Cotton Exchange and several other channels. We have between 1,500 and 3,000 men at work searching for bodies, clearing the streets and burning debris. Of this work, which ought to be done as fast as possible in the interest of the living, there is enough to keep 3,000 employed for forty days, although I believe we shall have the principal streets clear in ten days or two weeks.

"I hesitate to say how much it will take to put Galveston where her people can care for themselves. Certainly $5,000,000 will be a moderate estimate. There is not a building but is damaged, not a house of those left standing but will have to be re-roofed, and few that will not need to be straightened on their foundations. If Galveston could get $10,000,000 it would be used judiciously to enable the people to become self-sustaining.

"It is true Galveston is represented as being one of the wealthiest cities of the country. But our rich people had everything here and are crippled. The people of moderate means, who had homes and worked on salaries are, with scarcely an exception, ruined. The class dependent upon labor must be furnished something to do for wages or must suffer.

"Dr. Lord and others, who have been among the people more than I have, say there are 8,000 helpless who must be fed and clothed and carried along for some time to come, even after what might be called immediate needs have been met.

"There is no contagious disease and we do not anticipate any. But many are suffering from shock and exposure and from injuries received among the ruins. The City of Galveston, I am convinced, lost fully 5,000 persons. Down the island, outside of the city limits, were scattered between 2,000 and 3,000 persons. From the reports slowly coming in it appears that most of these people lost their lives. The island in the sparsely settled parts seems to have been swept clean of habitations."

The most motley crowd of United States regulars ever seen at attention lined up before Captain Rafferty the second Monday after the calamity. Battery O, First United States Artillery, the organization, was battered Battery O. No two men were dressed alike. Parts of uniforms and clothes which bore no semblance to any uniform were barely sufficient to cover nakedness, and in some cases there were bad rents, which showed the bare anatomy on dress parade.

Battery O came out of the storm with a loss of 28 out of 190 men, a loss seldom sustained in battle. One of these regulars floated fifty-two miles on a door; another was carried on an outhouse across the island and then across Galveston Bay. The survivors had been barracked in a shattered church since the Sunday after the storm. They were sent to San Antonio to be outfitted and armed. The officers and men lost everything and had to get clothes to cover them.

James Stewart, of St. Louis, had undertaken to see that Captain Benton Kennedy's boys did not suffer. It was believed the grain men of St. Louis would take a personal interest in this case. Captain Kennedy came to Galveston from St. Louis, Mo., where he was well known. He was superintendent of Elevator A. His family consisted of his wife, three boys and two girls. In August Captain Kennedy bought a nice home and moved into it. When the storm made the house no longer safe he placed Henry and Edwin, little fellows of 15 and 9, on a raft at the door and went back for the others. The raft was carried half a mile and the boys were rescued. Captain Kennedy and Mrs. Kennedy and the sisters and one brother were lost.

Adjutant-General Thomas Scurry said Monday evening, September 17:

"In my opinion the situation is rapidly growing better; the people found themselves dazed and shattered as a result of the storm. While there was an abundance of energy remaining, as might have been naturally expected, a vast amount of it was not concentrated. It has been the policy of this office to concentrate energies. These efforts have been most gratifying. We have a large number of men, possibly 2,000, at work.

"What is most needed for Galveston now is money. Thousands of persons who owned their little homes have had them destroyed. They are now dependent upon the generosity of the outside world and upon the Relief Committee to prepare for the rigors of winter and to refurnish their homes with necessities. No man who has not been an eye-witness to the desolation which has swept over this city can have the faintest conception of what it means.

"Galveston lies on an island about a mile wide from north to south, the city covering about six miles of this east and west. Along the southern side for a distance of two to five blocks every house has been absolutely demolished. Such of these unfortunates as were not drowned are now penniless."

# CHAPTER SIX:
## LOOKING TO THE FUTURE

Monday, September 17, Galveston presented a far different appearance than the Monday previous. Street cars were in operation in the business part of the city and the electric line and water service had been partly resumed. The progress made under the circumstances was little short of remarkable.

It must not be understood by any means that the remaining portion of the city had been put in anything like its normal condition, but so very great a change had been wrought, so much order and system prevailed where formerly chaos reigned, that Galveston and the people who had been giving her such noble assistance had good reason to be satisfied with what had been accomplished in the face of such fearful odds. According to statements made by General Scurry, Mayor Jones, Alderman Perry and others, there was equally good reason to believe that the progress of the work from that time on would be even more satisfactory.

On that morning the board of health began a systematic effort to obtain the names of the dead, so that the information could be used for legal purposes and for life insurance settlements. An agent was stationed at the headquarters of the Central Relief Committee to receive and file sworn statements in lieu of coroner's certificates. Persons who had left the city but were in possession of information concerning the dead were notified to send sworn statements to Mr. Doherty.

The steady stream of refugees from Galveston was kept up. There was not a departing train from across the bay which was not packed to its platforms. Refugees continued to leave for many days thereafter.

No sadder sight could be imagined than the picture presented by a boatload of refugees, when the ropes were cast off and the craft swung out into the bay and away from the desolate city. There was not a face that was not turned toward the ruin. There was not an eye that was not moistened by tears. So great had been the rush to leave behind the scene of the storm that the *Lawrence*, the boat which connected with trains at Texas City, had not left her wharf a single day without denying passage to a portion of those who wanted to get away.

The partings at the waterside were pitiful. Husbands came to the gangplank and kissed their weeping wives good-bye, turning back to the hard work of reconstruction which confronted them, with breaking hearts. Scores of women, overcome at the last moment, were cared for by strange hands, while those who loved them, bound to Galveston by necessity, could do no more than watch from afar and pray.

Instead of waiting until Galveston was reached to begin work, steps were taken to care for refugees at the bay terminal of the Galveston, Houston & Henderson Road, and during Saturday night and Sunday hundreds of hungry refugees were fed, while numbers of sick and wounded were cared for.

There was plenty of work on hand for ten times the force of laborers employed. The area which had not yet been touched embraced four and a half miles of frontage on the beach and bay.

There were enough provisions on hand ahead to feed everybody in Galveston for a week. There was a great deal of trouble in properly distributing supplies, the rush at the depots being as great as at any time since they were opened.

It was indeed a mercy that the weather since the storm had been clear and dry. Had it rained a single day the suffering would have been terrible, for there was not a whole roof in Galveston.

There were about 200 soldiers in Galveston doing guard and police duty. The camp on the wharf, between the Galveston Red Snapper Company and the foot of Tremont Street had been put into shape and the soldiers comfortably housed. There were five militia commands—the Dallas Rough Riders, Captain Ormonde Paget, with forty-five men; the Houston Light Guards, Captain George McCormick, with forty-five men; the Galveston Sharpshooters, Captain A. Bunschell, with thirty-five men; Battery D of Houston, Captain G. A. Adams, with fifteen men, and Troop A Houston Cavalry, commanded by Lieutenant Breedlove, with twenty men.

The fact that no money was available to pay the men who were engaged in cleaning the streets was a great detriment to preparing the way not only for rebuilding the city but in the efforts to prevent the spread of plague and pestilence.

General Scurry, general in charge of the operations at Galveston, made the following statement on Sunday, September 16:

> I have not a dollar to pay the men who are working in the streets all day long. I am not able to say to a single one of them "You'll be paid for your work." I have not the money to make good the promise. I hope and believe that the country will understand the situation. We must have this city cleaned up at any cost and with the greatest speed possible. If it is not done with all haste, and at the same time done well, there may be a pestilence, and if it breaks out here it will not be Galveston alone that will suffer.
>
> Such things spread, and it is not only for the sake of this city, but for others outside that I urge that above all things we want money. The nation has been most kind in its response to appeals from Galveston. From what I hear food and disinfectants sufficient for temporary purposes at least are here or on the way. The country does not understand. It cannot understand unless it could visit Galveston, the situation prevailing here.      SCURRY,
> Adjutant-General, State of Texas

As to the probability of a pestilence, General Chambers McKibbin, U. S. A., commanding the Military Department of Texas, said:

I am personally in favor of burning as much rubbish as possible, and of burning it as quickly as permissible. I do not predict a pestilence, but I think the things are coming to that point where a pestilence may be possible unless prompt measures are taken, and there is nothing so effective as fire. Burn everything and burn it at once.

All the churches in Galveston either being wrecked or ruined, with but one or two exceptions, divine services on Sunday, September 16, were in most cases suspended. Mass was celebrated at St. Mary's cathedral in the morning and was largely attended.

Father Kirwin preached an eloquent and feeling sermon, in which he spoke of the awful calamity that had befallen the people. After expressing sympathy with the afflicted, and distressed he advised all to go to work in burying the dead. The next day a census of the Catholic population was begun to ascertain the number of widows and orphans caused by the storm and the exact number of Catholics who perished.

Bishop Gallagher, who had been active in his efforts to mitigate suffering at Galveston, received a telegram from Archbishop Corrigan of New York, stating the diocese of that city would see that all Catholic orphan children sent to his care were kindly provided for.

Houston was the center of relief distribution, and also the key to Galveston. It was practically the only way in or out for weeks. Hundreds of refugees passed through every day. Houston was well filled with them, but the larger number went right through to points farther north. Free transportation was furnished to any point in Texas, provided they had relatives who would take care of them. Many of the refugees arrived at Houston scantily clothed and in a pitiful condition.

"Vast as the work is, all are being provided for," said Edward Watkins, chairman of the transportation division of the Relief Committee. "We have not let anybody go through uncared for."

Mere curiosity was at a discount here. People who had urgent business in Galveston found it hard to get permits to go there, and those who were simply curious could not get there at all. Camera fiends were absolutely barred. One man was shot for taking a picture of a nude woman on the beach, and three newspaper men who were taking views of the ruins were rounded up, their cameras smashed and themselves forced to go to work gathering up decomposed corpses.

Even Houston was in a similar state of martial law. Guards surrounded the depot of the International & Great Northern, the only road running south, and would not even allow curious crowds to gather to see the refugees come in. This was in enforcement of a proclamation issued by Mayor Brashear, copies of which, printed on large red cards, were posted conspicuously all over the city.

The catastrophe all but paralyzed shipping business in the storm-visited section. At Fort Worth all purchasing stopped. Cotton was just beginning to move, but it had to go by way of New Orleans, the additional freights eating up the apparent profit of the one cent a pound advance in price. Had the storm struck a few weeks later the loss would have been greatly increased, as the cotton would then have been upon the wharves.

Heavy financial losers were the fraternal societies. One known as the United Moderns, with headquarters at Denver, lost 100 out of a lodge of 500. Policies ranged from $1,000 to $2,000.

INSURANCE MATTERS CREATE A BOTHER

One hundred and fifty odd million dollars represented the value of the life insurance policies carried by the old-line companies in Texas at the time of the flood. It was estimated that $4,000,000 represented the life risks carried in Galveston by the regular companies, and that over $2,000,000 was carried by assessment and fraternal organizations.

Insurance men said it was probable that of the persons killed in the recent disaster 900 were men, and that, according to statistics, half of them had life policies of an average value of $2,000. On this basis $900,000 approximated the losses to be met in Galveston by the life insurance companies. Eighteen old-line companies and a great many assessment and fraternal companies divided the losses, and no reputable organization was crippled thereby.

Accurate figures of the losses were not made, but the above figures represented the calculations hastily made by George T. Dexter, superintendent of the domestic agencies of the Mutual Life Insurance Company of New York. In regard to this Mr. Dexter said:

"The most striking feature of the insurance situation at Galveston is the difficulty that will arise when the adjustment of claims is taken up. Hundreds of bodies have been buried without identification, hundreds more have been taken out into the gulf and many have been cremated. Whole families have been destroyed in many instances, and insurance papers have suffered in the general destruction of property. This state of affairs will make it difficult for the beneficiaries to establish their claims and will enable the organizations so disposed to escape payment. I have no doubt the level premium companies will adjust claims, in a large measure, on circumstantial evidence.

"Our agency property at San Antonio was destroyed, and we have no accurate reports of our Texas losses, so it is impossible to give other than general estimates of what they may be. The class of people insuring in the regular companies are in general surrounded by conditions that render them better risks in the event of such a calamity as this, but if my information is correct the better portion of the residence district suffered most, and we may hear of heavy losses. I think we carried between $300,000 and $400,000 insurance in Galveston. The insurance business in that part of the south has been exceptionally good of late because of the cotton values."

H. H. Knowles, southern manager of the Equitable Life of New York, said:

"We have two $100,000 risks in Galveston, and we are hoping that they are not among the lost. Our reports from Texas are not in, but I should think that our company will be fortunate if it gets off with less than a loss of $100,000. I believe that the assessment and fraternal insurance concerns will have the most losses because of the fact that in such a disaster the loss of life is greater among the poorer classes."

The accident insurance companies had heavy losses to meet.

## SERIOUS DANGER FROM FIRE

One of the serious dangers which Galveston faced for many days was fire. Not a drop of rain had fallen during the two weeks succeeding the hurricane, and the hot winds and blistering sun made the wrecked houses and buildings so much tinder, piled mountain high in every direction. In nearly all parts of the city the fire hydrants were buried fifty feet, in some places a hundred feet deep under the wreckage, and as yet the water supply at best was only of the most meager kind.

Galveston's fire department was small and badly crippled and would have been utterly powerless to stay the flames should they once start. There was no relief nearer than Houston, and that was hours away.

In view of all the then existing conditions it was no wonder that the cry was: "Get the women and children to the mainland; anywhere off the island," nor was it a wonder that with one small boat carrying only 300 passengers and making only two trips a day people fairly fought to be taken aboard.

All during Sunday, September 16, fears were entertained by the authorities that even this service would be cut off and Galveston left without any means of getting to the mainland owing to the trouble with the owner of the boat.

The sanitary conditions did not improve to any great extent. Dr. Trueheart, chairman of the committee in charge of caring for the sick and injured, was proceeding with dispatch. More physicians were needed, and he requested that about thirty outside physicians come to Galveston and work for at least a month, and, if needed, longer.

The city's electric light service was completely destroyed and the city electrician said it would be sixty days before the business portion of the city could be lighted.

A glorious and modern Galveston to be rebuilt in place of the old one, was the cry raised by the citizens, but it seemed a task beyond human power to ever remove the wreckage of the old city.

The total number of people fed in the ten wards Saturday was 16,144. Sunday the number increased slightly. No accurate statement of the amount of supplies could be obtained as they were put in the general stock as soon as received.

Galveston received another scare Sunday night, the 16th, when it became rumored that Houston, where all the relief trains were side-tracked, was burning with its precious supplies of food and clothing.

The scare grew out of a $400,000 fire in Houston, which destroyed the Merchants and Planters' oil mill, the largest in the world. The fire broke out at noon, but was not observable until nightfall, when the glow in the sky could be seen for a great distance.

Galveston was reassured by telegraph that a second southern Texas calamity was out of the question and that the relief supplies were safe.

A critical problem in the efforts to relieve the people of Galveston was the delay in getting supplies to the island city. Trainload after trainload was in Houston, which would have assisted materially in the work of relief, but on account of the limited transportation facilities they could not be hurried there. There was but one track and it was of light rails and was used only for terminal business. Even if the supplies were at Texas City they could not be moved fast, as there were not enough boats of light draft at Galveston. Buffalo Bayou could be used from Houston, but it was impossible to get the boats for the purpose.

## LABORERS IMPORTED INTO GALVESTON

The general committee of public safety at Galveston decided, on September 17, to import laborers. This action was taken with the consent of the local unions. Skilled mechanics had been busy burying the dead without pay, but were relieved of this work and replaced by imported unskilled labor.

According to Dr. William W. Meloy of Chicago, who has investigated the health situation, there was no fever in Galveston September 17.

"The water supply has been adequate," he said, "and is not liable to contamination. Nervous prostration, hysteria and mild dementia occur among the wealthy class, due to shock, exhaustion and grief. Among the poorer classes the use of spoiled food during the earlier part of the week has led to intestinal troubles. Several cases of heat prostration have occurred among the work men. The danger from the unburied dead is mostly to the people who handle them."

Major Frank M. Spencer arrived at Galveston on September 16 with $50,000 cash from Governor Sayers, to be expended in hastening the disposal of the debris and the burial of bodies. Major Spencer arrived too late to bank the money and for twenty-four hours it rested in the safe of the Tremont House, guarded by soldiers.

Galveston passed the first Sunday following the disaster burying the dead and clearing away debris. General Scurry's order that all men able to work should labor to the limit of their strength was carried out to the letter.

"We're thankful," said Mayor Jones on Monday, when told of the arrival of the Chicago relief train at Houston. "You can't make that statement too strong to the people of Chicago. We are thankful and thankful again. Chicago people are among the staunchest friends in the world in times like these. Yes, we'll build Galveston up again, and, like Chicago, we'll make it a better city than it was. We shall never forget the kindness of the people of Chicago in coming so generously to our relief, and we all thank them from the bottom of our hearts."

## GALVESTON AGAIN MADE A PORT

"Issue bills of lading to Galveston and through Galveston to other points."

On September 17, up and down the International & Great Northern, the Missouri, Kansas & Texas, the Santa Fe and their connections the wires were carrying the official information that Galveston would be a terminal, a sure enough port, as soon as the traffic could reach there. The Vice-Presidents and General Managers and General Agents had mastered the railroad wreck, they had set the time for the running of the first train into Galveston, and that time was Friday, September 21. By that date, according to the engineers, the temporary bridge would be ready for use. It was ready to the minute.

The news that the roads had declared readiness to accept freight for Galveston and through Galveston was received by businessmen as tidings of great joy. It added greatly to the improvement of spirit. For several days after the storm the prediction was that no trains would enter Galveston under thirty days and that the time might be sixty days.

Equally exhilarating with the action of the railroad men was the action taken by Secretary Bailey, of the Wharf Company, that exportation of wheat would be resumed tomorrow morning. The machinery of Elevator A was started up and was successful. Monday afternoon the wharf was cleared. A steamship was brought under the spout and loaded. James Stewart, Mr. Orthwein and other St. Louis grain men said almost the entire stock of wheat would be saved.

The number of persons who left Galveston up to September 17, it was stated at relief headquarters, was over 8,000, of whom about 5,000 were then in Houston being cared for. Others had gone on into the interior of the State or to other States. The number coming up on the trains showed no falling off.

New arrangements made at Galveston enabled people to get out without so much red tape and they took advantage of the opportunity to do so. Governor Sayers had now taken charge of the relief work here at all points, and money was being given out where needed, more than provisions and clothing.

## GOVERNOR SAYERS IN A HOPEFUL MOOD

"I look for the rebuilding of Galveston to be well underway by the latter part of this week," said Governor Sayers, of Texas, on September 18, at Austin. "The work of cleaning the city of unhealthful refuse and burying the dead will have been completed by that time, and all the available labor in the city can be applied to its rebuilding.

"If the laboring people of Galveston will only get to work in earnest prosperity will soon again smile on the city. Arrangements have been made to pay all the laborers working under the direction of the military authorities $1.50 and rations for every day they have worked or will work. An account has been kept of all work done and no laborer will lose one day's pay.

"The money and food contributions coming from a generous people have been a great help to the people of Galveston, as it has relieved them of the necessity of spending their money to support the needy, and it can now be applied to the improvement of their own property and putting again on foot their business enterprises.

"Five dollars a day is being offered to the mechanics who will come to Galveston, and, with the assurance from reputable physicians that there is no extraordinary danger of sickness, outside laborers will flock to Galveston and before many days a new city will rise on the storm-swept island.

"The telegraph and telephone companies and railroads have been exceedingly generous since the great calamity. They have not only given money, but everything has been transported to that city free of charge, while those desiring to get away from the harrowing scenes of Galveston have been transported free. The people of Texas will long remember with grateful hearts the kindness of these companies.

"It is now an assured fact that trains will be running into Galveston this week, and with uninterrupted communication with the outside world Galveston should soon assume her normal condition."

## WHY SHOULD GALVESTON NOT BE REBUILT?

The appalling nature of the wreck to which Galveston was reduced naturally led to some talk of abandoning the old site altogether and rebuilding the city somewhere on the mainland. An army officer concluded his report to Washington headquarters by expressing the opinion that Galveston was destroyed beyond the ability to recover, and the Southern Pacific railway was said to be in favor of leaving the flat island to the sport of the treacherous waves and heading a movement to rebuild the city at the mouth of the Brazos River.

It is natural that non-residents of Galveston should consider the advisability of abandoning such a perilous site, especially as there can never be any complete security against a disaster like that of Saturday, September 8. But it is safe to say that Galveston will be rebuilt on its sand island. Mankind is not wont to desert any spot of the earth's surface because of a sudden and rare convulsion of nature.

Lisbon was not abandoned because of the disastrous earthquake that killed 50,000 people in 1755. Similar earthquake disasters in Central and South America have not induced the survivors to abandon a single city.

When 100,000 Chinamen were swallowed up at Peking in the last century it did not change the site of the city nor have the still more disastrous floods along the Yellow River ever caused the survivors to change their habitat.

History shows Europeans and Americans to be quite as tenacious in this regard as any other races.

Italian peasants continue to cultivate the slopes of Vesuvius in spite of all past disasters, and the inhabitants of the Sea Islands along the Carolina coast were not disheartened when the elements committed fearful ravages.

The leading businessmen of Galveston emphasized a point when they began to talk of rebuilding which had escaped general attention until that time. They were exceedingly anxious that commercial bodies, steamship owners, brokers and those interested in the commerce of Galveston should be as considerate as possible in their treatment of the city, that is to say, there should be liberality in the commercial relations. These men urged that the extent of the calamity should be taken into account when adjustment of contracts took place and in all business arrangements until the city could regain its footing. Chapters provide by special mention for "Visitations of Providence," for the "Acts of God."

The Galveston businessmen hoped that their business connections would apply a like spirit to all commerce affected by the storm. They were not disappointed, as the result showed.

Galveston was just entering upon the busy season. There were from 200 to 300 ships under sailing contracts with that port for the months of September, November and December. Some of these ships were, when the storm came, on the high seas. Even a temporary paralysis of thirty days meant much loss and the derangement of many contracts.

It was a time which called for the generous policy, not for strict enforcements of the letter of agreements. Galveston only asked what her businessmen thought was just, that thereby the shock to commerce might be mitigated. When the time came Galveston found that she had not asked too much, as she received all the consideration she could wish.

Representatives of the railroad systems which connected Galveston with the outside world before the occurrence of the disaster agreed in saying, in a meeting held at New York, that her residents would rebuild on the same sand island in spite of the terrible experiences. They believed that Galveston, injured financially though her citizens had been, would be rebuilt by her citizens without the aid of outside capital.

A. F. Walker, Chairman of the Board of Directors of the Atchison, Topeka & Santa Fe, said he felt certain that Galveston would be rebuilt.

The new energy and courage displayed by the people of Galveston is what was to be expected in a city so full of American pluck. Though stunned and prostrate under the most fatal disaster that had ever overtaken an American community, Galveston took only a few days to regain its breath. It has simply reasserted the same indomitable courage and willpower by which Americans in times past built up a great nation where there was a wilderness a century ago.

The terse motto stuck up on every street corner of the wrecked city is "Clean Up." Behind its grim humor there lies a stern determination that is one of the proudest attributes of our race. There is no reason why a greater Galveston should not speedily rise on the site of the present ruins.

The report of an army officer that the city was ruined beyond recovery and the suggestions of other persons that Galveston should be rebuilt on another site find no sympathy among the citizens. Galveston will be rebuilt upon its former site.

Carpenters, masons and artisans are being called for by thousands, and, with the generous aid contributed by people all over the country, there will be a rapid transformation. The city has thrust its sorrow behind it and has its face set toward the future.

Since the danger of flood cannot be removed so long as the city stands at its present level, it is to be hoped its builders will begin a new era of security by raising the grade of the streets.

A few feet will materially decrease the danger from tidal waves. It will also be wise to construct the foundations of all permanent large buildings of stone to a height above the level reached by the recent inundation. In resolving to defy an untoward fate Galveston should begin by adopting all practical means for defying wind and waves.

Even though the expense and delay will be greater, it will pay to give the new buildings all possible safeguards of solidity.

Galveston will be rebuilt, as it was after the disaster of fourteen years previously. Its inhabitants will reason that the city had existed for two-thirds of a century in comparative safety, and that such a tidal wave is not likely to be repeated in a hundred years. The same commercial advantages that first tempted settlers to the island, and that made Galveston one of the most thriving cities on the gulf coast, are still present.

Men who own real estate on the island will not abandon it, even though the improvements thereon have been reduced to a wreck. They know that even if they did abandon it there would be plenty of others to take it—risks and all—and rebuild the city.

The federal government may hesitate about rebuilding its structures on so precarious a site, but private interests are not likely to abandon a city even for so terrible a disaster as that at Galveston.

## COASTAL CITIES IN DANGER

Galveston Island, with a stretch of thirty-five miles, rises only five feet above the level of high tide. To the south is an unbroken sweep of sea for 800 miles. Twelve hundred miles away is the nesting place of storms—storms that rise out of the dead calm of the doldrums and sweep northward, sometimes with a fury that nothing can withstand. Most of these storms describe a parabola, with the westward arch touching the Atlantic coast, after which the track is northeastward, finally disappearing with the storm itself in the north Atlantic.

But every little while one of these West Indian hurricanes starts northwestward from its island nest, moving steadily on its course and entering the gulf itself.

September and October are the months of these storms, and of the two months September is worse. In the ten years between 1878 and 1887, inclusive, fifty-seven hurricanes arose in the warm, moist conditions of the West Indian doldrums. Most of these passed out to sea and to the St. Lawrence River country, where they disappeared. But the hurricane of October 11, 1887, came ashore at New Orleans on October 17, and wrought havoc as it passed up the Eastern States to New Brunswick. The storm of October 8, 1886, reached Louisiana on the 12th, curving again toward Galveston on the Texas coast. It was in this storm that Galveston was flooded with loss of life and property while Indianola was destroyed beyond recovery.

With these non-recurring storms two conditions favor their passage into the gulf. A high barometric area lies over the Atlantic coast States, while a trough of low pressure leads into the gulf and northward into the region of the Dakotas. The hurricane takes the path of least resistance always, and it must pass far northward before it can work its natural way around the tardy high area that hangs over the central coast States. It was this condition exactly which diverted the recent storm to Galveston and the Texas coast.

The origin of a hurricane is not fully settled. Its accompanying phenomena, however, are significant to even the casual observer. A long swell on the ocean usually precedes it. This swell may be forced to great distances in advance of the storm and be observed two or three days before the storm strikes. A faint rise in the barometer may be noticed before the sharp fall follows. Wisps of thin, cirrus cloud float for 200 miles around the storm center. The air is calm and sultry until a gentle breeze springs from the southeast. This breeze becomes a wind, a gale, and, finally, a tempest, with matted clouds over head, precipitating rain and a churning sea below throwing clouds of spume into the air.

Here are all the terrible phenomena of the West Indian hurricane—the tremendous wind, the thrashing sea, the lightning, the bellowing thunder, and the drowning rain that seems to be dashed from mighty tanks with the force of Titans.

But almost in an instant all these may cease. The wind dies, the lightning goes out, the rain ceases, and the thunder bellows only in the distance. The core of the storm is overhead. Only the waves of the sea are churning. There may be twenty miles of this central core, a diameter of only one-thirtieth that of the storm. It passes quickly, and with as little warning as preceded its stoppage the storm closes in again, but with the wind from the opposite direction, and the whole phenomena suggesting a reversal of all that has gone before.

No storm possible in the elements presents the terrors that accompany the hurricane. The twisting tornado is confined to a narrow track and it has no long-drawn-out horrors. Its climax is reached in a moment. The hurricane, however, grows and grows, and when it has reached to 100 or 120 miles an hour nothing can withstand it.

It is this terrible besom of the Southern seas that so nearly has taken Galveston off the map. The great storm of 1875 frightened the city. The fate of Indianola in 1886 and the loss of ten lives and $200,000 worth of property on Galveston Island has kept Galveston uneasy ever since. Today, for it to suggest rebuilding, will meet with the disapprobation of many of the sympathizing Americans who are giving freely to the stricken people.

But the abandonment of Galveston could not be without a struggle. For fourteen years its old citizens had been admitting that twice in their memory the sea had come in on the island, causing death and destruction, but as sturdily as their conservatism prompted they had insisted that it never could do so again. They gave no consistent reason for their belief. The island was no higher; the force of the sea was as boundless as before; the doldrums of the West Indies still hung over the archipelago in storm-brooding calm. But their belief spread and the island city grew and developed as the old settler never had hoped to see it grow when he squatted there in the sand more than sixty years ago.

This settler stock of Galveston Island was of queer characteristics. The island settlement was of a sort of Captain Streeter origin. The only variation was that the Colonel Menard who founded it bought the island and established a townsite company to attract immigration. The mainland, as flat and desolate almost as the island, was three miles away. But deep water was there and to the north was an agricultural country that one day would have cotton to export. So the settlers waited. They held to their sand lots and traded with the "mosquito fleet" which sailed up and down the coast from Corpus Christi to New Orleans. This mosquito fleet was the only means for bringing outside traders to the town. As it grew it developed that the city's export trade was all it had. It did a wholesale business that was to its retail business in the proportion of 100 to 1!

In this way Galveston developed in growing propensities. It scoffed at the mainland for years after the gulf shore began to be peopled. It was satisfied with its railroad "bridges," which were mere trestlework mounted on piling driven into the shallow water of the bay. If the mainland wished to reach the city let it row out or sail out; the city would not go to the expense of a wagon bridge.

As a result, Galveston was the most somnolent city in Texas, save on the wharves where tramp and coastwise ships and steamers loaded. When the market house closed by law at 10 o'clock in the morning, and when Galveston's own local population had laid in its supplies for a midday dinner and for supper and breakfast, Strand Street took a nap.

In the 1880s, however, a new element had been attracted, which was dissatisfied with the mossback order of things. It was not satisfied to make change with a stranger and give or take bits of yellow pasteboard, representing street car rides, in lieu of nickels.

But these young immigrants were frowned upon by Galveston conservatism. They were a disturbing element. They kept the staid, mossback citizen awake in the afternoons and he did not like it. They were clamoring for sewers and artesian water in mains, whereas the conservative was content to build his rainwater cistern above ground out of doors and strain the baby mosquitoes out of the water through a cloth.

When a new waterworks and standpipe had been completed in 1889, and when some new mills had been established under difficulties, affairs had come to a pass when the new Galvestonian and the old found a great gap between. The visiting stranger was the confidant of both sides.

"This town isn't what it used to be," sighed the conservative. "As a matter of fact," the young businessman would say, "Galveston needs to bury about 150 of its 'old citizens' before it can get awake."

This was the situation when the government began to expend money upon the harbor. This was the situation, slightly altered by time, when the wagon bridge was built to the mainland, when the government appropriated $6,200,000 for the deepening of the harbor, and when export trade from Galveston approached the mark of $100,000,000 annually. And this, virtually, was the Galveston now in ruins.

In rebuilding Galveston, it has been suggested that the bay be dredged of sand and the island raised to a uniform level of fifteen feet above the tide. The plan is feasible in every sense, and it is contended that the value of the city as a port would more than justify the cost.

However the island city may decide, it will have departed from several notable instances of water-swept cities in rebuilding. In addition to the abandonment of Indianola, on the mainland of Texas, are the stories of Last Island in the Gulf of Mexico and of Cobb's Island, a great fishing resort in Chesapeake Bay.

Last Island was overwhelmed in 1856. Three hundred lives were lost in the hurricane. Lafcadio Hearn has put the

legend of "L'Isle Derniere" into print and his description
of the hurricane that swept in upon it is a description of the
storm that has laid Galveston waste:

"One great noon, when the blue abyss of day seemed to
yawn over the world more deeply than ever before, a sudden
change touched the quicksilver smoothness of the waters—
the swaying shadow of a vast motion. First the whole sea
circle appeared to rise up bodily at the sky; the horizon curve
lifted to a straight line; the line darkened and approached—
a monstrous wrinkle, an immeasurable fold of green water
moving swift as a cloud shadow pursued by sunlight. But it
had looked formidable only by startling contrast with the
previous placidity of the open; it was scarcely two feet high;
it curled slowly as it neared the beach and combed itself out
in sheets of woolly foam with a low, rich roll of thunder.
Swift in pursuit another followed—a third, a feebler fourth;
then the sea only swayed a little and stilled again.

"Irregularly the phenomenon continued to repeat itself,
each time with heavier billowings and briefer intervals of
quiet, until at last the whole sea grew restless and shifted
color and flickered green—the swells became shorter and
changed form.

"The pleasure-seekers of Last Island knew there must
have been a 'great blow' somewhere that day. Still the sea
swelled, and a splendid surf made the evening bath de-
lightful. Then just at sundown a beautiful cloud bridge
grew up and arched the sky with a single span of cot-
tony, pink vapor that changed and deepened color with
the dying of the iridescent day. And the cloud bridge
approached, strained and swung round at last to make
way for the coming of the gale—even as the light bridges
that traverse the dreamy Teche swing open when the
luggermen sound through their conch shells the long,
bellowing signal of approach.

"Then the wind began to blow from the northeast, clear,
cool. Clouds came, flew as in a panic against the face of the
sun, and passed. All that day, through the night, and into the

morning again the breeze continued from the northeast, blowing like an equinoctial gale.

"Cottages began to rock. Some slid away from the solid props upon which they rested. A chimney tumbled. Shutters were wrenched off; verandas demolished. Light roofs lifted, dropped again, and flapped into ruin. Trees bent their heads to earth. And still the storm grew louder and blacker with every passing hour.

"So the hurricane passed, tearing off the heads of prodigious waves to hurl them a hundred feet in air—heaping up the ocean against the land—upturning the woods. Bays and passes were swollen to abysses; rivers re-gorged; the sea marshes changed to roaring wastes of water. Before New Orleans the flood of the mile-broad Mississippi rose six feet above highest water mark. One hundred and ten miles away Donaldsonville trembled at the towering tide of the Lafourche. Lakes strove to burst their boundaries. Far-off river steamers tugged wildly at their cables—shivering like tethered creatures that hear by night the approaching howl of destroyers.

"And swift in the wake of gull and frigate bird the wreckers come, the spoilers of the dead—savage skimmers of the sea—hurricane-riders wont to spread their canvas pinions in the face of storms. There is plunder for all—birds and men. Her betrothal ring will not come off, Giuseppe; but the delicate bone snaps easily; your oyster-knife can sever the tendon. Over her heart you will find it, Valentio—the locket held by that fine, Swiss chain of woven hair. Juan, the fastenings of those diamond eardrops are much too complicated for your peon fingers; tear them out.

"Suddenly a long, mighty silver trilling fills the ears of all; there is a wild hurrying and scurrying; swiftly, one after another, the overburdened luggers spread wings and flutter away. Thrice the great cry rings through the gray air and over the green sea, and over the far-flooded shell reefs where the huge white flashes are—sheet lightning of breakers—and over the weird wash of corpses coming in.

"It is the steam-call of the relief boat, hastening to rescue the living, to gather in the dead. The tremendous tragedy is over."


GALVESTON BUILT UPON SAND

Galveston is built upon the sand. According to Professor Willis L. Moore, Chief of the United States Weather Bureau at Washington, not only Galveston was insecurely built upon the flat sands of the island, but other cities on the gulf and Atlantic coasts, lying at tide, are subject to the same dangers. The West Indian hurricane may strike almost anywhere from the southern line of North Carolina, on down the coast, around the peninsula of Florida, and anywhere within the great arc described by the western shores of the Gulf of Mexico. These storms, perhaps 600 miles wide, have a vortex of twenty to thirty miles in diameter. It is in this vortex that the land is laid waste.

It is this fact that will lead more strongly than any other to the rebuilding of Galveston. With an export business of $100,000,000 annually, the great West will bring pressure to bear upon the maintenance of the port. There is an island type of man in its population that will not be driven from that little ridge of sand three miles out in the gulf. There are 1,500 miles of gulf coast on which the vortex of such a storm may waste itself without touching Galveston, and both conservatism and commercialism will take the risk that a score of other cities at the tide level are taking.

At the same time there are those who see for Galveston only a commercial existence. It never can grow as it has grown; it never can be the home of people whose fortunes are not tied up in the island.

For fourteen years the city has had to contend with the fears of the incomer. The growth between 1890 and 1900 shows that these fears had been allayed in great measure, following the destruction in 1886. But years will not wipe out the black record of the last week. Hundreds will leave the island as a place of residence; thousands have been killed there and cremated in the sands or buried in the treacherous sea. A death rate of 200 in a population of 1,000 drove Indianola from the map of Texas. Five thousand or more deaths of the 35,000 population of Galveston must have its influence upon the living.

For with the assurances of the United States Weather Bureau, it is recognized that in natural phenomena there are cycle periods in which extremes are repeated from nature's great laboratory. Observation has put this period of repetition at twenty years. According to this, in the case of hurricanes, the range of maximum and minimum will be within such a period. Without question Galveston is in the track of a certain abnormal but not infrequent West Indian hurricane which fails to be deflected from the Georgia and Florida coasts. It keeps to its northwestward course and strikes the Louisiana, Texas or Mexico coasts, according to its impulse. In the Galveston storm a new maximum seems to have been established, yet its repetition may be looked for within the next twenty-year period. As a matter of fact, indeed, the average period between the recurrence of these maximum storms has been less than fifteen years.

Lyman E. Cooley, one of the original engineers in marking the route of the drainage canal, is an observer of periodic natural phenomena, and his theory holds in great measure with the observations of the United States weather service.

"It is a general proposition," said Mr. Cooley. "It means just this much: Suppose that Chicago has a snowstorm on June 15. Within a twenty-year period we may expect another phenomenon of the kind in the same calendar month. It may not snow in Chicago itself; the storm may be ten, twenty or thirty miles away, on any side of it. But in the same general territory, about the same time of the phenomenon, it will be repeated.

"Suppose a terrible rain or wind storm develops, its repetition may be looked for in the same period. So with extremes of temperature, influences on lake levels, and all the other phenomena of nature's forces. They have their cycles, and the twenty-year period covers most of them."

But in the case of Galveston, one of its great hurricanes was experienced in 1875, another in 1886, and the last only fourteen years later. These historic facts tend to confirm Mr. Cooley's observations.

Galveston's destruction and that of other towns similarly situated had been predicted. Writing in the *Arena* in 1890, Professor Joseph Rodes Buchanan said:

"Every seaboard city south of New England that is not more than fifty feet above the sea level of the Atlantic coast is destined to a destructive convulsion. Galveston, New Orleans, Mobile, St. Augustine, Savannah and Charleston are doomed. Richmond, Baltimore, Washington, Philadelphia, Newark, Jersey City and New York will suffer in various degrees in proportion as they approximate the sea level. Brooklyn will suffer less, but the destruction at New York and Jersey City will be the grandest horror.

"The convulsion will probably begin on the Pacific coast, and perhaps extend in the Pacific toward the Sandwich Islands. The shock will be terrible, with great loss of life, extending from British Columbia down along the coast of Mexico, but the conformation of the Pacific coast will make its grand tidal wave far less destructive than on the Atlantic shore. Nevertheless, it will be calamitous. Lower California will, suffer severely along the coast. San Diego and Coronado will suffer severely, especially the latter.

"It may seem rash to anticipate the limits of the destructive force of a foreseen earthquake, but there is no harm in testing the prophetic power of science in the complex relations of nature and man.

"The destruction of cities which I anticipate will be twenty-four years ahead—it may be twenty-three. It will be sudden and brief—all within an hour and not far from noon. Starting from the Pacific coast, as already described, it will strike southward—a mighty tidal wave and earthquake shock that will develop in the Gulf of Mexico and Caribbean Sea. It will strike the western coast of Cuba and severely injure Havana. Our sister republic, Venezuela, bound to us in destiny, by the law of periodicity will be assailed by the encroaching waves and terribly shaken by the earthquake. The destruction of her chief city, Caraccas, will be greater than in 1812, when 12,000 were said to be destroyed. The coming shock will be near total destruction.

"From South America back to the United States, all Central America and Mexico are severely shaken; Vera Cruz suffers with great severity, but the City of Mexico realizes only a severe shock. Tampico and Matamoros suffer severely; Galveston is overwhelmed; New Orleans is in a dangerous condition—the question arises between total and partial destruction. I will only say it will be an awful calamity. If the tidal wave runs southward New Orleans may have only its rebound. The shock and flood pass up the Mississippi from 100 to 150 miles and strike Baton Rouge with destructive force.

"As it travels along the gulf shore Mobile will probably suffer most severely and be more than half destroyed; Pensacola somewhat less. South Florida is probably entirely submerged and lost; St. Augustine severely injured; Charleston will probably be half submerged, and Newbern suffer more severely; Port Royal will probably be wiped out; Norfolk will suffer about as much as Pensacola; Petersburg and Richmond will suffer, but not disastrously; Washington will suffer in its low grounds, Baltimore and Annapolis much more severely on its waterfront, its spires will topple, and its large buildings be injured, but I do not think its grand city hall will be destroyed. Probably the injury will not affect more than one-fourth. But along the New Jersey coast the damage will be great. Atlantic City and Cape May may be destroyed, but Long Branch will be protected by its bluff from severe calamity. Rising waters will affect Newark, and Jersey City will be the most unfortunate of large cities, everything below its heights being overwhelmed. New York below the post office and Trinity Church will be flooded and all its water margins will suffer."

# CHAPTER SEVEN:
## COMPARISON OF GALVESTON & JOHNSTOWN

Until the elements wreaked their vengeance upon the fair City of Galveston and vented their wrath upon its unoffending population, the awful disaster at Johnstown, Pa., which occurred on the 31st of May, 1889, was the most frightful calamity known in the history of the United States. Johnstown was almost literally wiped from the face of the earth, the suddenness of the flood which created the havoc precluding the escape of anyone unfortunate enough to be in its path.

Unlike the Galveston catastrophe, the flood at Johnstown poured its waters upon the devoted inhabitants without warning and the slaughter was over within the space of a comparatively few minutes. The victims, that is to say, the majority of them, were drowned or dashed to pieces before they had time to realize the horror of it all.

At Galveston the people knew for hours what their fate was to be before the angry waters submerged the island and the resistless gale tore the business buildings and residences to pieces. They looked death squarely in the face hour after hour, suffering all the terrors dire certainty could inflict, their knowledge that they were absolutely powerless and beyond the reach of aid adding to their agonies.

Death was merciful to the people of Johnstown; he was cruel to his prey at Galveston, and delighted in the tortures he was enabled to impose before he placed his icy hand upon them and bade them come.

Perhaps the only parallel in history to the Galveston visitation was the destruction, in 79 A. D., of Pompeii and Herculaneum. The frightened pleasure-seekers of those doomed cities could see the red lava stream bearing down upon them as it was vomited up from the bowels of Vesuvius and thrown out from the mighty maw of the crater, but even then they were mercifully stifled by the tremendous, never ending shower of ashes which soon enveloped them and completely covered their homes.

They did not stand for hours, with the blackness of the night around them, listening to the roar of the volcano's eruption and hear their death knell sounded long before they were compelled to undergo the actual pain of an awful death; they were caught as they sought safety in flight and stricken down while endeavoring to get beyond the reach of the sickle of the grim reaper; they could move and act in accordance with their impulses which prompted them to make a flight for life, and they succumbed only after a desperate struggle.

It was different at Galveston. The men, women and children were not permitted even the small but precious boon of falling while battling with the grim destroyer; they were caught and imprisoned, even as those who were done to death during the time when the Inquisition reigned, and, on the way to execution, were, it might be said, compelled to bear the very cross upon which they were to be impaled.

There is no record since time began of such a long, drawn-out agony as that which the devoted people of Galveston endured during the period intervening between the advent of the hurricane in the Gulf of Mexico and the final imposition of the death penalty.

Fathers saw their wives and babes crushed by the wreckage flung aloft and around by the fury of the gale, or drowned in the swift running current; wives saw their husbands and children torn from them and swept from their sight forever; children saw their parents disappear in the murky, turbid waters of the flood.

Men saw the dead faces of their loved ones they would have deemed it a joy to save as they were borne along upon the bosom of the waters. Men invited destruction in their efforts at rescue, only to realize how weak and utterly futile was their strength in comparison to the irresistible power of the enraged elements. Men died desponding because they could not save those they had cherished and heretofore protected, and went down in despair and gloom.

At Johnstown the released waters tore their way through the beautiful valley of the Conemagh with the rush and speed of a giant avalanche and enfolded their victims in their merciless embrace; the inhabitants were, in the twinkling of an eye, borne from the sunshine of life to the gloom of the valley of the shadow; they may have felt a momentary terror before they succumbed, but it was all over in an instant.

At Galveston, the condemned simply waited for the inevitable; they clung to the brief remaining supports and died a thousand deaths before death claimed them; they stood upon the brink of eternity and cried in vain for the succor they well knew would not come; they prayed for mercy, but there was none.

When the waters of the gulf leaped upon the island where the beautiful city sat in all her glory the people fled to the high places and saw the flood creep higher and higher until it overcame them. Although it was not until the darkness of the night had long since settled upon them they had known in the afternoon that Galveston was doomed. The hurricane would not permit them to escape, but sundered all communication with the mainland and then laughed at their puny efforts at preservation.

The death roster in and around Galveston was fully 8,000; at Johnstown the known number of victims was a score less than 2,300. Many died at Johnstown of whom nothing was ever heard, and there were possibly 2,500 persons engulfed in the stream which all but destroyed the town, but at the same time the probabilities are that 10,000 people died at Galveston and in the immediate vicinity. Bodies were washed up and thrown upon the shore by hundreds for days after the disaster; how many were burned upon the many funeral pyres no accurate record was kept.

In one respect the two calamities were alike—the destruction of millions of dollars' worth of property, but the losses were not so great at Johnstown during those fearful two minutes as those occasioned by the beating of the winds and waves which for hours had Galveston at their mercy.

Johnstown was a city of 30,000, teeming with the industry of a manufacturing town. With not even a warning shout to apprise the inhabitants the dam of a lake high above the town broke and the flood sweeping down the Conemagh Valley engulfed the city and its inhabitants before they even knew of the danger. The whole place was a mass of debris and dead when the deluge subsided.

Galveston was a city of nearly 40,000 people, and had within its gates hundreds of strangers, and the fact that telegrams of inquiry from all parts of the United States poured into the mayor's office in a perfect stream for days after the flood indicated that scores were killed of whom the searchers knew nothing.

But Johnstown was not alone in its misery. In the southwest a tragedy was enacted a few years later which claimed hundreds of victims. A tornado, immeasurable in its force and fury, blotted out a section of St. Louis late in the afternoon of May 22, 1896. Nearly a thousand lives and tens of millions in property were sacrificed. Until the disaster at Galveston the St. Louis catastrophe was the second greatest disaster of its kind in the history of the nation.

The tornado destroyed dozens of the finest buildings in the city. It leveled massive structures to the ground. It tossed railroad locomotives about and crushed the eastern span of the Eads bridge, one of the strongest structures in the world. It made St. Louis a city of mourning for weeks and impoverished numberless families.

Yet Galveston surpassed these cities in the frightful nature of its calamity. Hundreds of insane people are being cared for, their reason having been overthrown by their great sufferings. This was one of the saddest features of the shocking visitation. These poor creatures, first bereft of home, family and property, are now living legacies of the most stupendous catastrophe this country has ever known.

# CHAPTER EIGHT:
## DEATH OF THE STORM

When the hurricane was through with Galveston and central and southern Texas it sped north through Missouri, Kansas and Nebraska—its path being 300 miles in width—and then turning toward the east, or slightly northeast, crossed northern Iowa, southern Minnesota, southern Wisconsin, southern Michigan, northern Illinois, northern Indiana, northern Ohio, northern New York and southern Canada, finally disappearing in the Atlantic ocean, creating wreck and havoc wherever it went. It caused great losses of life and property in Newfoundland and destroyed many vessels off the eastern coast of the United States.

The following dispatches show how widespread was its fury:

Buffalo, September 12—Immense damage was done here and at other lake ports by the Texas storm which traveled with great violence down Lake Erie last night. Reports from Crystal Beach, a summer resort on the Canadian side of Lake Erie, say that every dock has been destroyed, and all the boats of the Buffalo Canoe Club, together with several large seagoing yachts anchored there, were completely wrecked.

In this city the wind attained a velocity of seventy-two miles an hour, and seemed to regain some of the power which it exhibited in wrecking Southern cities. Reports of property loss and fatalities have come in.

St. Joseph, Mich., September 12.—The steamer *Lawrence* arrived here at 1 o'clock this afternoon from Milwaukee. She left that place at 8 o'clock yesterday morning, and the captain reports a fearful voyage. The captain's wife was here from Milwaukee and was on the dock waiting to meet her husband when the boat touched the dock. The meeting between the two was affecting. All this morning anxious watchers waited on the bluffs at the mouth of the river for a glimpse of the missing boat. Many people had friends among the passengers and crew, and as the morning hours wore on their anxiety became intense.

Cleveland, September 12—As a result of the furious gale which swept over the lake region last night telegraph and telephone lines were prostrated in all directions from this city today. During the height of the storm the wind reached a velocity of sixty miles an hour.

Today the storm is subsiding, the wind having dropped to twenty-six miles an hour. Up to noon today the big passenger steamers City of Erie and the Northwest, which left Buffalo last evening for this port, have not been heard from. They were due here at 6 o'clock this morning. The passenger steamer *State of Ohio*, due here about the same hour from Toledo, had not arrived at noon.

The wind blew sixty miles an hour across Lake Erie, but the warnings had been so thorough that few vessels were caught unprepared. The steamer *Cornell* of the Pittsburgh Steamship Company's fleet lost her smokestack off Fairport. Her barge anchored, but both came into port later. The Buffalo passenger boat has not yet arrived, having been in shelter at Long Point during the worst of the blow.

Detour, Mich., September 12—In the storm yesterday the schooner *Narragansett*, stranded near Cockburn island, was washed off the rocks, and shipping suffered greatly.

Sault Ste. Marie, Mich., September 12—The wind reached a velocity of thirty miles an hour from the northwest at midnight, the storm being accompanied by considerable rain. Many vessels were lost.

Amhertsburg, Ont., September 12—The tail end of the Galveston storm struck this section with great force about 11 o'clock last night and continued until early this morning. The loss to shipping is heavy.

Kingston, Ont., September 12—The Canadian steamer Albacore was driven ashore at 7 o'clock this morning, east of the life-saving station. The crew was saved. The wind is blowing a gale from the west, and shipping on Lake Ontario suffered seriously, many sailors being drowned.

South Haven, Mich., September 12—The storm did much damage to the docks here last night. Several vessels are reported lost.

Port Huron, Mich., September 12—The wind blew a gale until 11:30 last night. Three small schooners which left here bound for Sand Beach were wrecked.

The gale passed over Chicago September 11 and attained a velocity early in the afternoon of seventy-two miles an hour, destroyed many lives in the city and neighborhood, did great damage to property on the land and wrecked several vessels on the lakes.

The wind was fitful and blew in gusts. Its advance was met with frequent lulls and interruptions. An embankment of dark, ominous clouds rose steadily in the west. At first it was broken by an occasional rift which revealed the blue sky. But as the cloud bank rose it darkened and rolled over the plains toward Chicago with increasing speed. At 3 o'clock all the blue patches of sky had disappeared, the heavens had assumed a forbidding look and the lake rolled. The increased violence of the storm carried everything before it. No one disputed its rights to the streets, and it blew down wires innumerable, badly crippling the telegraph and telephone service. The Western Union's fifty-two New York lines were all down.

From Chicago the storm continued its progress across Lake Huron, but was steadily diminishing in intensity. The storm's velocity diminished after leaving Texas, but increased with wonderful rapidity after reaching the lake region. The wind reached the greatest velocity at Chicago it had attained since leaving Galveston.

## TAIL-END OF THE WEST INDIAN HURRICANE

On September 18 the remains of the tropical cyclone were present off the coast of Canada. The storm set in Monday morning, September 17, and was raging with increased severity the next day. Heavy cyclone rollers were sweeping in upon the coast and a strong northeast gale was blowing. All of the telegraph wires were blown down.

Southeast rollers began to wash the shores Sunday, but the barometer continued high. During the night, however, it commenced falling, showing 29.91 inches. At 7 o'clock in the morning the wind was rising. By noon it had reached gale force from the northeast and rain was falling. The barometer then recorded 29.71 inches. The storm continued to increase during the afternoon, and at 4 o'clock the wind was blowing more than sixty miles an hour, carrying away the telegraph wires. Heavy seas were rushing in upon the coast. The barometer continued to fall, recording only 29.32 inches, but the wind veered to the north, although it was still blowing with some violence.

A correspondent at St. John's, N. F., telegraphed as follows the same day:

"From all quarters of Newfoundland come reports of devastation wrought by the gale of last Wednesday and Thursday, the outcome of the Texas hurricane sweeping north. So far sixty-five schooners are reported ashore or foundered, over 100 more being damaged.

"Thirty-one lives have been reported lost so far. This small list of fatalities is due to the fact that most of the vessels have been in harbor latterly, as the fishing was poor. Several vessels are still missing, however, and it is feared the death roll may be enlarged. Labrador has suffered severely, fishing craft having been driven on the rocks by the shore, which fact, added to the bad fishing season, makes the condition of the coast folk pitiable in the extreme.

"In Belle Isle Strait the whole of the fishing premises has been destroyed. On the French shore over fifty vessels have been battered, ten being a total loss. The steamer *Francis* has been wrecked at St. George's. The bark, *Mary Hendry*, anthracite laden from New York, is dismasted and derelict off St. Mary's.

"On the Grand Banks the gale raged with the greatest fury. Twenty-four men from the Provincetown fishing schooner

*Willie McKay* were landed at Bay Bulls Monday morning, their ship having foundered from buffeting in the storm Wednesday, Thursday and Friday. The men drifted about on the sinking hulk, without food, water or shelter, and only by incessant pumping kept her afloat.

"The seas were constantly sweeping the decks and the entire crew were lashed about the rigging or bulwarks. They were ultimately rescued by the schooner Talisman of Gloucester, which landed them. One man perished from the exposure. The crew say the storm must have done awful damage on the banks. It seems certain many vessels could not escape the disaster when theirs, the finest of the fleet, succumbed."

## GREAT VALUE OF THE U. S. WEATHER BUREAU

The great value of the United States Weather Bureau and the remarkable correctness of its observations, all things considered, was demonstrated by the events preceding and succeeding the West Indian hurricane. It gave warning of the hurricane days before it manifested itself on the Texas coast. It anticipated its course from the vicinity of San Domingo until it reached Cuban waters, where it made a deflection no human skill could have foreseen.

The bureau was not caught napping, however. It sent out its hurricane signals both for the Atlantic coast and the gulf coast, and when the storm turned from the north of Cuba westward the bureau turned its attention to Texas, and on the morning of September 7, nearly thirty-six hours before the disaster, warned the people of Galveston of its coming, and during that day extended its signals all along the Texas coast, thus preventing vessels from leaving.

Of course the observers could not know what terrible energy it would gain crossing the Gulf of Mexico. Perhaps still greater accuracy in forecasting was displayed by the bureau in the warnings given out to mariners on the Great Lakes on

Tuesday morning, September 11. Though nearly all lines of communication in Texas were cut off, the bureau kept track of the storm as it swept through Oklahoma into Kansas, and gave timely warning that it would turn northeast, moving across northern Illinois and southern Wisconsin, and thence across Lake Michigan and the northern end of the southern peninsula of Michigan to Canada.

It further predicted the furious winds which prevailed the next day, their maximum velocity, the change caused by the northwest current from Lake Superior, and the fall of temperature yesterday to the nicety of a degree. Every vessel captain on the lakes had ample warning given him.

In times gone by it was the habit to jeer at Old Probabilities, and whenever a prediction failed of verification to condemn the Weather Bureau as unreliable and not worth the expense of its maintenance.

During the last few years, however, its operators have gained in skill and its record now is of a character of which its officials have every reason to be proud and which amply justifies whatever expense it may entail by its great saving of life and property.

# Chapter Nine:
## The Dead

The actual number of lives lost at Galveston will never be known, but over 4,500 bodies of victims of the frightful catastrophe were identified; and these, together with the hundreds of identified and unidentified corpses which were buried at sea, in the sands along the beach, in the yards and grounds of private residences; those bodies which must have been carried out into the gulf when the waters receded from the island Sunday morning; those cremated; the hundreds found on the gulf coast, on the shores of Galveston Bay, and those taken from the water; and, finally, those discovered in all sorts of places inland (the bodies found outside Galveston Island being buried where picked up)—all these served to swell the Galveston death list to possibly 7,000, which was the figure named by Mayor Jones the fifth day after the flood. He took every opportunity for obtaining reliable information on this point.

Until the cremation of bodies began the foremen of the various burial gangs made lists of the bodies disposed of by their men, but when it became necessary to burn the corpses, the danger of pestilence being so great that they had to be put out of the way at the earliest possible moment, the compilation of these lists was abandoned and a mere general estimate made. The work of clearing the business and residence streets proceeded but slowly, the men in the gangs assigned to this being enervated by the intense heat of the sun, sickened by the effluvia from the decomposing bodies, of dead human beings and animals, and depressed by the gloomy character of their surroundings. Most of the men thus employed were citizens of Galveston, many of whom were in comfortable circumstances before the storm swept away their belongings. In the majority of cases these workers had lost not only their earthly possessions, but members of their immediate families as well, and were heartsore and crushed in spirit. In the main, they engaged in this work because they wanted to help the city out in its desperate straits, and for the further reason that if not busied in mind and body they might possibly go mad.

The first of the lists of the identified dead was made out and made public on Tuesday following the disaster, and the lists compiled the succeeding days were given out as soon as completed.

The lists printed below comprise the first and only complete roster of the dead which has appeared anywhere to date:

## FIRST LIST OF IDENTIFIED VICTIMS - TUESDAY, SEPTEMBER 11

Aguilo, Joseph B., chairman of the Democratic county executive committee

Allen, Charlotta M., Seventeeth Street and Avenue A

Allen, E. and wife

Amundsen, mother of Deputy Chief of Police Amundsen

Burrows, Mrs. M.

Bross, Mrs. Kate, Twenty-second Street, near beach

Burnett, Mrs. George, and child, Twenty-fourth Street and Avenue P

Barbon, Mrs.

Baxter, Mrs., and child, lost in Magia store

Bell, Mrs. Dudley, wife of *Galveston News* compositor, and child

Beveridge, Mrs., and two children

Betts, Walter, cotton broker, and wife

Bird, the family of police officer Bird

Broecker, John F., wife and two children

Bowe, Mrs. John, and three children. Police officer John Bowe attempted to save his family on a raft but they were swept away and drowned

Burnett, Gary, and wife and mother

Caddom, Alex, and four children

Clark, Mrs. C. T., and infant

Compton, A. J., and wife

Correll, Mrs. J. R., and family

Collins, daughter of Mrs. Collins

Cline, Mrs., wife of Dr. L. M. Cline, local forecast official of the United States Weather Bureau

Coryell, Patti Rosa

Coates, Mrs. William, wife of William A. Coates, of the *Galveston News*

Cramer, Miss Bessie

Daly, W. L., grain exporter and steamship agent for Charles F. Ortwein & Co.

Day, Alfred

Davies John R., and wife

Delaney, Mrs. Jack, wife of United States bridge officer of the port, with two children

Delyea, Paul, ex-sergeant, police

Davenport, W., wife and three children

Davis, Lessie

Dorian, Mrs., and five children; had taken refuge with nine other persons on the roof of a house which was destroyed and all lost. The Dorian house withstood the elements

Dorin, Mrs.

Ellison, Mrs. and two children of Captain Ellison, one of them drowned in its mother's arms

Engelke, John, wife and child

Evans, Mrs. Kate, and two daughters

Eichter, Edward, Thirteenth Street and Avenue N

Ewing, Miss

Fordtran, Mrs. Claude J., 1919 Tremont Street

Fix, C. H.

Fisher, W. F., wife and two children

Flash, William, and daughter. Twenty-fifth Street and Avenue P; Mrs. Flash was saved

Foster, Harry, wife and three children

Frederickson, Violet

Frederickson, Mrs., and baby

Gernand, Mrs. John F., and two children

Guest, Mamie

Gordon, Mrs. Abe, and five children

Gernaud, John H., wife and two children

Hamburg, Mrs. Peter, and four children

Hansinger, H. A., daughter and mother-in-law

Harris, Mrs. (colored)

Harris, Mrs. J. H.

Harris, Mrs. Rebecca

Hobeck, —, and boy

Howe, —, police officer and family

Howth, Mrs. Clarence

Hughes, Joe

Hawkins, Mattie Lea

Hesse, Mrs. Irene, Broadway and Sixth Street

Hunn, F., streetcar motorman

Hunter, Albert, and wife

Jones, Mr., and wife

Johnson, Richard, struck by flying timber and instantly killed

Jones, Mrs. W. R., and child

Keller, Charles A., prominent cotton man

Kelly, Barney

Kelly, Willie

Labbat, Joe

Lackey, Mrs., and two children of Leon J. Lackey, telegraphy operator

Lafayette, Mrs., and two children

Lassocco, Mrs., Twenty-first Street and Avenue P. Twenty-five persons are reported to have been lost in the store building of Mrs. Lassocco

Lisbony, W. H.

Longnecker, Mrs. A.

Lord, Richard, traffic manager for George H. McFaden Brothers, cotton exporters

Lynch, John

Magia, Mr., two daughters and son; grocery at Eleventh Street and Avenue A

Masterson, B. T., and family

McCauley, Miss Annie

McKenna, five members of the P. J. and J. P. McKenna families

Monroe, Mrs., and three children (colored)

Mordon, Miss

Morton, Mrs., and two babies

Motter, Mrs., and two daughters

Munn, Mrs. J. W., Sr.

Nolly, Mrs. Sam, and four children, in the Nolly house on Fortieth Street and Avenue T. Mr. Nolly and another man were saved after a bitter struggle.

O'Dell, Miss Nellie, and brother, daughter and son of James O'Dell

O'Harrow, William

O'Keefe, Mrs. Michael, and brother

Palmer, J. B., and baby

Parker; an entire family living at Thirty-ninth and Avenue Q, consisting of Angeline Parker and grandchild, Tommy Lesker

Parker, Mrs. Frank, Thirty-first Street and Avenue Q

Parker, Mrs. Mollie

Peek, Captain R. H., city engineer, wife and five children

Plitt, Harmon

Porette; thirteen persons killed in a house at Eighth Street and Broadway. Dominick Porette is the only one of the party who lives to tell the tale

Porfree, Henry, a tailor

Ptolmey, Paul

Quester, Bessie

Quester, Mrs. W., little son and daughter

Regan, Mike, wife and mother-in-law, lost at Porette house

Rhymes, Thomas, wife and two children

Rice—, proofreader on the *Galveston News*, and child

Richards, —, police officer

Ripley, Henry, son of H. S. Ripley

Roll, J. F., wife and four children

Rose, Mrs., wife of Commissary Sergeant Franklin Rose of the United States Army

Roudaux, Murray

Rowan, —, police officer, and family

Rust, Charles, knocked from a dray while attempting to carry his family to safety; instantly killed

Sailor, Spanish, of the steamship *Telesfora*, which drifted against Whitehall at pier 15

Schaler, Mrs. Charles, and four children

Schofield, Miss Ida, lost in Magia store

Schroeder, Mrs. George M., and four children

Schuler, Mr., wife and five children

Schultz, Mr., and wife

Schwartzback, Joseph

Sharp, Miss Annie

Sharp, Mr., and wife

Shaw, nephew of M. M. Shaw

Sherwood, Charles

Smith, Mrs. Mamie

Somers, Miss Helen

Spencer, Stanley G., local representative of Demster & Co.'s steamship lines and North German Lloyd steamship lines

Stickloch, Miss Mabel, Mechanic Street

Summers, Sarah

Swain, Mr., and wife

Sweil, George, mother and sister

Sylvester, Mrs.

Taylor, Mrs. (colored)

Thompson, mother-in-law and sister-in-law of William Thompson of the fire department

Toothacker, wife and daughter of Jesse W. Toothacker, contractor and builder

Tovrea, —, police officer

Treadwell, Mrs. J. B., and infant

Trebosius, Mrs. George, wife of George Trebosius of the *Galveston News*, and two sisters of Mr. Trebosius, at the home at Fortieth Street and Avenue R.

Unidentified —Two sisters-in-law and a niece

Unidentified —White girl, 12 years old, found in the yard of J. Paul Jones

Unidentified —Four white and seven colored persons found in the first story of W. J. Reitmeyer's residence. Reitmeyer family, in the second story, escaped

Unidentified—A lady and her daughter from St. Louis

Unidentified—Thirteen inmates and three matrons at the Home for the Homeless

Wakelee, Mrs. Davis

Wallace, —, and four children

Walter, Mrs. Charles, and three children

Watkins, S. W., Thirty-first Street and Avenue Q. Mr. Watkins was drowned and it was reported that about twenty other persons in the same house met a similar fate.

Webster, Edward, and two sisters

Webster, Thomas Sr., secretary of the grain inspector of the port, with family of four

Wenman, Mrs. J. W., and two children

Wensmor, several members of the family residing in the east end; one of the family, an old man, was saved

Wilson, Mrs. Mary Ann, and baby

Wolfe, Charles, police officer, and family

Wollam, C., drowned after saving several women and while trying to save others

Wood, Mrs., mother of United States Deputy Marshal Wood

Woodward, Miss Hattie

Wootam, —

Wren, James, wife and six children; drowned at the Porette house

—, Francois, a well-known waiter, and twenty-two persons who had taken refuge in his house.

# HITCHCOCK

At Hitchcock, thirty lives were lost. Two Italian families of thirteen people met death by drowning. The following were killed by falling timbers:

Dominico, a child

Johnson, Hiram, and wife

Montelona, Mary

O'Connor, T. W.

Palmero, —, wife and seven children

Pietze, Mrs., and three children

Robinson, William

Young, Mrs., wife of C. W. Young, two sons and two daughters. In addition, members of two families from Alvin who were visiting the Young family.

Seven unidentified persons found on the prairie, supposedly from Galveston.

# SEABROOK

Five Houston people perished at Seabrook in the hurricane. They were:

Lucy, Mrs. C. H., and two small children

McIlhenny, Haven, and the 5-year old son of David Rice

# ALVIN

Appelle, Miss

Collins, Mrs. J. W., killed by falling timbers

Collins, Mrs.

Glaspy, John S.

Hawley, W. P.

Johnson, J. M.
Johnston, Mr. J. S.
Lewis, Mrs. O. S.
Mebam, W. C., and wife
Richardson, B.

## ROSENBERG

Herman, B. S.
Ontrall, Mrs. I. J.
Watson, Rev. A.

## OYSTER CREEK

Arnold, A.
Carlton, H.
Jones, Tom
Marshall, Lucy
Smith, Connie
Smith, S.
Stephens, Tom (colored)

## ARCOLA

Wofford, Mrs. A., aged white woman

## MORGAN'S POINT

Vincent, Mrs., and two children

## GALVESTON DEATH LIST - WEDNESDAY, SEPTEMBER 12

Almers, Mrs. P.

Anderson, M., and family

Andrew, Mr., and three children

Annudsen, Louis

Armstrong, Mrs. Dora, and four children

Bell, Guy

Bell, Mrs. A. C.

Berger, W. L., wife and child

Bodden, Mrs., and Mrs. J. F.

Brockelman, three children of J. T. Brockelman

Bures, —, wife and sister

Burge, William, wife and child

Burnett, Mrs. Gary, and two children

Burnett, Mrs. Mary

Carigan, Joseph

Childs, K. T.

Cleveland, George, and family

Connett, Mr. and Mrs. William, and two children

Cornett, Charles, and wife

Craig, George

Dailey, K.

Darby, Charles

Delcie, Mrs. Henry R., and child

Dilz, M., and two sons

Dorian, George, and wife

Dowell, Mrs. Sam

Ducos, —, two children

Edmunsen, Mrs.

Edwards, Miss Eliza

Eggerett, William, and son Charles

Eideman, H. E.

Ellis, Mrs., and family

English, John, wife and child

Everhart, J. H., wife and daughter

Fabey, Sumptey

Falke, Joseph, and three children

Farmer, Mrs. I. P.

Faucett, Mrs. Belle

Faucett, Robert

Fegue, Lillie; with Esther and Laura May, children of Mrs. Lillie Fegue

Floehr, Mrs.

Fox, Thomas

Fritz, —

Gaulters, J.

Grathcar, Mrs. John, and child

Harrah, Martin

Harris, Mrs. John, and three children

Hayman, Mrs. John A., and five children

Heck, Mrs., and son

Herman, Martin, and two children

Hinke, August, Richard and Johanna

Holbeck, Mrs. L. L.

Homburg, Peter

Hock, Mrs., and son

Johnson, A. S., wife and three children

Jones, Robert

Junemann, Charles, wife and daughter

Junter, William, and six children

Kampe, Charles

Kauffman, H., wife and children

Kelso, Munson, Jr.

Kelso, Roy, baby boy of J. C. Kelso

Kirby, Mrs. J. H., and three children

Klein, Mrs. E. V.

Kleincke, H., and wife

Koepler, Mrs. Fred, and family

Kraus, Mr. and Mrs. J. J.

Krauss, Joseph J., and wife and daughters

Krausse, I., wife and two daughters

Lorance, Mrs. T. A.

Louis, Poland, carrier for the *News*

Lucas, Mrs. H., and two children and white nurse

Malrs, O. M., wife and child

Malter, J.

Maree, —, employed by James Fascher

Martin, Mrs., wife of Policeman Martin

Masterson, B. T., and family

McManus, Mrs. William

Miles, Colson

Miller, William, and family (business partner of Childs)

Miner, Lucia

Mitchell, Mrs. W. H., and child

Mongon, John

Morrow, Dotlo, wife and seven children

Muttie, A.

Neill, —, and family

Nolan, Mrs.

Odelle, O.

Olsen, Mrs. Matilda, and two children

Olson, Mrs. Mattie, and two children

Opperman, Miss May, and Marguerite and Gussie of Palestine

Palmer, J. B., and baby

Park, Miss Alice

Park, Miss Lucy

Park, Mrs. M. L.

Parker, Mrs. D., and two children

Pasker, Miss Ethel

Pauls, Nellie and Cecilia

Peters, Mrs.

Pix, C. H.

Plitt, Harmon

Ratissa, Mrs. W. L., and three children

Rattizan, Mrs. Leon, and four children

Raymond, Mr. and Mrs., and two children

Reagan, J. N.

Rhaes, T. F., wife and two children

Roan, Mrs., and three children

Roberts, —, watchman for GH&NRR

Rudger, C., wife and child

Runter, A., mother and father

Sayers, Dr. John B.

Sayers, Tom

Schwoebel, George, wife and daughter Lulu

Seixas, E., and two daughters Anna and Lucile

Severet, J., and wife

Sherwood, Thomas, wife and three children

Shilke, Mrs., son and infant

Siegler, Mrs. Fred

Smith, Jacob

Sommers, F., wife and three daughters, and his son, Joseph, wife and child

Stetgel, Mr., and family

Stockfleth, Peter, wife and six children

Stowinsky, Mr., and wife

Swanson, Mrs.

Tarpey, Joseph

Thomsen, Mrs. W. D., and two children

Tillebach, Charles, wife, mother-in-law and two children

Toothacker, Miss Jennie

Torrea, Sam, policeman, wife and four children

Tow, T. C., wife and five children

Villeneve, Mrs., and child, from Hitchcock

Vogel, Mrs. Henry, and three children

Vondenbaden, Mrs., and two children

Walden, Mr.

Warmarvosky, Adolph, mother and sister reported missing

Warneke, Mrs. A. W., and five children

Warren, James, wife and six children

Webber, Mr., family missing

Webster, Edward, Sr.

Webster, George

Webster, Joe

Webster, Mrs. Julia

Webster, Mrs. Sarah

Wedges, Judge, justice of the peace, and wife

Wilsh, Joseph, wife and two children

Wincott, Mrs.

Windman, Mrs.

Yeats, —, child

Youngblood, L. J., wife and child

Zipp, Mrs., and daughter

## GALVESTON DEATH LIST - THURSDAY, SEPTEMBER 13

Adams, Mrs.

Adams, Toby

Agin, George

Albertson, A.

Albertson, Mrs.

Allen, Mrs. Alex

Alpin, George

Alpin, Mrs.

Anderson, Mrs. S.

Ashe, George Jr.

Ashe, George Sr.

Bell, Alexander

Bell, Henry

Berger, Mrs. Lucy

Bland, Mrs.

Bodecker, Charles

Boss, Charles

Brooks, J. R.

Cain, Mrs.

Cain, Rev. Thomas W.

Calhoun, Mrs. Thomas

Carter, Corinne

Casey, Mrs. Annie

Chaffee, Mrs.

Clark, C. Y.

Cuney, R. C.

Dammel, Mrs.

Dammell, W. D.

Davis, Gabe

Davis, Henry T.

Day, Alfred

Day, Willie

Dempsey, Mr. and Mrs.

Direkes, Henry

Dorrfe, Mr. and Mrs.

Dowell, Mrs. Samuel

Dunning, Mrs. H. C.

Dunning, Richard

Dunton, Mrs. Annie

Evans, Mrs.

Falkenhagen, Mr. & Mrs.

Feither, Mrs. F.

Ferget, Julius

Frank, Mrs. Aug.

Freitag, Harry

Gentry, Charlotte

Gibson, Professor

Goth, A. E.

Goth, Mrs.

Gottleib, Mrs.

Green, Mrs. Lucy

Harris, Effie

Higgins, Mrs.

Hoffman family

Holland, Mrs. James

Homes, Florence

Hughes, Robert

Jasters, Perry

Jefferbrook, August & Mrs.
Johnson, Mrs.
Johnson, Mrs. W. J.
Jones, W. R.
King, Mrs.
Knowles, Mrs. W. T.
Kuhn, Mrs. H. Clem
Kuhnel, Mrs.
Lawson, Charles
Lawson, Mrs.
Lemmon, Virgie
Levin, P.
Lewis, Agnes
Lewis, Mrs. Maria
Lindquist, Mrs. O.
Lloyd, Buck
Lloyd, Mrs.
Lockman, Mr. and Mrs. H.
Ludwig, Albert
Ludwig, Alfred
Manley, Joe
Martin, Herman
McDade, Ed
McGuire, John
McPherson, Robert
Menzel, John
Menzel, Mrs.
Moore, Mrs. Nathan
Morse, Arthur P.
Morse, Mrs.
Nelson, Mrs.

Patrick, Cora
Patrick, Ida
Pierson, Alice
Pierson, Frank
Pierson, Mrs. Mary
Piner, Mrs. Ella
Piney, Mrs.
Powers, Mrs.
Randolph, Edith
Ravey Family
Reuter, Henry
Reuter, Otto
Roehle, John
Roehle, Mrs.
Roehm, Mrs.
Roehm, William
Roukes, Mrs. Charles
Rowe, Ada
Rowe, Hattie
Rowe, George
Ruehrmond, Mrs.
Ruehrmond, Professor
Schultze, Charles
Schulz, Charles C.
Schulz, Fred
Schulz, Mrs.
Schutte, E. R.
Schutte, Mrs.
Schwotsel, George
Scott, Annie
Scull, Mrs. Mary

Shaw, Frank
Shilhe, Mrs.
Seidenstricker, Henry
Seixas, Miss Anna
Seixas, Miss Lucille
Seixas, Cecilia
Thurman, Mrs.
Tix, Herman
Torr, T. C.
Torr, Mrs. T. C.
Tresvant, Jordan
Trostman, Mrs.
Turner, Mr.
Turner, Mrs.
Turner, Mrs.
Uleridge, Adelaide
Van Buren, Herman
Van Liew, Mollie
Waring, Mrs. of Chicago
Warren, Celia
Washington, Mrs.
Weidemann, Fritz
Weiss, Professor
Wilke, Mr. , city electrician
Wilke, Mrs.
Williams, Mrs.
Williams, Mrs. E. C.
Williams, Sam
Woodrow, Matilda
Yeager, William
Zweigel, Mrs.

## GALVESTON DEATH LIST -
## FRIDAY, SEPTEMBER 14

Aberhart, T., and wife

Ackermann, Herman, wife and daughter

Adameit, Mrs. G., and seven children

Adams, M. and Mrs. Tobey (colored)

Akers, C. B., and wife and three children

Albertson, A., wife and two children

Allardico, R. L., wife and three children

Allen, Cornelia

Allen, Daisy

Allen, Elve

Allen, Zerena

Alphonse, John, wife and family

Anderson, Andrew, wife and children

Anderson, Oscar, wife and children

Andrew, Mrs. A., and family

Armitage, Miss Vivian

Armour, Mrs., and five children

Artisan, John, wife and nine children

Bankers, Mrs. Charles

Barnard, Mrs.

Bass, John, wife and four children (colored)

Baulch, Will, wife and two children

Beach, Miss Nina of Victoria

Beal, Mrs. Dudley, and child

Becker, John, wife and daughters, Mae and Vida

Bedford, Cushman (colored)

Bell, Alexander, wife, two sons and daughter

Bell, Henry

Bellew, Mr. and Mrs. J., and daughter

Bentley, and family

Bercer, Mrs. Lucy

Bittell, Mrs.

Bland, Mrs., and seven children (colored)

Bockelman, C. J.

Boedecker, Charles

Boedenker, H., father, brother and sister-in-law

Bohn, Dixie

Boss, Peter, and wife

Bowen, —

Bradley, Miss Ethel

Bradley, Mannie

Briscoll, A. M.

Brooks, J. T.

Brown, Joe, and family

Brown, Winnie M.

Buckley, Blanche

Buckley, Selma

Buckley, mother and daughter

Buckley, Mrs. and daughter

Burgee, William, wife and child

Burrell, Mrs. (colored)

Catholic Orphan Home, Ninety persons

Cato, William (colored)

Childs, William, and wife

Christian, John

Caddoe, Alex, and five children

Campbell, Miss Edna

Campbell, Will

Carnett, —, and wife, of Orange, Texas

Carson, Frank C.

Carter, Adeline

Carven, Mrs. and daughter

Clark, Tom

Clausen, Charles, and family of four

Clinton, Mrs. Mary, and children: George A., Horace, Lee W., Joseph B., Willie B. and Freddie

Colsen, —

Connor, Captain D. E.

Conner, Edward J.

Corbett, James J., and four children

Cowen, —

Crawford, Rayburn

Credo, Will

Cromwell, Mrs., and three children

Crook, Ashby

Crouse, J. J., wife and children

Crowley, Miss Nellie and brother

Cuneo, Mrs. Joseph of New Orleans

Curry, Mrs. E. H., and child

Curry, Mrs. Martha J., and Miss Louisa

Dammill, W. D., and wife (colored)

Darfee, Mr. and Mrs., and two daughters

Darrell, —, and five children

Davis, Miss Emma

Davis, Mrs. Mary and children: Carrie, Alice, Lizzie and Eddie

Davis, Mrs. T. F.

Deltz, M., and two sons

Demesie, Mrs., and two sons

Dinter, Mrs., and daughter

Dirke, Henry, and family

Doll, Frank and family

Doll, George, and wife

Donahue, Ellen, Utica NY

Donahue, Mary, Utica NY

Donnelly, Nick

Doty, John

Dowles, Samuel, wife and one child

Doyle, Jim

Drewa, H. A.

Ducos, Madeline and Octavia

Dunham, George R., and wife

Dunham, George R., Jr., and two children

Dunnin, Mrs. Howard C., and three children

Dunningham, Richard E.

Eads, Sumpter

Eckett, Charles

Eckett, Fred

Edward, James, and family

Eismann, —, wife and child

Eismann, Howard

Ellas, James, and two children

Emmanuel, Joe

English, John, wife and child

Eppendorf, Mr. and Mrs.

Faby, C. S., wife and two children

Fanchon family

Farrer, Miss Nannie of Sullivan's Island

Fedo, Joe

Feither, Mrs. Fritz

Ferwedert, Peter

Fickett, Mrs., and four children

Fiegel, John

Figge, Mrs., and four children

Forbush, John and Freddie

Forget, Julius

Fornkesell, T. C.

Foster, Mr. and Mrs. Harry, and three children

Foster, Mrs. August

Foster, Mrs. S. F.

Fox, Thomas, wife and four children

Frank, Anton, wife and two daughters

Frankovich, Charles and John

Franks, Mr., and daughter

Frau, Mrs. August, and daughter

Fredericks, Corinne

Freise, Mr. and Mrs. Charles M.

Fretwell, J. B., Mrs. and boy

Furst family

Gabel, Mr. and Mrs. (colored)

Gaines, Captain Edward, and wife

Gaires, Mrs. Lillie, and two daughters

Gait, A. E., and wife

Gallishaw, and five children

Ganth, —

Garnett, Robert F.

Garrigan, Joe

Garbaldi, August

Gecan, Matt

Genning, Tim, and wife

Gentry, Charlotte (colored)

George, H. K., and family

Gibson, Mary C.

Gibson, Professor and family

Gonzales, Andrew, wife and daughter Pauline

Goodwin, two girls

Gordon, Oscar

Graham, Mrs. H., and baby

Gregg, —, and four children

Grey, Randolph, four children and sister-in-law

Grief, John, wife and three children

Grosscup, Mrs.

Gruetsmicher, Louis, wife and two daughters

Guilett, Colonel, of Victoria

Haines, sister of Mrs. Captain Haines

Hall, Charles (colored)

Hannamann, Mrs. August

Harris, L.

Harris, Miss Rebecca

Harris, Mrs. W. D. and son

Harrison, Tom, and wife

Hasselmeyer family

Hassler, Charles, and wife

Haughton, Mrs. W. W.

Haughton, Willie O.

Heidmann, William, Jr.

Helfenstein, Sophie and Willie

Hennessy, Mrs. M. P., and two nieces

Herman, Martin, and two children

Hersey, Mrs. John

Hildebrand, Fred

Holmes, Mrs. (colored)

Hoskins, T. D., wife and three children (colored)

Hubbell, Misses Maggie and Emma

Huebener, Mrs. A., and boy

Hull, Charles (colored)

Hull, William (colored)

Humberg, Mrs. Peter, and four children

Hunter, George

Jaecke, Mrs. Curt, and three children

Jackman, Ada, and two children

Jaeger, John, and wife

Jaeger, Walter H.

Jaeger, William H.

Jennings, James A., and wife

Jennssen, Mrs. and Mr., and five children

Johnson, Asa, wife and son

Johnson, child

Johnson, Julian

Johnson, Mrs. C. S.

Johnson, Odin, wife and child

Johnson, V. S.

Johnston, J. B., wife and two children

Johnston, Mrs.

Johnston, Mrs. Alice

Johnston, Mrs. E. E., and four children

Johnston, Mrs. W. J.

Jones, J. H., and wife

Junka, Mrs. Paulina

Junker, Mrs. Colina

Junkf, Martha

Karvel, Mrs. Jack, and four children

Keats, Tom, and wife

Keeton, J. C., wife and three children

Keiffer, wife and daughter

Keis, L., wife and four children

Kelmer, Charles L., Sr.

Kely, —, wife and three children

Kelly, Thomas, wife and two children

Kemp, Tom and wife

Kemp, W. C., and wife

Kennelly, Mrs. Annie

Kester, Fred, and daughter

Kimlo, Mrs. John, and two children

King, Mrs.

Kirby, James, and three men

Kirby, Mrs. George, and two children

Kleinicke, Mrs., and family

Kleinmann, Henry and wife

Klenmann, Fred and wife

Klindlund, Newton and Carl

Knowles, Mrs. W. T., and three children

Konstantopolos, F.

Kotte, William

Kreckrecek, Joe, wife and three children

Kreywell, David and daughter

Kuder, Ed, and wife

Kuhn, Oscar, wife and three children

Labatt, H. J.

Labatt, Louisa C. and sister Nellie E.

Lackey, and children, Leon and Pearl

Lackey, Mrs., father and mother

Lanahan, Laura, Francis, Terrence and Claude: children of John Lanahan

Lane, Rev. Mr. and family

Lang, F. A., four sons and daughter and colored nurse

Lang, five children

Lapeyre, James, wife and four children

Larson, H., and two children

Laukhuffe, Genevieve

Lawson, Charles, wife and child

Lawson, Mrs. W., and one child

Learman, H. L.

Legate, Christian

Legate, Louis, wife and son

Legate, Mrs. Peticles, two sons and two daughters

Leibe, Mrs. Mary

Lemier, Joe, and four children

Leon, —, and two children

Lepehear, J. H., wife and three children

Leslie, Mrs. Gracie

Letterman, W., wife and two children

Leverman, Professor

Levine, Mrs. P. A., daughter and two sons

Levy, Miss, of Houston

Levy, W. T.

Lewis, Mrs. J., and six children

Little, Mrs. J. A.

Livingston, Mrs.

Lloyd, Charles H., wife and one child

Loasberg, Miss Maggie

Locke, Mrs. Mary

Lockstadt, Albert, wife and three children

Londer, John, wife and seven children

Lorance, Mrs. E. A.

Love, Ed G.

Luca, Mrs. J.

Luddeker, —

Ludeke, Henry, wife and son

Ludwig, Alfred, mother and sister-in-law

Lyle, William, grandmother and sister

Manley, Joe, mother and two nieces

Manley, Mrs. S. R.

Marcotte, Miss Pauline

Marlo, Alex

Martin, Miss Annie

Massey, E., wife and child

Mati, Amendio

Maybrook, Mr., wife and five children

McAvay, Mrs. E. C.

McCamish, R., wife and two daughters

McCluskey, Mrs. Charles, and two daughters

McCormick, Mrs. B., and four children

McMillan, Mrs. E. and family

McNeill, Miss J. and Miss Ruby

McPeters, Mr., wife and children

Mealy, Joseph and Mrs.

Medzel, John, and wife and five children

Mesley, Charles (colored)

Mielhulan, Mrs.

Milan, wife and four children

Miller, Leslie

Miller, Mrs., and five children (colored)

Mitchell, Louis R. (colored)

Mitchell, Mrs. Annie, and son

Moffett, —, wife and two children

Monoghan, John and wife

Monoghan, Mike and family

Morley, D., and wife

Moore, —

Moore, E. W.

Moore, Miss Maggie

Moore, Mrs. Nathan (colored)

Moore, O., wife and seven children

Moore, two children

Morris, Harry, wife and three children

Morrow, Mrs., and four children

Morse, Albert T., wife and three children

Morton, Hammond, and four children

Mulcahey, two children

Mulsburger, Tony, and wife

Munn, Mrs. J. W., Sr.

Murie, Annie and Murine

Myer, Hermann, wife and son

Myers, Mrs. C. J., and one child

Neimann, Mrs., and one daughter

North, Miss Archie

O'Connolly, Miss Mamie

O'Connor, Mamie

Oakley, F.

Ohlsen, Mr. and Mrs.

Olds, Charlotte (colored)

Opperman, Albert L., and wife

Ormond, George, and five children

Paisley, William

Palmer, Mrs. Mae, and son Lee, 6 years old

Park, Mrs., and two daughters

Park, Mrs. M. L.

Patterson, Florence

Pellins, Mrs. M.

Penny, Mrs. A., and two sons

Perry, Jasper Jr., wife and two children

Peterson, Charles, wife and two children

Peterson, Mrs. J., and children

Pett, Mrs.

Phelps, Miss Ruth

Powers, Mrs., and child

Pruesmith, Mrs. F., and three children

Quinn, John

Raab, George W., and wife

Randolph, Edith

Raphael, Nick

Reader, —, and family

Reagan, Mrs. Patrick, and son

Reagan, John P.

Redello, Angelo, wife and four children

Rhea, Mrs. and Miss Mamie of Giles County, Tennessee

Rhodes, Miss Ella, trained nurse

Rice, Fisher (colored)

Richardson, William (colored)

Ricke, Tony, and wife

Riesel, Mrs. Lula, and children Ray and Edna

Riley, Solomon, and wife

Ring, J., proofreader at *Galveston News*, and two children

Riordan, Thomas

Riser, Henry, wife and three children

Roach, Annie

Robbins, Mrs. H. B. of Smith's Point

Roberts, —, watchman

Roberts, Herbert N.

Rodefeld, William Jr.

Roe, K. (colored)

Rose, C. M.

Rotter, A. J., wife and two children

Rowe, Ada (colored)

Rowe, Hattie (colored)

Rohl, John, wife and five children

Roll, Mrs. A., and four children

Rosenberg, —, and baby

Ross, daughter of Mrs. Ross of Houston

Roth, Mrs. Kate, and three children

Rudder, Robert, wife and four children

Rudger, C., wife and child

Rughter, Lena

Ruhler, Frank, Mrs. K, Leon and Albert

Ruce, Ida (colored)

Rutter, H., wife and five children

Sandford, S., and family

Sargent, Thomas, Arthur and Allen

Sawyer, Dr. John B.

Sawyer, Mrs. Robert, and three children

Sawyer, Tom

Schadermantle, Maud and Randle

Scheirholz, W., wife and five children

Schook, Mr. and Mrs. Robert Jr.

Schoolfield, D. (colored)

Schrader, Mary

Schuler, Mr. and Mrs., and five children

Schutte, R., wife and two children

Schwartz, Marie, Maggie and Willie

Scull, Mrs. Mary

Seidenstucker, John

Simpson, W. R., and two children, James and Berry

Skarke, Charles F., and son

Sladeyce, R. L., wife and three children

Smith, Charles L.

Smith, Jacob

Smith, Mary

Smith, Mrs. Mary, and baby (colored)

Smith, Professor F. C., wife and five children

Smith, Wiley, wife and children (colored)

Sodiche, L.

Solomon, Frank and family of six

Solomon, Julius and wife

Spann, J. C., wife and daughter

Stacker, George

Stacker, Miss Alfreda

Stacker, Mrs. Sophie

Stackpole, Dr., and family

Stanford, Mrs. Emma

Steding, Mr., wife and children (seven in family)

Stenzel, wife and three children

Stewart, Captain T. and family

Stewart, Miss Lester

Stewart, Miss Mamie

Strabo, Nick, and family, except one

Strickhausen, Mrs.

Summers, Miss Sarah of Cading, Ky.

Sweigel, George, mother and sister

Symms, two children of H. C.

Tayer, Verma and M. C.

Taylor, Mrs. J. W.

Thomas, —, wife and six children

Thomas, Nolan and Nathan

Thomason, Mrs. W. B., and two children

Thornton, two children of Leigh

Thurman, Mrs.

Tickel, Mrs. James Sr.

Trahan, Mrs. H. V., and child

Travers, Mrs. H. C. and son, Sheldon

Trizevant, Jordan

Trostman, Mrs. E., and three children

Turner, Mr. and Mrs.

Turner, Mrs.

Ulridge, Adelaide (colored)

Unger, Mrs. E. and five children

Van Buren, Ethel

Van Buren, Herman, wife and three children

Vaught, Edna, child of W. J. Vaught

Vitocitch, John, and family

Waldon, son of Henry

Walker, Joe

Walker, Louis D.

Wallace, Earl

Wallace, Scott

Wallis, Lee, wife, mother, four children and a little orphan girl
    formerly of Palestine

Walsh, J., wife and child

Warren, Martha

Warner, Mrs. A. S.

Warner, Mrs. Flora

Watkins, Mrs. F., Stanley, Arthur and Berna

Webber, Mrs. F., and family

Weber, Mrs. Anna

Weber, Mrs. Charles T.

Weight, Jennie T., and Lula

Weinberg, Otto, wife and five children

Weiss, Oscar, wife and child

Wenderman, Mrs.

Westway, Mrs. George

Wharton, —

White, —

White, family of Walter

Whittle, Tom

Wilde, Mrs., and Miss Freida

Williams, Alex

Williams, Frank, wife and child

Williams, Mrs. E. C. (colored)

Williams, Rosanna (colored)

Wilson, Annie

Winberg, Mrs. F. A. and Fritz

Windberg, Otto, wife and child

Windmann, Mrs.

Winmoore, James, wife and two children

Winn, Mrs., and child

Winscoatte, Mrs. W. D.

Wisrodt, August Jr., and wife and two children

Withey, H. M.

Wood, William (colored)

Woodrow, Matilda

Woods, Miss, from Joliet Ill.

Woods, Mrs. Julia and Miss Nannie, of Joliet

Wright, Lulu and John

Wurzlow, Mrs.

Yeager, William

Yuenz, Lillie and two children (colored)

Zeigler, Mrs., and two daughters

Zwigel, Mrs., and two daughters


At the Catholic Orphanage:

| | |
|---|---|
| Sister Camillus, Superior | Mary Finbar |
| Mary Vincent | Evangeline |
| Mary Elizabeth | Ranignus |
| Raphael | |
| Catherina | |
| Genevieve | |
| Felicitus | |

## GALVESTON DEATH LIST - SATURDAY, SEPTEMBER 15

Allison, S. B.

Antonovitch, P.

Augustial, P.

Allen, E. B.

Banneval, Mrs. A.

Barry, Mrs. M. E.

Bearman, T.

Bell, Clarence

Bellew, J.

Bellew, Mrs. J.

Benston, T.

Bereckman, Edward

Bergeron, Mrs.

Blum, Mrs. Isaac

Blum, Mrs. Sylvan

Bourdon, Mrs. L. A.

Bowles, Samuel

Bowles, Mrs. S.

Brown, Adolph

Buckner, Mr.

Carlton, Charles

Cleary, Dan

Clupp, Mrs. C. P.

Coddard, Alex

Cook, Mrs. Scott

Cook, William

Copps, Charles

Cowan, Mr.

Cratz, Jack

Davis, Mrs. Thomas

Dawler, Mrs. Samuel

Demsie, John and Mrs.

Dorrin, Mrs. C.

Duett, Miss M.

Edwards, A. R. C.

Esteman, Paul

Falk, Mrs.

Fuger, Frank

Garabaldi, August

Goldman, Theo

Hayman, John A.

Hegman, Edward

Herr, Leonard

Higgins, Mrs.

Hoffman, H. H.

Holland, Mrs. J.

Irvin, Joseph

Jefferbrook, August & Mrs.

Johnson, H. P.

Jones, J. H. and Mrs.

Kaiser, Louis

Kalb, August

Kalif, Mrs. John

Karvel, Mrs. Jack

Keefe, T. J.

Kelly, Florence

Kimpman, Paul

Kinds, Joseph

King, Mrs.
Kinsfader, Joe
Kirky, George
Levy, Major W. T.
Lindner, Mrs. L.
Lossing, Mrs. H.
Marcoburro
Marcotte, Miss P.
Martin, Herman
Martin, Jim
Martyn, Mrs. R.
Massey, Tom
McEwan, John H. Jr.
McGovern, James
McGuire, John
McHale, John
McPherson, Robert
McVay, Mrs. E. C.
Mellor, Robert
Menard, Miss Mary
Meyer, Joe
Miller, Joe
Miller, Mrs.
Morton, Henry
Morton, Mrs. A.
Mott, Mrs. Frank
Nelson, Mrs.
Nick, oysterman
O'Keefe, Mrs. C. J.
Olsen, Steve
Olson, Thomas H.

Opiliz, Anita
Peco, Leon
Peklinge, Mrs.
Phelps, Ruth
Pierson, Alice
Pierson, Frank
Pinto, Mrs. Tony
Plotomey
Potoff, Charles
Provost, James
Quarrovich, —
Raleigh, Miss Nellie
Randolph, Edith
Ravey, —
Reagan, H. J.
Reamann, Mrs.
Redford, Mattie
Riesel, Mrs. Lulu
Riser, Hy and Mrs.
Ritter, Mrs. W. M.
Roehm, W. W. F.
Rosenberg, —
Rummelin, Ed
Rurehmond, Professor
Rurehmond, Mrs.
Sargent, Allen
Sargent, Arthur
Schuler, A.
Schultz, Charles
Schultz, Charles C.
Schultz, Fred

Schultz, Mrs. F.

Scull, Mrs. Mary

Senott, Maggie

Simpson, W. R.

Steager, J.

Smith, O. P.

Stanford, Mrs. E.

Tayer, M. C.

Tayer, Verma

Tuckett, Walter

Walker, L. D.

Wallis, Lee

Wallis, Mrs. L. C.

Walters, F. A.

Waring, Mrs.

Watkins, Arthur

Watkins, Berna

Watkins, Mrs. F.

Watkins, Stanley

Wegner, Fritz

Weight, Jennie T.

Weight, Lula

Wicke, Mrs.

Williams, Mrs. E. C.

Williams, R.

Williams, Rosanna

Wisrodt, August Jr.

Wisrodt, Mrs. A., Jr.

Woodward, E. C., Jr.

Woodrow, Matilda

Zippi, J. M.

Zumberg, Gus

## MEMBERS OF BATTERY "O"
## FIRST ARTILLERY, U. S. A. LOST

Andrews, George F. - private

Andrews, William L. - private

Cantner, James W. - cook

Delaney, William A. - private

Downey, Peter - private

George, Hugh R. - first sergeant

Glaffey, John - private

Hess, Fred - private

Hunt, Frank W. - private

Kelly, John - private

Lewis, Everett A. - private

Link, George - mechanic

Marsh, James A. - sergeant

Mitchell, Benjamin D. - private

McArthur, Malcolm - mechanic

Peterson, George - private

Rander, Leopold - private

Roberts, Samuel - corporal

Sauerber, William S. - private

Seffers, Otto - private

Vantilbruch, Benjamin - private

Wheeler, Wadsworth B. - private

White, Herbert R. - private

Wilhite, Carvan M. - private

Wright, Sidney - private

HOSPITAL CORPS:

Forrest, Samuel - private

Gossage, Joseph - private

McIlvene, Elright - private

Few of the bodies of the dead regulars were found. Twelve miles down Galveston Island the following were killed:

John Schneider's family

Henry Schneider's family

Fritz Opper's family

William Schroeder's wife and seven children

Sam Kemp's (colored) family

Fritz Boehle's wife

Ansie Boehl, wife and three daughters

Ostermayer and wife

## Revised List of the Dead
## Outside Galveston

(The number of those who met death outside of Galveston is aggregated at 1,000)

### Arcadia

James Bodecker and son

James Wofford

(eleven total lives lost)

### Alvin

Misses M. and S. M. Johnson

Mrs. Wilhelm, sister of Misses Johnson

Mrs. Hawley, killed by being blown against a post

### On Chocolate Creek

Mr. Gilaspey

Mrs. J. W. Collins

Mrs. S. O. Lewis

Mrs. Proctor, of Rosenberg, killed in Santa Fe wreck

### Marvil

Mr. Bumpass

H. H. Richardson, Jr.

Mrs. Jules A. Tix, of Galveston County

### On Mustang Creek

J. McLain

(total of twelve lives lost)

### Angleton

Feklin Williams

E. J. Duff and son

Three unknown

## BROOKSIDE

W. B. Smith's daughter, aged 16

Alice Leonard (colored)

## COLUMBIA

Perry Campbell and three unknown negroes

## DICKINSON

Three ladies, mother & two daughters, and seven unknown men

## HITCHCOCK

William Johnson and wife

William and Robinson Linnie

Mrs. Pietze

Mary Monenla

Mr. Palmero, wife and five children

Unknown woman, aged 45

Unknown boy, aged 14

George Young, wife and four children

T. W. O'Connor and wife of Alvin

Mrs. J. W. Collins

W. P. Hawley

Son of Joseph Bodecker

Son of James Bodecker

Hiram Johnson and wife

William Robsinson

Domenio child

Mrs. Joe Meyer

*Several unknown found on the prairie.

*Three unknown found on a fence

## League City

W. A. Williams

Miss Letitia Schultz and Mrs. Sophia Schultz

## Morgan's Point

Louis Bracquail

"Billy" Jones

## Patton

B. Landrum, wife and five children

— Aikins, wife and child

Mrs. Slatom and child

Traney Lenton, wife and five daughters

A. Vinson, wife and child, of Liverpool, Texas

John Gluspey

## Quintana

Fifteen convicts

Six bodies on beach believed to have floated over from Galveston

## Rosenberg

J. L. Cantrell

Rev. Mr. Watson

Coleman Norman, of Needville

Mrs. Robert Dawson's infant

Child of Mrs. Graggiss

Child of Mrs. Kirkpatrick

Child of Mrs. Palmer

Charles Scott

Mary Hughes

## RICHMOND

Eighteen unknown

## SANDY POINT

Eight negroes, names unknown

## SEABROOK

Mrs. Fred May

Mrs. P. Pflinger

Mrs. Vincent and three children

Mrs. S. K. Milhenny

Haven Milhenny

Child of Rice Davids

Mrs. Dr. Nicholson

Mrs. Jane Woodlock

Two unknown

## VIRGINIA POINT

Two children of Mrs. Wright

Mrs. Leon Cleary and three children

James Sylvester

Louis Domengeux

Three unknown negro men

Two unknown negro women

## MOSSING SECTION

Foreman Kirby, with fourteen white men

## Velasco

Rev. Father Keene

L. W. Perry

"Sam" Bliss

Mrs. Parker and granddaughter

## Waller

Mrs. Mary Proctor, of Rosenberg, killed in Santa Fe wreck.

# GALVESTON DEATH LIST -
## SATURDAY & SUNDAY, SEPTEMBER 15 & 16

Agin, George, and child

Alaway, Fred, and family

Alexander, Annie and Christian

Almeras, children of Thomas

Alpin, George, and wife

Amundsen, Emil, wife and child

Anderson, Amanda (colored)

Anderson, Henry

Anderson, Mrs. Carl, and four children

Anderson, Nelson

Anizen, Mrs. Frank, and two children

Armstrong, Mrs. Dora, and four children

Augustine, Pasquila, and wife

Azteanza, Captain Sylvester

Badger, Otto

Balje, Otto

Balliman, Gus, Irene and John

Balseman, Mrs.

Barns, Mrs. Louise

Barry, Mrs., and six children

Batteste, Horace

Baubch, William, wife and two children

Baxter, Mrs. George, and two children

Bell, George, wife and four children

Bell, Henry (colored)

Bell, Miss Mattie

Berger, Theodore, wife and child

Bergman, Mrs. E. J., and daughter

Bernerville, Mrs. Antonio, and two children

Bierman, Frederick

Blackson, baby of William

Block, son of Charles

Blum, Isaac

Blum, Sarah and Jennie

Borden, J. M., and wife

Bornkessel, T. C. of United States Weather Bureau, wife and child

Boske, Mrs. Charles, and two sons

Bourke, J. K.

Bowen, —

Boygoyne, Mrs. Francis, and son

Bradford, F. H., and family

Branch, Allen (colored)

Brandies, Fritz, wife and four children

Brandon, Lottie

Britton, James (colored)

Brooks, J. T.

Brown, Adolph, wife and two children

Bryan, Mrs. L. W. and daughter

Buckley, Selma and Blanche

Burgoyne, Douglas

Burke, J. G., and wife

Burns, Marco, wife and four children

Burrell, Elivie, and two children (colored)

Burrell, Mrs. C. (colored)

Chambers, Ada

Chenivere, Mrs.

Christian, Paul and wife

Clancy, Pat, wife and three children

Clauson, Katie

Cleary, Mrs. Dan, and five children

Cleary, Mrs. Leon, and one child

Cleveland, George, and wife

Cleveland, Roy and Seneca

Close, J. M.

Coleman, Mandy, and child (colored)

Connell, William

Cook, W. S., wife and six children

Cornell, Mrs. Porter, and two daughters (colored)

Cort, infant of E. L. (colored)

Cramer, Miss Bessie

Credo, child of Anthony

Cromwell, Mrs., and three daughters

Curtis, Jane, two children and her mother-in-law (colored)

Curtis, Lula (colored)

Curtis, Mrs. J. C., and one child (colored)

Cushman, John Henry

Daley, Nicholas

Daniels, Mrs. E., three girls, one son, two grandchildren

Darby, Charles

Darkey, John, wife and daughter Belle

Davis, Annie N.

Davis, Henry T. (colored)

Davis, Irene

Deegan, Joe

Delano, Asa P., wife and children

Deltz, M., and two sons

Dempsey, Mr. and Mrs. Robert

Dinsdale, Mr., wife and two children

Dittman, Mrs. F., and son

Dixon, Mrs. Louisa, and children

Dore, —, an old Frenchman

Dore, Deo, Jr., wife and two children

Dorsett, B., and family of five

Dotto, Mike, wife and six children

Doyle, Jim

Dreckschmidt, H.

Drew, H. A.

Duffard, A.

Duffy, Mrs.

Dunant, Frank Sr.

Dunkins, Mrs.

Dunton, Mrs. Adelaide

Duntonovitch, John and Pinckey

Eberhard, F., and wife

Eberg, Mrs. Kate

Eckel, William, wife and son

Edmonds, Mrs.

Edmondson, Fred, and father

Eichler, Mrs. A.

Eichler, W.

Eisman, Howard

Ellis, John, and family of four

Ello, Joseph, wife and two children

Englehart, G. C.

Englehart, Louis

Englehart, Mrs. Ludwig

Evans, Mrs. Katy, and two daughters

Everhart, J. H., wife and Miss Lena and Guy

Falke, Joseph, and three children

Faucette, Mrs. Robert

Feigle, John, Sr., and wife

Feigle, Mabel

Ferrell, Mrs., wife of Rev., and three children

Flanagan, Mrs. Martin and child

Foreman, Mrs. Mamie, Cassie, Thomas, Amos and Webster

Franck, Mrs. Augusta

Franklin, George

Freidolf, —, wife and son

Freilag, —, and son Harry

Frohne, Mrs. Charles, and two children

Frye, Mrs. W. H.

Fryer, Bessie Bell

Gabell, Mr. and Mrs. (colored)

Gaines, Mrs. Tillie J., and two daughters

Gallishaw, five children

Garrett, Ed

Garrigan, James

Garrigan, Joseph

Garth, Johnnie and Gussie

Gensen, four children

Genter, Robert

George, Charles, and wife

George, first sergeant of Battery "O"

Gillis, Dan

Gordon, Asker, and baby

Gordon, Sol, and two children

Gother, Mrs. Fred

Grant, Fred (colored)

Grant, Mamie E. (colored)

Grumberg, Alex - supposed to belong to live-saving station

Gwynn, Mrs. D.

Haag, three children of Mrs. B.

Hagen, George W.

Hall, Joe and family (colored)

Hansel, Dick, wife and three children

Harris, George

Harris, Mrs. W. R. and son

Harris, Robert, wife and one child

Harris, Tim

Harris, Thomas, wife and three children

Harry, Mrs. (colored)

Hayes, child of Mrs. Eva of Taylor, Texas

Helfstein, John Jr. (child)

Helfstein, Sophie and Lily, children of W.

Hemann, Mrs. R. M. and child

Hess, Bugler

Hester, Charlie

Hoarer, Martin, wife and son

Hoch, Mrs. and three sons: Mike, Willie and Louis

Holland, — (colored)

Holland, James H., wife and son Willie and grandson Otis

Holmes, child of Laura (colored)

Hubner, Edward and Antoinette

Hudson, Mrs.

Hughes, John

Hughes, Mrs. Mattie

Hughes, Stuart C.

Hull, Charlie (colored)

Huzza, Charles, wife and four children

Hybach, Charles, and son

Hyman, Anthony

Jackson, Mrs. J. W., and two children

Jaeger, Mr. and Mrs., and two children

Jamoneck, Ed, wife and two children, all of Dallas

Jasper, two children of Perry (colored)

Jefferbock, Mr. and Mrs. Augusta

Jerrel, J., wife and four children and mother-in-law

Johnson, A. S., wife and six children

Johnson, Harry

Johnson, Mike, wife, child and mother-in-law

Johnson, Mrs. Genevive, and daughter

Johnson, Mrs. H. B.

Johnson, Mrs. P., and children

Johnson, Peter, wife and five children

Johnson, R. D., wife and two children

Johnson, W. J., wife and two children

Jones, Frank, son and Fred (colored)

Jones, Mrs. Matilda and daughter

Junemann, Charles, wife and daughter

Kace, Mrs. John, and four children

Kaiser, Louie, wife and three children

Kehler, Mrs. Fred, and two sons

Keiffer, wife and daughter

Keiss, Miss Judie

Keiss, Mrs. John

Keiss, Mrs. Louise, and four children

Kelsy, James

Kemp, Mrs. (colored)

Kemp, Pearl C. (colored)

Kennedy, Benton, wife and three children

Kerpan, Mr. and Mrs. Paul

Kimley, Mrs. John and family

Kindlund, Edgar

King, Mrs. (colored)

King, Rosa J. (colored)

Kinsell, E.

Knowles, Mrs. W. T., and three children

Kreza, Joseph, wife and three sons

Kunker, William, wife and child

Lackey, Alma

Lackey, Miss Pearl

Lackey, Mrs., four children and daughter-in-law

Lackey, Robert

Lafayette, Mrs., and two children

Lapierce, James, wife and five children

Larson, H., and two children

Lashley, Mrs. Dave

Laukhuff, Genevieve

Lausen, August, and three children

Lawson, Mr. and Mrs., and child

Lawson, Mrs. W. and Miss Oralie

Lee, Captain G. A., and wife

Legue, three children of Mrs. Lillie

Lemira, Joseph, wife and four children

Lenker, Tom

Lennard, Fred

Leon, —, and two children

Leslie, Miss Gracie

Lewis, Anges (colored)

Lewis, Mrs. C. A. (colored)

Lewis, Mrs. Jake, and six children

Lindgren, John, wife and seven children (eldest Miss Lillie, saved)

Lloyd, Buck, and wife

Locke, Mrs. Mary

Lockhart, Mrs. Charles, and two children

Losica, Mrs. F., daughter, three children and son-in-law

Lucas, John, and two children

Lucas, Mrs. William and two sons

Lucas, two children of Mrs. David

Ludewig, E. A. and mother

Ludke, Henry, wife and son

Lumber, Gus, wife and nine children

Lynch, A.

Lynch, Ed, and family

Lynch, James, and wife

Lyster, W. W.

Macklin, W. L., wife and three children

Maquelte, Mrs. Pauline

Martin, Frank, wife and son

Matson, Grace, and three children (colored)

Maudy, Mrs., and daughter (colored)

Maxwell, Mrs.

McAmish, S. A., wife and two daughter

McAughlar, Ira (colored)

McCauley, J. B., and wife

McCulloch, A. R. (colored)

McManus, Mrs. W. H.

McMillan, Mrs. M. J.
McNeal, Mrs. James and child
McNeill, Mrs. and baby
McPeters, wife and two children
McPherson, Robert (colored)
Mealy, Joseph
Megna, child of Mike
Megna, Mrs. Joe
Menzella, John, wife and five children
Meric, Eugene, and mother
Meric, John, wife and children
Merley, Mrs. John
Mestry, Charlotte (colored)
Meyer, Chris - missing
Meyer, Herman, wife and son Willie
Miller, Joe, and children
Miller, wife and six children
Moore, —
Moore, Estelle (colored)
Moore, Mrs. Nathan
Moran, James and wife
Morley, D., and wife
Morris, Harry, wife and three children
Morrow, Mrs. and four children
Morton, Hammond, and four children
Mott, B. F.
Mulcahey, two children of J., of Houston
Mulholland, Mrs. Louise
Mullock, Henry, wife and child
Mundyne, Mrs. Maria

Munn, Mrs. S. S.

Murie, Mrs. Annie, and daughter

Myers, Mrs. C. J., and one child

Napoleon, Henry, wife and sister (colored)

O'Dowd, D. J.

O'Keefe, C. J. and wife

O'Shaughnessy, Pauline

Olsen, Ed

Oterson, A. A. and wife

Otis, Charlotte (colored)

Paetz, Mrs. Lena

Pashelag, Miss Louisa

Pashela, Mrs. E., and three children

Paskall, August and wife

Pauly, Mr. and Mrs.

Paysee, Mrs. Henry, and two children

Peetz, Mrs. Captain J. J. and eldest & youngest daughters

Pellenze, Mrs., and mother

Perkins, Albert (colored)

Perkins, Arthur (colored)

Perkins, Mr., wife and grandson (colored)

Perry, Mrs. H. M., and son Clayton of Houston

Peterson, K. C., wife and child

Peterson, Mrs. J., and children

Pettingill, W. H., and wife and three sons: Walter W., James and
Norman (missing)

Pettit, W. B.

Pilford, W., Mexican Cable Company, and children: Madele, Willie, Jack and Georgianna

Puesnutt, Mrs. Fred, and three children

Quester, Bessie

Quinn, John, engineer (missing)

Quinn, Thomas

Quowvich, John, and four others unknown

Raleigh, Miss Lelia

Rattisseau, A., wife and three children

Rattisseau, Mrs. W. L., and three children

Rayburn, Crawford

Reagan, Mrs. John J.

Reagan, W. J., wife and three children

Redelli, Angelo, wife and four children

Rein, Mr., wife and daughter

Reinhart, Agnes and Helen, daughters of John

Rhone, Lulu L. (colored)

Rhymes, Thomas, wife and two children

Richamderes, Mrs. Irene and baby

Richardson, S. W., and wife

Riley, Mrs. W. and two children

Rimmelin, Edward H., and wife

Riordan, Thomas

Ritchford, Ben and wife

Ritzeler, Mrs.

Roach, Annie

Roberts, "Shorty"

Rockford, William and wife

Roehm, Mr. and Mrs. William, and two children

Roemer, Elizabeth, wife of A. C.

Rogers, Blanch Donald, niece of D. B.

Ross, 9-year old child of Mrs. Ross of Houston

Rossalee, B., wife and three children

Rosse, Mrs. L.

Roth, Mrs. Kate, and three children

Rowe, Mrs., and three children

Rudder, Robert, wife and four children

Rudger, C., wife and child

Ruenbuhl, Johnnie

Ruhrmond, Professor, wife and two children

Rust, Henry, and three children

Ruther, A., mother and father

Ryan, Joseph, wife and child

Sanford, Southwick, wife and child

Schmidt, Mrs. F., and son Richard

Schmidt, Richard J.

Schneider, J. F., wife and six children

Schoolfield, — (colored)

Schoolfield, Isaac

Schutte, —, wife and two children

Schutze, Mr. and Mrs.

Scott, Hugh (colored)

Seals, Wallace D. (colored)

Seats, Sarah N. (colored)

Sedgwick, child

Seibel, Lizzie

Seibel, Mrs. Jacob and son Julius

Seibel, Mrs. Julius

Seixas, Mrs. E., Anna, Lucille and Cecilia

Severt, John, and wife

Shaper, Henry, wife and two sons

Sharke, Charles F.

Sherman, Albert

Simerville, S. B., and wife (colored)

Simms, two children of H. G.

Skelton, Mrs. Emma, and two children

Slayton, Mrs. Carey B. (colored)

Smith, Jim, prize fighter

Sourbien, —, Battery "O"

Steeb, J., and wife and two children

Stevens, Frank, Leo, Jerold and Edward - sons of T. J.

Stewart, Captain P., and family

Stilkolitch, Mannie

Stimman, Robert, wife and child

Strabe, Nick and family, except one

Strickhausen, Mrs.

Strunk, William, wife and six children

Sudden, Clara (colored)

Swartsbach, child of A.

Swickel, mother and three sisters of John

Sylvester, Miss

Tavinette, Antoinet

Terrell, Mrs. Q. V., and four children (colored)

Thomas, Miss Daisy

Thomas, Newell and Nathaniel

Thompson, Mr., wife and three children

Thurman, Mrs. (colored)

Tiggs, Lavina, and daughter (colored)

Tilsman, Robert, wife and five children

Tinbush, and family

Trickhausen, Mrs.

Trostman, Mrs., and three children

Tucker, Mr. and Mrs., and one child

Turner, Mr. and Mrs.

Udell, Oliver, wife and child

Uhl, Mrs. Christopher and six children

Ulridge, Val and Mrs., and six children

Van, Miss Mary

Vining, Mrs. Annie, and four children

Viscavitch, Magdelena, daughter of Mrs.

Wade, Hettie and husband (colored)

Wade, Mrs. Hillie (colored)

Walden, Samuel, son of W. H. (colored)

Waldgren, Mr.

Walker, Mrs. H. V.

Wallace, Scott and Earl

Walsh, Joseph, wife and three children

Walsh, Mrs.

Walter, Mrs. Charles, and three children

Walters, Gus

Waring, Mr. (colored)

Warrah, Martin

Waters, three nephews of James

Watkins, child of P.

Watson, Judge, wife and two children

Weber, W. J., wife and two children

Webber, Mrs., and family

Weidmang, Fritz and wife, Paul and mother

Weiss, Professor

Wemberg, O. M., wife and five children

Westaway, Mrs. George

Wester, George and Joe

Westerman, Mrs. A.

Westman, Mrs.

White, James, wife and baby

Wicke, Lena

Wilke, C. O.

Wilcox, child

Wilde, Miss Freda

Williams, Mrs. Mary

Wilson, Bertha (colored)

Winn, Mrs. and grandchild

Withey, H.

Witt, C. H., wife and two children

Wood, Eddie and Burley (colored)

Wood, Mrs. Caroline, and two daughters, Mary and Kate

Wood, Mrs. R. N.

Wuchnach, M., wife and two children

Young, Mrs., two daughters and one son


The following, previously reported dead, were saved:

Coddou, Alex, Jr., Ray and Eugene, whose father and three brothers were lost

Cato, William

Hunter, Mrs. J. J.

Sommer, Miss Helen T.

## GALVESTON DEATH LIST - MONDAY, SEPTEMBER 17

Allen, Mrs. Kate

Allen, Mrs. Alex, and five children

Anderson, Mrs. Dora

Anderson, Mrs. Sam (colored)

Anderson, Nick, and two sons

Andrel, Mrs., and three children

Anlonovich, Eddie

Baker, Florence (colored)

Baker, Mrs., and three children (colored)

Baldwin, Sallie (colored)

Bastor, Mrs. Clara

Bostford, Edwin and wife

Bostford, Kate

Boyd, Andy, and family, on beach

Brady, —, and wife

Brandus, Fritz, wife and four children

Brophey, M., and mother of Peter

Burns, Mrs.

Bushon, Hisom

Calvert, George W., wife and daughter

Campbell, Mrs. Emma

Caroline, Mrs. Alice, and three children

Carter, A. J.

Carter, Mrs. Celeste

Cheles, William, and wife

Chester, Paul, and wife

Christian, John

Crain, Anna M.

Crain, Charles

Crain, Maggie McCree

Crain, Mrs. C. D.

Dagert, Mrs., and children

Davis, E.

Debner, William, wife and three children

Doherty, Mrs.

Floehr, Mrs.

Hoesington, H. A.

Hurt, Walter, wife , two children and two servants

Iwan, Mrs. A.

Johnson, Leonard, wife and four children

Jones, E. B.

Jones, John A. , and wife

Joughin, Tony

Kaufman, Mrs. Eliza

Keller, and family

Kleiman, Joe, wife and two workmen

Kolbe, infant of C. B.

Kroener, Will, Sophie and Florie

Kupper, —

Larson, H., and two children

Lott, Walker C., wife and two children

Luckenbell, B. E., and wife

Manly, Joen Sr., mother and two nieces

Martin, Miss Annie

McCauley, J., and wife

Neuwiller, William, wife and three children

Newton, Mrs. J. M., and child

Oakley, F.

Patrick, Mariah

Patter, C. H., and baby

Poland, Ed, and sister

Powers, Carrie V.

Pryor, Ed, wife and four children of St. Joseph, Missouri

Quinn, Mrs. Frank, and son Claude

Ripley, Henry

Roberts, John T.

Scholea, Richard, wife, son Frank, and adopted daughter, Tilla Meyer

Simons, two children of H. G.

Slayton, Mrs. Carrie (colored)

Sommer, Joe, wife and child

Spaeter, Mrs. Fred

Spaeter, Otilla

Steeb, —, wife and child

Steinbunk, Edward, George and Arthur

Sweikel, mother and three sisters of John

Steinforth, Mrs. Emma

Stevens, Frankie and Lee, two boys of T. J.

Stewart, Miss Lester

Stillman, Lily

Swenson, Mrs. Mary K.

Tavenett, Anton

Thompson, Milton

Thompson, Mr., wife and four children

Tickle, H. P., wife and two children

Told, Subie

Toothacre, Miss Etta

Torr, T. C.

Tozen, Mrs. G. M. and Miss Bella

Washington, John, and five children

White, family of Walter

White, Willie

Wiede, Mr., wife and five children

Williams, Ed

Zickler, Mrs. Fred, and two children

Zinkie, August, and two children

Zwansig, Adolph Sr., Richard, Herman and three daughters of Adolph

## GALVESTON DEATH LIST - TUESDAY, SEPTEMBER 18

Allardyce, Mrs. R. L., and three children

Allen, Claude

Allen, Herbert

Allen, Lucy

Allen, William, wife and three children

Anderson, C. L., wife and children

Andrews, Mrs.

Bernardoni, John

Boening, William, wife and three children

Bradfoot, William

Briscal, Alfred, and two children

Buren, Larzen, wife and five children

Burkhead, Mrs., and daughter

Burns, Mrs. M. E., and daughter

Burns, Mrs. P., and daughter Mary

Burwell, T. M.

Byman, Mr. and Mrs. George

Calloum, Antona, wife and four children

Chester, Frank, Ellen and Mary (colored)

Chouke, Mrs. Charles, and child

Christianson, Miss Annie of Shreveport (visiting George Dorian)

Clancy, Pat, wife and five children

Colmer, H. H., wife and five children

Colsberg, Frank G., wife and baby

Connolly, Mrs. Ellen

Cook, Henry (colored)

Cook, Mrs. Ida (colored)

Cornell, Mrs. Eliza

Costly, Sanders, and wife and child of Alexander Costly (colored)

Cowan, Isabella, and daughter

"Dago Joe", and wife Mary

Dazet, Mrs. Leon, and child

Dearing, William, wife and six children

Deboer, P. G., and wife

Devoti, "Doc"

Devoti, Joe, and three children

Devoti, Louis

Devoti, Mrs. Julia, and two children

Dickinson, Mrs. Mary, and children (colored)

Doyle, James

Dumond, Joseph, and wife

Durrant, Frank

Eaton, F. B.

Edwards, Mrs. Jane, and daughter (colored)

Ellis, Mrs. Henry (colored)

Fachan, family gone; he is alive

Fagan, Frank

Fager, Mrs. Frances

Falco, J. A. C.

Falk, Gustavo

Falk, Mrs. Julius, and five children

Felsmann, Richard (blacksmith), wife and five children

Frank, Miss Anna

Fritz, Mr., wife and two children

Galmer, H. H., and wife

Geist, Mr., wife and daughter

Graus, Mr., wife and two children

Hall, Chase (colored)

Harris, John, wife and two children

Hass, Professor Carl, and family

Haucius, Mrs., and one child

Heare, L., wife and twelve children

Herman, Mrs., and five children

Hermann, W. J.

Heusse, W. A., and wife

Hoch, Mike

Homburg, Joe, wife and four children

Homberg, William, wife and five children

Hurlbert, Mrs. Victoria, Miss Minnie, Walter & Hattie (colored)

Hylenberg, Jacob, wife and child

Jackson, Mr., wife and daughter Mabel

James, Mr., and children

Jay, J. J.

Jerrel, J., wife and four children

Johnson, A., and wife

Johnson, Dan (colored)

Jordan, Charles

Kaper, August, wife and one child

Keats, Miss Tillie

Keogh, John, wife and four children

Keogh, Mrs., and three children

Kessner, August, Lena, Emma and James H.

Koch, William Sr.

Kothe, William Q.

Leaget, Mrs. Celia, and family of six

Leagett, Mrs., and three children

Lehman, Charles, and son

Lemere, T., and wife

Letts, Captain, wife and two children and sister

Lisbony, Mrs. W. H. Jr., and Miss Eunice, daughter of C. P.

Lynch, Peter

Mackey, Mrs. W. G., and four children

Maclin, J. D., wife and seven children

Manning, Mark

Maupin, Joseph

McCann, Billy, wife and four children

McConnelly, H., and wife

McDonald, Mrs. Mary, and son

McEwen, John

McGown, Jim

McGraw, Peter, and wife

McNeil, Hugh, and baby and Miss Jennie McNeil

McPeters, Mrs., and two children

McVeagh, Mrs. J. M.

McVeigh, Miss Lorena

Mead, James

Mellor (better known as Miller), Robert

Meyer, Henry, and four children

Middleburger, George, wife and three children

Midlegge, August, wife and five children

Miller, E. O.

Miller, Frank

Miller, Mr., wife and four children

Mitchell, W. P.

Moore, Cecelia, Loraine, Vera and Mildred - children of Mr. and
Mrs. Louis Moore

Moore, Mrs. Dock

Morseburger, Antonio, and wife

Moserger, —

Neal, a fisherman

Neimeier, Henry, wife and five children

O'Neill, James and Frank, sons of James

O'Neill, Lawrence

O'Neill, Mr., wife and five children - oysterman - with four hired
men

Panleick, Matthew

Parobich, Michael, wife and four children

Patterson, H. J.

Patterson, Miss S. (colored)

Perkins, Lucy and Lotta (colored)

Perkins, Mrs. L., and two children (colored)

Peterson, George (soldier), wife and four children

Peters, Robert

Peters, Rudolph

Pischos, Mr. and Mrs.

Platt, Mrs. S.

Potter, C. H., and little daughter

Praker, William

Preussner, Henry

Preussner, Mrs., and three children

Quinn, Robert, wife and six children

Radeker, Mrs. Herman, and child

Rattiseau, C. A., wife and seven children

Rattiseau, J. B., wife and four children

Rattiseau, Mrs. J. L., and three children

Rattiseau, P. A.

Raw, Mr.

Ray, Miss Susie

Rehm, William, wife and two children

Reymanscott, Louis

Richardson, William

Ricker, John

Roberts, Herbert M.

Rose, baby of Mrs.

Rose, H., and wife

Rosen, Mrs., and four children

Rudireker, Mr., and three women

Ruther, Robert, wife and six children

Ryan, Mrs. Mary

Scarborough, Harry (fisherman)

Schroeder, Mrs. Lottie A.

Scott, Hughie (colored)

Seible, O. J. Jr.

Speck, Captain

Steerholz, W., and wife

Summers, Mrs. M. S.

Swan, George, wife and four children

Terrell, G., and wife

Tian, Mrs. Clement, and three children

Tripo, Bosick (an oysterman)

Varnell, James, wife and six children

Vuletach, Andrew, wife and daughter

Wallace, Mr. and Mrs.

Warnke, Mr. and Mrs., and three children

Warren, Mrs. Flora

Washington, Johnnie and family (colored)

Weit, Mr., and three children

Walker, L. D., stepson and W. J. Hughes

Weeden, Lou, wife and four children

Wilkinson, George, wife and son

Wurzlow, Mrs. Annie

Zurapanin, Mrs. N., and eight children


One laborer at Dr. Fry's dairy

www.ingramcontent.com/pod-product-compliance
Lightning Source LLC
Chambersburg PA
CBHW020338100426
42812CB00029B/3172/J